Lecture Notes in Computer Science 8743

Commenced Publication in 1973
Founding and Former Series Editors:
Gerhard Goos, Juris Hartmanis, and Jan van Leeuwen

Sjouke Mauw
Christian Damsgaard Jensen (Eds.)

Security and Trust Management

10th International Workshop, STM 2014
Wroclaw, Poland, September 10-11, 2014
Proceedings

 Springer

Volume Editors

Sjouke Mauw
University of Luxembourg
Luxembourg
E-mail: sjouke.mauw@uni.lu

Christian Damsgaard Jensen
Technical University of Denmark
Lyngby, Denmark
E-mail: christian.jensen@imm.dtu.dk

ISSN 0302-9743   e-ISSN 1611-3349
ISBN 978-3-319-11850-5   e-ISBN 978-3-319-11851-2
DOI 10.1007/978-3-319-11851-2
Springer Cham Heidelberg New York Dordrecht London

Library of Congress Control Number: 2014949608

LNCS Sublibrary: SL 4 – Security and Cryptology

Typesetting: Camera-ready by author, data conversion by Scientific Publishing Services, Chennai, India

Printed on acid-free paper

Springer is part of Springer Science+Business Media (www.springer.com)

Preface

These are the proceedings of the 10th International Workshop on Security and Trust Management (STM 2014). They mark the second lustrum of a workshop series that started in 2005 with the foundation of the ERCIM Security and Trust Management group. This is a Working Group of the European Research Consortium in Informatics and Mathematics (ERCIM) with the aim of providing a platform for researchers to present and discuss their ideas and foster cooperation. One of the means to achieve these goals is the organization of the annual STM workshop. This year's workshop was held during September 10–11, 2014, in conjunction with the 19th European Symposium on Research in Computer Security (ESORICS 2014) in Wrocław, Poland.

The STM 2014 workshop received 29 submissions that were evaluated on the basis of their significance, novelty, technical quality, and appropriateness to the STM audience. After intensive reviewing and electronic discussions, 11 papers were selected for presentation at the workshop, giving an acceptance rate of less than 38%. In addition, the Program Committee selected six short papers, based on their potential to initiate interesting discussions or to highlight novel research directions.

As in previous editions, the program of the STM 2014 workshop also featured a talk by the winner of the ERCIM-STM best PhD thesis award, Juraj Somorovsky, for his thesis entitled "On the Insecurity of XML Security."

We would like to thank all the people who volunteered their time and energy to make this year's workshop happen. In particular, we thank the authors for submitting their manuscripts to the workshop and all the attendees for contributing to the workshop discussions. We are also grateful to the members of the Program Committee and the external reviewers for their work in reviewing and discussing the submissions, and their commitment to meeting the strict deadlines. Last but not least, our thanks also go to all the people who played a role in the organization of the event: Pierangela Samarati (chair of the STM working group) for her energy, support, and the many useful pieces of advice; Mirosław Kutyłowski, Jaideep Vaidya, and Giovanni Livraga (co-chairs and publicity chair of ESORICS 2014) for their support; Piotr Kordy for managing the STM 2014 website; and Rolando Trujillo Rasua for taking care of the publicity of the workshop.

August 2014

Sjouke Mauw
Christian Damsgaard Jensen

Organization

STM (Security and Trust Management) is a working group of ERCIM (European Research Consortium in Informatics and Mathematics).

Program Chairs

Sjouke Mauw	University of Luxembourg, Luxembourg
Christian Damsgaard Jensen	Technical University of Denmark, Denmark

Publicity Chair

Rolando Trujillo Rasua	University of Luxembourg, Luxembourg

Web Chair

Piotr Kordy	University of Luxembourg, Luxembourg

STM Steering Committee

Theo Dimitrakos	British Telecom, UK
Javier Lopez	University of Malaga, Spain
Fabio Martinelli	IIT - CNR, Italy
Sjouke Mauw	University of Luxembourg, Luxembourg
Stig F. Mjølsnes	Norwegian University of Science and Technology, Norway
Pierangela Samarati (Chair)	Università degli Studi di Milano, Italy
Babak Sadighi	Axiomatics AB, Sweden
Ulrich Ultes-Nitsche	University of Fribourg, Switzerland

Program Committee

Rafael Accorsi	University of Freiburg, Germany
Gildas Avoine	IRISA Rennes, France
Cas Cremers	University of Oxford, UK
Jorge Cuellar	Siemens AG, Germany
Christian Damsgaard Jensen	Technical University of Denmark, Denmark
Sabrina De Capitani Di Vimercati	Università degli Studi di Milano, Italy
Roberto Di Pietro	Bell Labs, France
Josep Domingo-Ferrer	Universitat Rovira i Virgili, Spain

Carmen Fernández-Gago	University of Malaga, Spain
Simone Fischer-Hübner	Karlstad University, Sweden
Sara Foresti	Università degli Studi di Milano, Italy
Sascha Hauke	Technische Universität Darmstadt, Germany
Michael Huth	Imperial College London, UK
Bart Jacobs	Radboud University Nijmegen, The Netherlands
Martin Johns	SAP Research, UK
Günter Karjoth	Lucerne University of Applied Sciences and Arts, Switzerland
Dogan Kesdogan	Universität Regensburg, Germany
Marek Klonowski	Wrocław University of Technology, Poland
Yang Liu	Nanyang Technological University, Singapore
Giovanni Livraga	Università degli Studi di Milano, Italy
Javier Lopez	University of Malaga, Spain
Fabio Martinelli	IIT-CNR, Italy
Sjouke Mauw	University of Luxembourg, Luxembourg
Catherine Meadows	Naval Research Laboratory, USA
Silvio Ranise	Fondazione Bruno Kessler, Italy
Michael Rusinowitch	Inria Nancy-Grand Est, France
Pierangela Samarati	Università degli Studi di Milano, Italy
Jan-Philipp Steghöfer	Augsburg University, Germany
Rolando Trujillo Rasua	University of Luxembourg, Luxembourg
Jie Zhang	Nanyang Technological University, Singapore

Additional Reviewers

Cristina Alcaraz	Leanid Krautsevich
Clara Bertolissi	Aliaksandr Lazouski
Vincent Cheval	Francisco Moyano
Yannick Chevalier	Simone Mutti
Alessio Coletta	Tobias Müller
Florian Hahn	Saša Radomirović
Sara Hajian	Albert Sabaté
Roger Jardí	Giada Sciarretta
Ravi Jhawar	Santiago Suppan
Markus Karwe	Mathieu Turuani
Barbara Kordy	

Table of Contents

Short Papers

Integrating Trust and Economic Theories with Knowledge Science for Dependable Service Automation

Vangalur Alagar[1] and Kaiyu Wan[2]

[1] Concordia University, Montreal, Canada
[2] Xi'an Jiaotong-Liverpool University, Suzhou, PRC
alagar@cse.concordia.ca, Kaiyu.Wan@xjtlu.edu.cn

Abstract. This paper examines the necessity to integrate Economic Theories and Trust Theories with Knowledge Science for trustworthy service automation in modern day society's technology-driven environment. Current demands for open user-centric distributed service systems far outweigh the capabilities of existing systems in application areas such as health care, e-business, and consumer-centric power and water distribution systems. The basis of service transactions, whether in traditional market place or on-line system, is trust and lack of trust will have diminishing effect on the economic value. It is essential to identify user perspectives and relate their social psychology to meaningful trust determinants in the system to be automated. Since the systems are typically large, distributed, and deal with many heterogeneous collection of sensory devices and actuators that are specific to each service domain, it is necessary that the experts of the application domain and system developers share their knowledge and wisdom in the creation of the system. Sharing knowledge requires trust, and using the acquired knowledge requires creativity, born out of tacit knowledge, to go beyond risks. Motivated by this triangular web of Economics, Trust, and Knowledge that impacts on consumer-centric service automation, this paper explores their interesting connections, explains the different kinds of trust to be distilled from it, and identifies the design stages where the appropriate trust determinants are to be fostered in order to achieve a dependable service automation system.

Keywords: Service Automation, Economic Theory, Trust Theory, Knowledge Science.

1 Introduction

In this paper we explain the necessity and the means for harmoniously integrating *consumer trust* with domain knowledge, which is the basis for developing the system with which the consumer interacts. The different trust determinants of the consumer group should be identified and integrated with the requirements for developing the system. The system must be developed in a rigorous manner in order to enable both the developers of the system and the consumers of the system validate the trust determinants in the system behavior. We explain the challenges in achieving this goal, and as a means to achieving it we offer insight into different trust factors that must be integrated with and propagated through service automation layers.

S. Mauw and C.D. Jensen (Eds.): STM 2014, LNCS 8743, pp. 1–16, 2014.

Trust is a fundamental concept in human behavior. Human relationships and the interactions of humans with organizations are enabled by trust. In modern day global computing environment, interactions between humans and organizations are being *implemented by programs*, communicated through *complex networks*, and are mostly analyzed and validated by *mechanical means*. In order to translate the implicit meaning of trusting behavior in society to a trusting interaction among a network of humans and computers, we need to understand the many sources from which trust arises in global computing networks, their nature and influence on the subjects and objects in the network, and then synthesize them through trust policy-based decisions that satisfy the consumer group. This research is particularly relevant to many service-oriented systems such as health care networks [23], e-commerce systems [25], power distribution networks [24], and systems that provide emergency services [15]. Not surprisingly the factors that influence consumer trust are very different in these application domains. It is reported in the study [23] on consumer behavior for health care that "the look and feel of a web site influences the user whether or not to trust the web site". The same work (dated 2004) has remarked that for e-commerce "most published studies (before 2014) do not investigate the *act of trusting*, but rather investigate the *intention to trust*". The methods proposed in 2012 [25] have remedied this situation, however there is no evidence that this user-centric context-aware approach has been experimentally evaluated. For power grids [24] trustworthiness is a system property, as originally proposed in [3], and is pinned on the properties *security*, *safety*, *reliability*, and *availability*. This view is consistent with the study [2] on trust in computer science and semantic web. User-centric demands on context-aware power distribution, automated smart meters, and mechanisms for on-demand power supply are not studied as part of this cyber power system. For emergency services sought during a crisis [15], the trust is squarely dependent on the system's ability to provide sensitive information without violating privacy concerns for the "first responders". Without it, the ability to save lives and property cannot be guaranteed. The policy-based methods proposed in [15] and the method for information flow control across mutually distrusting partners [20] provide effective solutions. However, these published works have not investigated methods to integrate the different dimensions of consumer trust in service automation.

We posit that a total automation of a service-oriented system may not be possible and desirable. For example, online systems that integrate patients, medical devices, physicians, and clinical staff with medical devices used by patients will always need a "supervisory control" to manage crisis situations and offer expert opinions. That is, medical data and information accessed through interoperable medical devices are not sufficient to reason about health status. The "knowledge and wisdom" of medical experts are required for a dependable diagnosis. Often a team of experts may need to share their knowledge and experience in deciding the treatment process. Such a collaboration among experts uses *tacit knowledge*, whereas the phase preceding that might use *cognitive knowledge*. In order to share and use these two types of knowledge, trust is required [11]. In e-commerce and other business transaction-oriented systems, trust must exist between business partners, and between service providers and service requesters. The basis of exchange of goods between business partners must be trust [21], which builds confidence. The essence of trust is that the confidence it builds does not happen instantaneously, rather it is built gradually over a series of stages. Initially, its effect is to make consumers comfortable in believing the quality of advertised products. This is "trust intention" stage. Once the initial trust is formed, consumers ultimately purchase the item through the seller whom they trust. This is "trusting action" stage. Following this stage, consumers share personal information with business firms with total confidence. This stage denotes "trusted privacy". Next, they share their experience among social groups, acting as agents for recommending the seller and the product. This aspect is "social trust". These trusting stages have been have been well studied in the Economic Theories [8], which concludes trust adds economic value. From the consumer side, as revealed by the experimental studies in [23], trust is largely *behavioral* which is dominated by *performance* of the system (such as responsiveness, relevance) and emotion (such as liking the presence of familiar images, prominent logos, and promotional features). Many of the consumer groups may also be quite knowledgeable in the sense that they "know what they want" (purpose) and "know how to validate certain claims" (process). Motivated by this study, in [10] the three trust dimensions *purpose*, *process*, and *performance* are associated with consumer behavior. Because some consumer groups might be more knowledgeable about the application domain and technology than other consumer groups, we must add *cognitive* and *affective* trust to *behavioral* trust and generate additional trust dimensions.

1.1 Contributions and Significance

Given this mixture of trust notions, we need to synthesize consumer trust determinants into the trust dimensions coming out of knowledge domain (of experts developing the system) [11], and the trust dimensions propounded by the three Economic Theories [8] in the design and implementation of a service automation system. This we structure in the rest of the paper as follows.

We introduce a simplified conceptual model of a service automation system in Section 2. This model is layered into three levels, respectively called *Service Creation Facility* (SCF), *Service Provision Facility* (SPF), and *Service Transaction Facility* (STF). We explain the functionality for each layer in order to motivate the trust determinants that are appropriate for each layer.

We discuss *cognitive*, *affective*, and *behavioral* trust dimensions of consumer in Section 3 and explain the kinds of trust to be carried over into the three layers. Our approach follows the social psychology perspective of Johnson and Grayson [13], who remark that *behavior* trust is projected in actions that flow from a combination of *cognitive*(C) and *affective*(A) trust. Consequently, our approach to determining consumer trust is more general than the approach [10], in which only behavioral trust aspects are considered.

In Section 4 we review the DIKWE (Data, Information, Knowledge, Wisdom, and Ethics) hierarchy and motivate that the intelligence and creativity of the development team members should be shared and used in developing large service automation systems. Sharing and using knowledge also require both *cognitive* trust and *affective* trust. Trust among developers, experts, and designers is the basis for sharing and using this knowledge. This kind of trust is essential in SCF. However, the set of antecedents of cognitive and affective trusts for consumer trust are very different from the set of antecedents of trust for the development teams. Only with trusted partnership they can play the roles of (1) integrating consumer domain knowledge with application domain knowledge, (2) sharing their expertise in system development, and (3) using them in innovative ways to build automated systems. These reasons and the fact that consumer (and developers) trust dimensions vary across application domains suggest that reuse technology can play only a limited role in the creation of large service automation systems.

In [8], the trust relationship between partners in a transaction has been classified broadly into three areas, called *Transaction Cost Economics* (TOC), *Information Economics* (INE), and *Socio-Economics* (SOE). From this market research and economic perspective, we understand that trust adds economic value to partners in a transaction. In Section 5 we briefly review these three Economic Theories and suggest how the trust attributes relevant to adding economic value can be integrated in the three service layers SCF, SPF, and in STF. We conclude the paper in Section 6 with a summary of trust distribution across the three service automation layers, and give an outline of future work.

The significance of our work is that consumer trust dimensions carried over to SCF will be used in two stages. These are

- [1.] Some of them are to be integrated into the *dependability criteria*, which the developers of the system will determine during (application) domain analysis. The development teams should choose those trust dimensions for which verifiable implementations are possible and implement them. This approach is in line with the work of Jackson [12] on dependability. He emphasizes that (1) dependability criteria is to be determined at domain level, and (2) a verification of the dependability claim is necessary. Because we have included the verifiable trust elements of consumer in the dependability criteria, once the system is verified to satisfy this criteria then it can be certified to be dependable in the sense it behaves according to those user expectations that are integrated in dependability criteria.
- [2.] The trust determinants of consumers and those collected from market research that may not be verifiable may be included with non-functional requirements in SPF and in the *contract* part for providing the service at STF.

Thus the identification of trust dimensions from consumers, developers, and market research play an important role in linking *dependability*, defined as system attributes in [3,12,17], with the definition of trust in automation [14]. In this respect our approach differs from the approach in [10], where dependability and trust for service automation are regarded as two separate concepts.

2   Conceptual Model of Service Automation

Services in typical service domains, such as Health Care, Power Distribution, On-line Banking, and On-line Shopping, involve heterogeneous object types and service requirements. Consequently, services in such domains can not be created as services in small embedded systems. We need a rich service definition. We need to build such systems in a modular fashion in order to tackle the complexity arising from the creation, deployment, and delivery of complex services in rich application domains. Layered architectures, as those explained in [4,9], are effective ways to break the complexity barrier and promote component-based development across all layers. Conceptually,

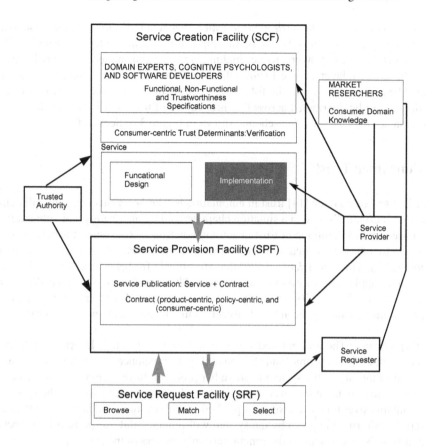

Fig. 1. Conceptual Model of Service Automation

service automation involves service creation, service publication, service selection and negotiation, and service delivery. The service creation activity is done by the teams of service developers in *Service Creation Facility* (SCF). They collaborate with domain experts, market research teams, and cognitive psychologists to respectively gather domain-specific knowledge and consumer-centric requirements. Based on this collective knowledge they define service functionality, non-functional requirements, and dependability criteria. They create designs, and implementations for services. In Section 4 we discuss the roles of teams that collaborate in SCF. The implemented services are verified to satisfy the dependability criteria by an independent Trusted Authority (TA). After a service provider (SP) has consulted the TA, the SP may buy the service from SCF and publish it in *Service Publication Facility* (SPF). That is, SPF is shared forum for all SPs to publish the services they buy (with a right to sell to consumers) from SCF. The other three activities are essentially done by consumer groups (and by any service requesting organization) in *Service Request Facility* (SRF). The SRF has well-defined interfaces for consumers to interact with SPs and services published in SPF. Thus the model has a clear separation of concerns, activities within each layer are *autonomous* and *conform to norms of the institutions to which members in the layer belong*. Another significant feature of the model is the set of simple well-specified interfaces which facilitate interaction between layers, while shielding a layer from changes that may happen within the adjacent layer. Figure 1 shows the three layers in service automation and the stakeholders for each layer. In the following three sections we discuss trust types and how they are to be distributed across the three layers of this model. The result of this discussion is a trust propagation schema, shown in Figure 3 of Section 6.

3   Consumer Trust

According to Lee and See [14] trust in automation is "the *belief* that an agent will help achieve an individual's goal in a situation characterized by uncertainty and vulnerabilities". Based on this definition of trust in automation, trust of consumer (the believer) in the system (agent) is classified into one of three dimensions *Performance*, *Process*, and *Purpose* (PPP). The *antecedents* of PPP that are suitable for behavioral trust definition in ubiquitous applications are enumerated in [10]. Although these sets of antecedents for PPP are mutually disjoint [10], our analysis, given below, based on their semantics reveal some relationships among the antecedents across the the three dimensions of PPP.

-   *Performance:* The four antecedents included are Competence, Information Accuracy, Reliability over time, and Responsibility. Competence is consumer's estimate of the suitability of the system to solve her problem. Information accuracy is consumer's judgment on the level of precision of the information given by the system. Reliability over time is consumer's prediction on how long (and how far) in the future the information given by the system will remain valid. Responsibility reflects consumer's assessment on the functional completeness of the system.
-   *Process:* The four antecedents included are Dependability, Understandability, Control, and Predictability. Dependability is consumer's assessment (say, by validation) on the consistency and reliability of system reactions. Understandability reflects the consumer's ability to grasp the functionality of the system. Control stands for the consumer's gut feeling "am I in control or not?". Predictability is consumer's assessment of "whether or not expectations are met".
-   *Purpose:* The three antecedents included are Motives, Benevolence, and Faith. Motives assess "whether or not the developers truthfully communicated the intended use of the system". Benevolence is an estimate of consumers on "whether or not the developers had their interests in mind while developing the system". Faith is the belief that the system can be relied upon in future.

This definition of consumer level behavior trust has been well researched in social norms of trust [16,25]. From the semantic affinities we observe the four sets of relationships G_1 = {Competence, Benevolence, Predictability, Control}, G_2 = {Information Accuracy, Predictability, Motives}, G_3 = {Reliability, Faith, Dependability}, and G_4 = {Responsibility, Understanding, Faith}. This observation is significant because it suggests that some of the behavior trust determinants from different dimensions may be exported to the same layer in the service automation design.

Building from social psychology literature Johnson and Grayson [13] remark that *behavior* trust is projected in actions that flow from a combination of *cognitive*(C) and *affective*(A) trust. According to Moorman [18] cognitive trust is a customer's confidence and willingness to rely on the *competence* and *reliability* of the SP, and affective trust is characterized by the confidence one places on the partner based on "emotions" generated by the level of care and concern demonstrated by the partner. Since services, whether they are offered through traditional market places or automated systems, must add economic value by "owning" and "expanding" the customer base, we must consider cognitive trust and affective trust as the basis for service automation. Behavior trust that results from the actions that flow out of the combination of actions that are consequences of cognitive and affective trust should then exhibit the antecedents in PPP. If this can be convincingly demonstrated we can say that the *cognitive-affective trust* (CA) model subsumes the PPP model. To achieve this goal we start with the CA model of consumer trust [13], relate it to PPP model, and explain to which service automation layer the consumer trust determinants should be exported.

In the CA model [13], the antecedents for cognitive trust are *SP Expertise, Product Performance, Firm Reputation*, and *Satisfaction with Previous Interactions*, and the antecedents for affective trust are *Firm Reputation, Satisfaction with Previous Interactions*, and *Similarity*. The three consequences of cognitive trust are that it has a positive influence on (1) sales effectiveness, (2) anticipatory future interactions, and (3) affective trust in SP. The consequence of affective trust is that it has a positive influence on anticipatory future transactions. Below we discuss these findings in order to relate them to PPP model and export them to service automation layers.

SP Expertise: This is an antecedent of consumer's cognitive trust. The consumer assesses the expertise of SP by evaluating (1) the depth of knowledge of SP about the service provided by it, and (2) the identifiable actions of SP in service announcement and service delivery. The consumer might pose questions to SP on the nature of service and assess SP's domain knowledge from the responses. Such a conversation typically happens at the time the consumer is intending to buy a service, that is when browsing the service publications before selecting the service. In our service automation model we have separated the SP from SCF where services are created. Hence, this consumer trust should be addressed at SCF, verified by the TA, and fulfilled by SP at SPF. That is, the SP learns about the service from the teams in SCF and the TA tutors SP on the verified properties. This way, the SP gains the necessary depth of knowledge on the service provided by it. Thus, "SP expertise" antecedent of the CA model relates to the PPP antecedents competence, understanding, faith, and motives.

Service/Product Performance: This is an antecedent of consumer's cognitive trust. Service functionality (process) and service provision (outcome) are two distinct stages in service automation. In our service automation model, the quality attributes of the service functionality are to be defined and implemented by service developers in SCF, and the quality of service provision is to be associated with the contract for providing the service which is drafted by the SP. The SP packages a service with a contract and publishes it in SPF, and delivers the published service in STF. Consequently, the antecedent "service provision" must be exported to SPF and STF in order to be fulfilled by the SP. We can group the PPP antecedents competence, reliability, responsibility, benevolence, faith, dependability, and understandability as the set of antecedents for process, and group the PPP antecedents information accuracy, reliability, motives, and control as the set of antecedents for outcome.

SP (Firm) Reputation: In general, consumer groups are not aware of the firm that creates services, rather they interact only with SPs. The reputation of SP (the business firm) who provides the service depends on (1) the reputation of the TA who certifies the dependability attributes of the service that the SP buys, and (2) his own reputation in accurate service publication and dependable service provision. Since consumers are not aware of SCF, the antecedent here refers only to "SP reputation". It is an antecedent for both cognitive and affective trust. The consumer will use the on-line system features to assess whether or not the SP has (1) described the service functionality correctly, (2) truthfully posted the rankings and recommendations of peer groups, and (3) precisely stated the contractual obligations. So, the SP has to act in a fair manner, respect the contract, and never feed inaccurate or ambiguous information. We export SP reputation trust to SPF. Once the consumer is convinced (cognitive/analytic) of such high ratings of SP, the consumer is likely to reciprocate through a long-term customer of the SP. Hence, the PPP antecedents "information accuracy, responsibility, dependability, understandability, predictability, motives, benevolence, and faith" arise out of a combination of cognitive and affective trust, and collectively relate to SP reputation.

Satisfaction with Previous Interaction: This antecedent refers only to SP. It is common to both cognitive and affective trust because satisfaction involves both emotions (affective) and cognitive process during the comparison of service performance with consumer expectation. Cognitive process involves comparison of service quality and verification. Affective trust is triggered by "social" factors. An on-line service system might advertise that (1) first-time buyers get a reward, or (2) regular buyers are rewarded with some privileges, such as points accumulation for free flights or hotel stays. As consumers participate in this "socialization" they and SPs go into trusting bonds. This kind of trust may be included in SPF, in the description of "non-functional attributes" of service and in the contract part of service. The PPP antecedents related to this CA antecedent are responsibility, faith, and motives.

Similarity: This is an antecedent for affective trust because the consumer observes that certain goals and interests are common between him and the SP. Once the consumer detects this affinity a trusting environment for SP is created. This trust aspect is exported to SPF and STF. The PPP antecedents that are related to this CA antecedent are control, motives, benevolence, and faith.

4   Knowledge Hierarchy and Trust

In this section we examine the trust factors for the groups that collaborate in developing a service automation system. The groups and their roles are as follows.

- *Domain Experts:*(DE) Typically, services provided by a system are specific to one application domain. However, the domain knowledge might come from different related domain. Domain experts have the knowledge specific to each domain.

They will assist the system designer in identifying the requirements, constraints, and dependability criteria for an application.

- *Software System Designers:*(SSD) Software systems design is the process of defining the architecture, components, modules, and interfaces for a software system to satisfy specified requirements. A software system designer consults the experts, clients and software developers about required specifications, and produce designs. The developers collaborate among themselves during implementation, testing, and refinement stages.
- *Market Researchers:*(MR)   Their role is to establish, maintain, enhance, and commercialize consumer relationships. They will acquire knowledge on what consumers want, who are potential competitors and what are their plans, what are environmental constraints, and construct models based on them to enhance service type and quality. From economic theory point of view (see Section 5) they determine the trust factors that add economic value and assist the DE and SSD in formulating a dependability criteria. They collaborate with SSD in the design of SCF interfaces through which consumers will be able to browse accurate and precise information on services in a level that they can understand. On demand, they may assist the SPs in the drafting of service packages (contract and service descriptions) that will be announced in SPF.
- *Social Psychologists:* (SS) They will assess the trust determinants of consumers (as explained in Section 3 and synthesize it with the knowledge gathered by the market researchers.

The above groups should be formed at SCF before domain analysis starts towards constructing a software automation system. We conceptualize the collaboration between these groups in three stages. In the first stage the groups MR and SS collaborate to reach a decision on the consumer trust profile and communicate it to both the groups SSD and DE. In the second stage the group DE constructs the domain models, integrates the consumer trust input received from MR and SS into dependability criteria, and communicates these results to the group SSD. In the third stage the group SSD develops the service system, collaborates with the group MR in determining the information content to be included in SPF and STF layers. An in-depth discussion on the nature of collaboration within the members of each group and across different groups is beyond the scope of this paper. We only discuss the nature of collaboration within the groups DE and SSD and emphasize that trust is the basis for a collaboration.

4.1 Collaboration among Domain Experts

A domain is a set of applications that share similar requirements, capabilities, and data. Each domain expert has the knowledge that is specific to one application. They have the skills to define, model, construct, and catalogue a set of artifacts specific to the domain. The artifacts include a domain model, architectures and components that are suitable for the domain model, dependability criteria for the domain, and the specific contexts of operations of an application in each domain.

The core of domain engineering is domain analysis, in which domain knowledge is captured and represented. This model includes application domain concepts, their attributes, and their associations. This knowledge, together with the set of requirements

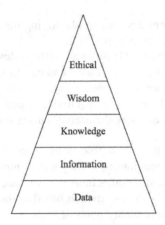

Fig. 2. DIKWE Hierarchy

specific to an application, the set of non-functional requirements, the set of quality attributes, and user expectations forms the foundation on which an application is to be developed. In addition, the dependability criteria developed for domain applications will be specialized for each specific application, taking into account the consumer expectations. In this process, the domain-specific data and information gathered during domain analysis should be included with the data and information on the application environment. As an example, the design of *Autonomous Vehicle* will need knowledge from different related domains such as *Automotive Engineering*, *Transportation Networks*, *Social Aspects of Engineering*, *Embedded System Development*, and *Communication Networks*. The domain experts from all these domains are expected to *share* and *use* their knowledge for a common goal. This activity requires mutual trust among the creative partners who are experts.

4.2 Collaboration among Software Developers

It is remarked in [5] that information technologists view knowledge as an object to be possessed. They also remark that "the preoccupation of organizations with information technology for managing *explicit* knowledge may have led to neglect the more important and challenging task of facilitating the sharing and use of *tacit forms* of knowledge". In knowledge management study [1,6,22], *Data* (D), *Information* (I), *Knowledge* (K), *Wisdom* (W) (called DIKW hierarchy) are placed in a pyramid structure, with D at the bottom of the pyramid and W at the peak of the pyramid. To this pyramid we add *Ethics* (E) on top of W and get the hierarchy DIKWE shown in Figure 2. The lower part of the pyramid (DIK) can be called *cognitive or explicit* knowledge, because all of data, information, and some parts of knowledge (for information processing) can be reduced to writing. They take the form of reports, manuals, policies, patents, and formulas. This type of knowledge can be represented for mutual use among a set of developers. The higher part of the pyramid (KWE) can be called *tacit* knowledge because some aspects of knowledge for reasoning about information (know-how and know-why), wisdom, and ethical principles (arising out of wisdom) are rooted in individual's experience and values can not be put in writing. From many publications on DIKW hierarchy [6,22] it is clear that wisdom is intended for the well-being of others, and it involves a balanced coordination of mind and ethics. The group intelligence in creating large service systems is reflected in the "intelligent behavior of the system". So, intelligence and wisdom are perceived similar to each other. With respect to the development of large service automation systems the DIKWE hierarchy suggests that practical problem solving, goal-orientation and achievement, balanced intellectual discussions and integration, ability to reason, learning from other group members, learning and adapting from the flaws of earlier systems, and sagacity are the ideal traits for SSD members. Face-to-face human interaction is the primary method for acquiring such traits and transferring tacit knowledge. Building knowledge hierarchies for each subdomain of an application domain must be a joint effort of the groups DE and SSD.

The level of risk in storing and transferring explicit knowledge can be reduced by applying security mechanisms involving trusted cryptography, authentication, and information flow controls [20]. However, to reduce the level of uncertainty associated with tacit knowledge transfer trusting relationship is essential. Tacit knowledge transfer requires willingness to share and capacity to communicate. The main barriers for tacit knowledge transfer are (1) difficulty in identifying the persons who have tacit knowledge on a specific topic (domain), (2) unwillingness of a group member to share and his incapacity to communicate, and (3) a feeling of competitive disadvantage (risk) in sharing. To overcome these barriers trust relationship must be promoted among the members of the SSD group at SCF. The two kinds of trust studied towards improving trust are (1) affect-based trust, and (2) cognition-based trust. Affect-based trust is grounded in mutual care and concern for members of the group, and in the ability to reach a compromise on the goal-oriented creative process of the system. Cognition-based trust is grounded on the competence of individuals in the group, and their reliable cooperation among themselves in using explicit knowledge. Based on the statistical evidence [11] we may say that affect-based trust has a positive effect on the willingness to share tacit knowledge, while cognition-based trust has a positive effect on the willingness to use tacit knowledge. With trusted collaboration among themselves, the group SSD develops the service system. The trust determinants included by SSD in service implementation at SCF are precisely those that are included in the dependability criteria. The trust determinants to be placed in SPF and STF are collaboratively determined by the groups SSD and MR.

5 Economic Theories and Trust

The basis of exchange of goods and services between business partners must be *trust* [21], which builds confidence. The essence of trust is that the confidence it builds will make consumers comfortable in believing the quality of advertised services, which they may ultimately purchase that adds economic value for the service provider. In society, trust is defined [16] as one party's *belief* that the other party will not *exploit* its *vulnerabilities*. With respect to the Internet Friedmnan [7] remarks that "*the greatest difference between trust online and in all other contexts is that when online, we have more difficulty (sometimes to the point of futility) of reasonably assessing the potential harm and good will of others, as well as what counts as reasonable machine performance. That is why people can engage in virtually identical online transactions, yet reach widely disparate judgments about whether the interactions are trustworthy.*" The term 'judgment' refers to the conclusion of a consumer after evaluation of a relation that exists between the consumer and the system behavior. The result of this evaluation leads to either trust or mistrust. That is, the consumer-centric 'judgments' are to be expressed and evaluated against the "trustworthiness assertions" expressed by the service provider. In our approach, detailed in Section 4, consumers have a say in the definition of 'trustworthiness'. So, their judgments are likely to be more favorable. A service-oriented system, owned by a business firm, is governed by a well-defined set of its institutional policies formulated with significant input from market research. Such policies will be aligned with Economic Theories [8] in order to maximize economic gain and user satisfaction. It is essential that consumers are made aware of these policies. This is an essential step to educate as well as convince the consumer that the system behavior is consistent with the announced policies, which in turn creates economic value. This means that 'consumer level judgment' will tend to be more rational rather than ad-hoc. As a result, the system level dependability property and the trust coming out of 'consumer level judgment' have the Economic Theory (ET) as the meeting point.

5.1 Trust Aspects of Economic Theory

In this section we explain the trust relationship between consumers (SR: service requesters) and SPs from market research perspective. In [8] the Economic theory has been classified into three broad areas, respectively called *Transaction Cost Economics* (TCE), *Information Economics* (INE), and *Socio-Economics* (SOE).

The theory of TCE states that every service transaction has a quantifiable direct and indirect cost, as well as an unquantifiable cost. The direct cost is the cost involved in negotiations, contract drafting and service implementation. The indirect cost may include cost of information dissemination, and monitoring the different transaction phases. The unquantifiable cost is usually the "cost of disadvantage" in the event of posting inaccurate or irrelevant information, contract violation, and not meeting service provision rules in certain contexts. The TCE theory postulates that the following trust building behaviors will offset the cost of disadvantage.

– Information should be disseminated to consumers *without interruption in a proactive manner*. This requires the inclusion of system availability and reliability in dependability definition.
– The communicated information must be *correct and current*. That is, integrity of information must be assured. Sometimes, service is to be delivered in total confidence. That is, security and privacy should be included in dependability definition.
– A service whose quality violates the ethical and social values in an environment should not be provided. That is, safety is an important feature of dependability.
– Every service provision must be monitored for contract consistency.

In summary, the trust attributes related to TCE theory are safety, security (privacy and integrity included), availability, accountability (transaction monitoring), and reliability. Not all of these may be relevant for an application. The teams at SCF have to sort out those TCE trust attributes that are required for an application. Hence, TCE trust attributes are exported to SCF.

The INE theory postulates that the relationship between a SR and any SP is *asymmetric*, because a SP has the knowledge about its services, whereas the SR may have little or no knowledge on what to expect from a SP. Since the consumer is most likely to accept only services that have economic value, the SPs should try to provide knowledge-intensive tutoring to the SRs before selling the services. Here is where the human-computer interface niceties arise. It is not sufficient for the SP to make the web site attractive. It is essential that the web site is easy to navigate for any SR, enabling them to "browse" and search for "relevant" information, facilitating them to understand the authenticity of information provided, and advising them on the procedures for selecting/querying services, completing the contract and getting the services delivered according to their preferences. So, SPs should employ sophisticated, yet simple to use, interfaces to convey the knowledge to consumers in order that they may be able to evaluate the value potential of offered services. The INE theory postulates that feeding more information to buyers may not help to sell products in an asymmetric relationship. The theory suggests that in order to overcome *information asymmetry*, information must be filtered, screened, and delivered *directly* to buyers before selling products. Another important implication of INE theory is that even if user-friendly interfaces to the web pages of sellers are added, it may not help disseminate information to SRs because of the steep learning curve required by them to understand the product metrics from the web pages. In other words, the *learning curve* required by consumers must be made "less steep" through "long term" contacts and tutorials. In essence, INE theory emphasizes trust building through direct interaction. The teams SSD and MR should collaborate to fulfill INE trust at SCF (interface design). Both SP and MR collaborate in fulfilling INE trust at SPF (service and contract description), and STF (delivery of service to satisfy user preferences).

The theory of SOE studies the role of social networks and cultural aspects in influencing consumer behavior. SOE concludes that trust arising out of social and independent business research affiliations plays an important role in the evolution of service-based systems. Consumers may seek recommendations from social groups [16], and consult independent experts and trusted authorities (such as Better Business Bureau) to guide them in choosing best vendors. A service provider may be ranked by independent trusted authorities and by consumers. Thus, in SPF a service publication lists two kinds of recommendations. These are "peer rankings" from trusted authorities and experts who have verified (or evaluated) the announced service, and "consumer rankings". To sustain consumer trust, the SP will ensure that these trust recommendations are both truthful and verifiable.

6   Conclusion

In general, a domain has a family of related applications. For any one application in a particular domain there exists a consumer domain. Services automated for the chosen application should earn the trust of consumers from its corresponding consumer domain. The developers of the service application system might formulate a dependability criteria to convince the consumers that the system can be depended upon. In order that the

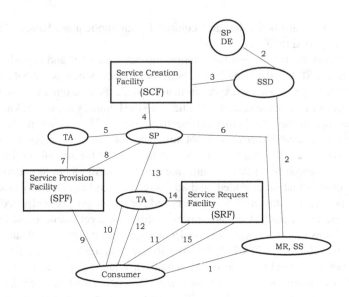

Fig. 3. Trust Propagation Across the Layers of Service Automation System

consumers trust the system it is essential that the equation $DC \vdash CT$ holds, where CT is the consumer trust expression, DC is the system dependability criteria, and $\vdash$ is "satisfaction relation". To achieve this goal we have attempted to integrate consumer-centric trust determinants CT with system-centric dependability criteria DC. In this attempt to bind CT within DC, we have brought in marketing research team of SPs to assess CT, application domain experts and software developers of SPs to craft DC. For a seamless binding, we have postulated the different kinds of trust and knowledge that are to be shared among these stakeholders. We have also postulated that as a result of this approach trust is propagated to different stages in the development process of a service automation system.

The theoretical approach that we have suggested has two stages. In the first stage the combined effect of existing theories in Economics, Trust, and Knowledge Science on consumer-centric service automation has to be understood and exported into the development process of the system. In the second stages the understanding gained in the first stage is put together to trust building, and export appropriate trust determinants to the different stages of service automation system development. Our investigation has led to the trust propagation schema shown in Figure 3. In the diagram, each edge is labeled by a number and reading them in sequence will guide us in the manner trust determinants are fostered and propagated. Table 1 shows the different cognitive and affective trust determinants of the consumer that are exported to the different layers of service model. This table, combined with the service automation model shown in Figure 1 should convince us that our approach leads to integrating consumer-centric trust with system-centric dependability criteria. In this context we emphasize that the verification box in SCF of Figure 1 can be automated by following the rigorous component-based development methodology [17]. We believe that the trust propagation model in Figure 3 is also consistent with the theoretical issues raised on trust and human interaction of automated systems [19].

Table 1. Exporting Consumer Trust

Consumer Perception	Interpersonal Trust	Action	Export Layer
SP Expertise	Cognitive Trust	Include Attributes for Correctness,Security, Safety, Privacy And Evaluate Dependability ⇔ Consumer Expectation	SCF, SPF
Performance	Cognitive Trust	State Verifiable Actions Ensure Correctness And Timeliness	SCF, SPF, STF
Firm Reputation	Cognitive Trust	Doing Things Right Doing the Right Things	SPF, STF SCF
Satisfaction	Cognitive Trust	Check: Reliability Accountability Availability	SCF, SPF, STF SPF, STF SPF, STF
Firm Reputation Affinity	Affective Trust Affective Trust	Referring Peers Groups Observation/Perception	SPF SPF

Our work has largely been theoretical. In our opinion, our findings in this paper should be regarded as a set of hypotheses that need statistically based experimental verification. Hypothesis testing approach is the ideal approach to follow. Such an approach has been followed in the two works [11] and [13]. Hypothesis testing for our theory will require sample spaces of stakeholders, the systems constructed by them, and market surveys. Given this complexity, large software industries have the ability to pursue this research.

Acknowledgments. We want to thank the referees whose insightful comments helped us to improve the paper presentation. The research work reported in this paper has been supported by research grants from China and Canada. The first author is supported by a grant from Discovery Grants Program, Natural Sciences and Engineering Research Council of Canada (NSERC). The second author is supported by Research Grants from National Natural Science Foundation of China (Project Number 61103029), and Research Development Funding of Xi'an Jiaotong-Liverpool University (Project Number RDF-13-02-06).

References

1. Ackoff, R.L.: From Data to Wisdom. Journal of Applies Systems Analysis 16, 3–9 (1989)
2. Art, D., Gil, Y.: A Survey of Trust in Computer Science and the Semantic Web. Web Semantic Sci Serv Agents World Wide Web 5(2), 58–71 (2007)
3. Avizienis, A., Laprie, J.C., Randell, B., Landwehr, C.: Basic concepts and taxonomy of dependable and secure computing. IEEE Transactions on Dependable and Secure Computing 1(1), 11–33 (2004)
4. Broy, M.: Service-Oriented Systems Engineering: Modeling Services and Layered Architectures. In: König, H., Heiner, M., Wolisz, A. (eds.) FORTE 2003. LNCS, vol. 2767, pp. 48–61. Springer, Heidelberg (2003)

5. Cross, R., Baird, L.: Technology is Not Enough: Improving Performance by Building Organizational Memory. Sloan Management Review 41(3), 69–78 (2000)
6. Fricke, M.: The Knowledge Pyramid: a critique of the DIKW hierarchy. Journal of Information Science 35(2), 131–142 (2009)
7. Friedman, B., Khan, P.H., Howe, D.C.: Trust Online. Communications of the ACM 43(12) (2000)
8. Fritz, M., Hausen, T., Schefer, G., Canavari, M.: Trust and Electronic Commerce in the Agrifood Sector: a trust model and experimental experience. Presented at the XIth International Congress of the EAAE (European Association of Agricultural Economists), The Future of Rural Europe in the Global Agri-Food System, Copenhagen, Copenhagen, Denmark, August 24-27 (2005)
9. Herzberg, D., Broy, M.: Modelling layered distributed communications systems. Formal Aspects of Computing 17(1), 1–18 (2005)
10. Hoffmann, H., Söllner, M.: Incorporating Behavioral Trust Theory into System Development for Ubiquitous Applications. Pers. Ubiquit. Comput. 18, 117–128 (2014)
11. Holste, J.S., Fields, D.: Trust and Tacit Knowledge: sharing and use. Journal of Knowledge Management 14(1), 128–140 (2010)
12. Jackson, D.: A direct path to dependable software. Communications of the ACM 52(4), 78–88 (2009)
13. Johnson, D., Grayson, K.: Cognitive and Affective Trust in Service Relationship. Journal of Business Research 58, 500–507 (2005)
14. Lee, J.D., See, K.A.: Trust in Automation: Designing for Appropriate Reliance. Human Factors 46(1), 50–80 (2004)
15. Levin, T., Irvine, C., Benzel, T., Nguyen, T., Clark, P., Bhaskara, G.: Trusted Emergency Management. Technical Report (NPS-CS-09-001), Naval Postgraduate School, Monterey, California, USA (2009)
16. McKnight, D.H., Chervany, N.L.: Trust and Distrust Definitions: One Bite at a Time. In: Falcone, R., Singh, M., Tan, Y.-H. (eds.) AA-WS 2000. LNCS (LNAI), vol. 2246, pp. 27–54. Springer, Heidelberg (2001)
17. Mohammad, M., Alagar, V.: A Formal Approach for the Specification and Verification of Trustworthy Component-Based Systems. Journal of Systems and Software 84, 77–104 (2011)
18. Moorman, C., Zaltman, G., Deshpande, R.: Relationship between Providers and Users of Marketing Research: the dynamics of trust within and between organizations. J Mark Res 29, 314–328 (1992)
19. Muir, B.M.: Trust in Automation: Part I: Theoretical Issues in the Study of Trust and Human Intervention in Automated Systems. Ergonomics 37(11), 1905–(1922)
20. Myers, A., Liskov, B.: A Decentralized Model for Information Flow Control. In: Proceedings of the 16th ACM Symposium on Operating System Principles, Saint Malo, France (October 1977)
21. Pavlou, P.A.: Consumer Acceptance of Electronic Commerce: Integrating Trust and Risk with the Technology Acceptance Model. International Journal of Electronic Commerce 7(3), 101–134 (2003)
22. Rowley, J.: The wisdom hierarchy: representation of the DIKW hierarchy. Journal of Information Science 33(2), 163–1805 (2007)
23. Sillence, E., Briggs, P., Fishwick, L., Harris, P.: Trust and Mistrust of Online Health Sites. In: ACM SIGCHI Conference on Human Factors in Computing Systems, Vienna (2004)
24. TCIPG. Trustworthy Cyber Infrastructure For The Power Grid, http://tcipg.org/
25. Wan, K., Alagar, V., Ibrahim, N.: An Extended Service-oriented Architecture for Consumer-centric E-Commerce. International Journal of Information and Communication Technology Research 3(1), 1–28 (2012)

Privacy Architectures: Reasoning about Data Minimisation and Integrity

Thibaud Antignac and Daniel Le Métayer

Inria, University of Lyon, France
{thibaud.antignac,daniel.le-metayer}@inria.fr

Abstract. Privacy by design will become a legal obligation in the European Community if the Data Protection Regulation eventually gets adopted. However, taking into account privacy requirements in the design of a system is a challenging task. We propose an approach based on the specification of privacy architectures and focus on a key aspect of privacy, data minimisation, and its tension with integrity requirements. We illustrate our formal framework through a smart metering case study.

1 Introduction

The philosophy of privacy by design is that privacy should not be treated as an afterthought but as a first-class requirement in the design of IT systems. Privacy by design will become a legal obligation in the European Community if the Data Protection Regulation [11] eventually gets adopted. However, from a technical standpoint privacy by design is a challenging endeavour: first, privacy is a multi-faceted notion stemming from a variety of principles[1] which are generally not defined very precisely; in addition, these requirements may be (or may seem to be) in tension with other requirements such as functional requirements, ease of use or performances. To implement these requirements, a wide array of privacy enhancing technologies (PETs) are available[2]. Each of these techniques provides different guarantees based on different assumptions and therefore is suitable in different contexts. As a result, it is quite complex for a software engineer to make informed choices among all these possibilities and to find the most appropriate combination of techniques to solve his own requirements. Solutions have been proposed in different application domains such as smart metering [14,29], pay-as-you-drive [2,18], or location-based systems [20] but the next challenge in this area is to go beyond individual cases and to establish sound foundations and methodologies for privacy by design [9,33]. In this paper, we advocate the idea that privacy by design should be addressed at the architectural level, because it makes it possible to abstract away unnecessary details, and should be supported

---

[1] These principles include collection limitation, data quality, purpose specification, use limitation, security, openness, individual participation, accountability, etc.

[2] For example homomorphic encryption, zero-knowledge proof, secure multi-party computation, private information retrieval, anonymous credentials, anonymous communication channels, etc.

S. Mauw and C.D. Jensen (Eds.): STM 2014, LNCS 8743, pp. 17–32, 2014.

by a formal model. The fact that not all aspects of privacy are susceptible to formalisation is not a daunting obstacle to the use of formal methods for privacy by design: the key issue is to be able to build appropriate models for the aspects of privacy that are prone to formalisation and involve complex reasoning. Data minimisation, which is one of the key principles of most privacy guidelines and regulations, is precisely one of these aspects. Data minimisation stipulates that the collection and processing of personal data should always be done with respect to a particular purpose and the amount of data strictly limited to what is really necessary to achieve the purpose [11].

In this paper, data minimisation requirements are expressed as properties defining for each stakeholder the information that he is (or is not) allowed to know. Data minimisation would not be so difficult to achieve if other, sometimes conflicting, requirements did not have to be met simultaneously. Another common requirement, which we call "integrity" in the sequel, is the fact that some stakeholders may require guarantees about the correctness of the result of a computation. In fact, the tension between data minimisation and integrity is one of the delicate issues to be solved in many systems involving personal data.

In Section 2 we propose a language to define privacy architectures. In Section 3, we introduce a logic for reasoning about architectures and show the correctness and completeness of its axiomatisation. This axiomatisation is used in Section 4 to prove that an example of smart metering architecture meets the expected privacy and minimisation requirements. Section 5 discusses related work and Section 6 outlines directions for further research.

2   Privacy Architectures

Many definitions of architectures have been proposed in the literature. In this paper, we adopt a definition inspired by [4][3]: *The architecture of a system is the set of structures needed to reason about the system, which comprise software and hardware elements, relations among them and properties of both.* The atomic components of an architecture are coarse-grain entities such as modules, components or connectors. In the context of privacy, the components are typically the PETs themselves and the purpose of the architecture is their combination to achieve the requirements of the system.

The meaning of the requirements considered here (minimisation and integrity) depends on the purpose of the data collection, which is equated to the expected functionality of the system here. In the sequel, we assume that this functionality is expressed as the computation of a set of equations[4] Ω such that $\Omega = \left\{ \tilde{X} = T \right\}$ with terms T defined as shown in Table 1. $\tilde{X}$ represents (potentially indexed) variables and X simple variables ($X \in Var$), k index variables ($k \in Index$), Cx constants ($Cx \in Const$), Ck index constants ($Ck \in \mathbb{N}^{5}$), F functions ($F \in Fun$)

---

[3] This definition is a generalisation (to system architectures) of the definition of software architectures proposed in [4].

[4] Which is typically the case for systems involving integrity requirements.

[5] Set of natural numbers.

Table 1. Term Language

$$
\begin{aligned}
T &::= \tilde{X} \mid Cx \mid F(T_1, \ldots, T_n) \mid \odot F(X) \\
\tilde{X} &::= X \mid X_K \\
K &::= k \mid Ck
\end{aligned}
$$

and $\odot F(X)$ is the iterative application of function F to the elements of the array denoted by X (e.g. sum of the elements of X if F is equal to $+$). We assume that each array variable X represents an array of fixed size $Range(X)$.

In the following subsections, we introduce our privacy architecture language (Subsection 2.1) and its semantics (Subsection 2.2).

2.1 Privacy Architecture Language

We define an architecture as a set of components C_i, $i \in [1, \ldots, n]$ associated with relations describing their capabilities. These capabilities depend on the set of available PETs. For the purpose of this paper, we consider the architecture language described in Table 2.

Table 2. Privacy Architecture Language

$$
\begin{aligned}
A &::= \{R\} \\
R &::= Has_i\left(\tilde{X}\right) &&\mid Receive_{i,j}\left(\{S\}, \{\tilde{X}\}\right) \\
&\mid Compute_i\left(\tilde{X} = T\right) &&\mid Check_i\left(\{Eq\}\right) \\
&\mid Verif_i^{Proof}\left(Pro\right) &&\mid Verif_i^{Attest}\left(Att\right) \\
&\mid Spotcheck_{i,j}\left(X_k, Eq\right) &&\mid Trust_{i,j}
\end{aligned}
$$

$$
\begin{aligned}
S &::= Pro \mid Att &&& Att &::= Attest_i\left(\{Eq\}\right) \\
Pro &::= Proof_i\left(\{P\}\right) &&& Eq &::= T_1 \; Rel \; T_2 \\
P &::= Att \mid Eq &&& Rel &::= \; = \mid < \mid > \mid \leq \mid \geq
\end{aligned}
$$

Subscripts i and j are component indexes and the notation $\{Z\}$ is used to define a set of terms of category Z. $Has_i(\tilde{X})$ expresses the fact that variable $\tilde{X}$ is an input variable located at component C_i (e.g. sensor or meter) and $Receive_{i,j}(\{S\}, \{\tilde{X}\})$ specifies that component C_i can receive from component C_j messages consisting of a set of statements $\{S\}$ and a set of variables $\{\tilde{X}\}$. A statement can be either a proof of a set of properties P (denoted by $Proof_i(\{P\})$) or an attestation (denoted by $Attest_i(\{Eq\})$), that is to say a simple declaration by a component C_i that properties Eq are true. A component can also compute a variable defined by an equation $\tilde{X} = T$ (denoted by $Compute_i(\tilde{X} = T)$), check that a set of properties Eq holds (denoted by $Check_i(\{Eq\})$), verify a proof of a property Pro received from another component (denoted by $Verif_i^{Proof}(Pro)$), verify the origin of an attestation (denoted by $Verif_i^{Attest}(Att)$), or perform a spotcheck. A spotcheck, which is denoted by $Spotcheck_{i,j}(X_k, Eq)$, is the request from a component C_j of a value X_k taken from array X and the verification that this value satisfies property Eq. Primitive properties Eq are simple equations on terms T. Last but not least, trust assumptions are expressed using $Trust_{i,j}$ (meaning that component C_i trusts component C_j). In the sequel, we use Γ to denote the set of architectures following the syntax of Table 2. Architectures can also be defined using graphical representations. As an illustration, Figure 1 displays a simple architecture involving a meter M and the central server of a provider P. The meter plays both the role of a sensor providing the input consumption values ($Has_M(Cons)$) and the role of a secure element computing the fee. Because the provider trusts the meter ($Trust_{P,M}$), it merely checks the certificate $Attest_M(\{Fee = \odot + (y), y_t = F(x_t), x_t = S(Cons_t)\})$ sent by the meter.

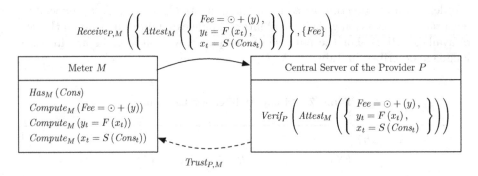

Fig. 1. Example of smart metering architecture

Strictly speaking, we should introduce a notion of actor and a relationship between actors and the components that are under their control but, for the sake of brevity (and without loss of generality[6]), we do not distinguish between components and actors here.

Architectures provide an abstract, high-level view of a system: for example, we do not express at this level the particular method (for example, a zero-knowledge proof protocol) used by a component to build a proof ($Proof_i(\{P\})$) or to verify it, or to check that another component has actually certified (attested) a property ($Verif_i^{Attest}(Att)$). Another main departure from protocol specification languages is that we do not have any specific ordering or notion of sequentiality here, even though functional dependencies introduce implicit constraints in the events of the system, as discussed below. The objective is to express and reason about the main design choices rather than to cover all the development steps.

---

[6] The fact that an actor controls several components can be expressed through a trust relationship.

2.2   Privacy Architectures Semantics

The definition of the semantics of an architecture is based on its set of compatible traces. A trace is a sequence of high-level events occurring in the system as presented in Table 3. Events can be seen as instantiated relations of the architecture. For example, a $Receive_{i,j}\left(\{S\},\{\tilde{X}:V\}\right)$ event specifies the values V of the variables $\tilde{X}$ received by C_i. Similarly, $Spotcheck_{i,j}\left(X_{Ck}:V,\{Eq\}\right)$ specifies the specific index Ck (member of $\mathbb{N}$) chosen by C_i for the spotcheck and the value V of X_{Ck}. All variable indexes occurring in events, except for variables occurring in the properties of $Receive_{i,j}$, $Verif_i^{Proof}$, $Verif_i^{Attest}$, and $Spotcheck_{i,j}$, must belong to $\mathbb{N}$.

Table 3. Events and traces

$$\theta ::= Seq(\epsilon)$$
$$\epsilon ::= Has_i\left(\tilde{X}:V\right) \qquad \mid Receive_{i,j}\left(\{S\},\{\tilde{X}:V\}\right)$$
$$\mid Compute_i\left(\tilde{X}=T\right) \quad \mid Check_i\left(\{Eq\}\right)$$
$$\mid Verif_i^{Proof}(Pro) \qquad \mid Verif_i^{Attest}(Att)$$
$$\mid Spotcheck_{i,j}\left(X_{Ck}:V,\{Eq\}\right)$$

In the following, we consider only consistent architectures and consistent traces. An architecture is said to be consistent if each variable can be computed (or can be initially possessed, as expressed by Has_i) by a single component, a component cannot receive a variable from different sources, a component computing a variable or checking a property can receive or compute all the necessary input variables (variables occuring in T for $Compute_i(\tilde{X}=T)$, in Eq for $Check_i(Eq)$), a component can only verify properties that it can receive from another component, etc. The same kind of consistency assumptions apply to traces, in addition to ordering consistency properties (variables and properties are not used before being received or computed).

We use *Event* to denote the set of events ϵ and *Trace* to denote the set of consistent traces θ.

Definition 1 (Compatibility). *A trace θ of length $\overline{\theta}$ is compatible with an architecture A if and only if:*

$$\forall a \in [1,\overline{\theta}], \ if \ \theta_a \neq Compute_i\left(\tilde{X}=T\right) \ then \ \exists \alpha \in A, \mathcal{C}(\theta_a, \alpha) \ and$$
$$if \ \theta_a = Spotcheck_{i,j}\left(X_{Ck}:V,\{Eq\}\right)$$
$$then \ \forall b \in [1,\overline{\theta}], b \neq a \Rightarrow \forall k', V', Eq',$$
$$\theta_b \neq Spotcheck_{i,j}\left(X_{k'}:V',\{Eq'\}\right)$$

where $\mathcal{C}(\epsilon, \alpha)$ holds if and only if ϵ can be obtained from α by adding specific values V for variables and instantiating index variables to integer values.

The first condition in the definition of compatibility states that, except for compute events, only events which are instantiations of components of the architecture A can appear in the trace θ. The rationale for excepting compute events is the need to express the potential actions of a curious agent trying to derive the value of a variable $\tilde{X}$ from the values of variables that he already has. As a result, compatible traces may include computations that are not contemplated by the architecture, provided that the component possesses all the variables necessary to perform this computation (consistency assumption). The adversary model considered here includes computation of new variables, erroneous computations, and communication of incorrect values, which corresponds to Dolev-Yao attacks for internal stakeholders (except they cannot break the protocol). The second condition expresses the fact that spotchecks can be performed only once. This condition could be relaxed through the introduction of an additional threshold parameter t to express the fact that up to t spotchecks are possible. We denote by $T(A)$ the set of compatible traces of an architecture A.

In order to define the semantics of events, we introduce first the notion of state of a component:

$$State = (State_V \times State_P \times State_P) \cup \{Error\}$$
$$State_V = (Var \to Val_\perp)$$
$$State_P = \{\{Eq\} \cup \{Trust_{i,j}\}\}$$

The state of a component is either the error state $Error$ or a triple made of a variable state assigning a value (or the undefined value $\perp^7$) to each variable and two property states: the first one defines the set of properties known by the component and the second one the set of properties believed by the component (after a spotcheck). In the sequel, we use σ to denote the global state (state of the components $\langle C_1, \ldots, C_n \rangle$) defined on $State^n$. The initial state for an architecture A is denoted by $Init^A = \langle Init_1^A, \ldots, Init_n^A \rangle$ with:

$$\forall i \in [1, n], Init_i^A = (Empty, \{Trust_{i,j} \mid Trust_{i,j} \in A\}, \emptyset)$$

where $Empty$ denotes the empty variable state ($\forall X \in Var, Empty(X) = \perp$). The only information contained in the initial state is the trust properties specified by the architecture.

The semantics function S_T is defined in Table 4. It specifies the impact of a trace on the state of each component C_i. It is defined as an iteration through the trace with function S_E defining the impact of each type of event on the states of the components.

The notation $\epsilon.\theta$ is used to denote a trace whose first element is ϵ and the rest of the trace is θ. Each event modifies only the state of the component C_i. This modification is expressed as $\sigma[\sigma_i/(v, pk, pb)]$ (or $\sigma[\sigma_i/Error]$ in the case of the error state) that replaces the variable and property components of the state

---

[7] Please note that $\perp$ is used to denote undefined values, that is to say values which have not been set, as opposed to error values (e.g. division by zero or type errors). We do not consider computation error values here.

Table 4. Semantics of traces of events

$$S_T : Trace \times State^n \to State^n$$

$$S_E : Event \times State^n \to State^n$$

$$S_T (\langle\rangle, \sigma) = \sigma$$

$$S_T (\epsilon.\theta, \sigma) = S_T(\theta, S_E(\epsilon, \sigma))$$

$$S_E \left(Has_i \left(\tilde{X} : V\right), \sigma\right) = \sigma[\sigma_i/(\sigma_i^v[\tilde{X}/V], \sigma_i^{pk}, \sigma_i^{pb})]$$

$$S_E \left(Receive_{i,j} \left(\{S\}, \{\tilde{X} : V\}\right), \sigma\right) = \sigma[\sigma_i/(\sigma_i^v[\{\tilde{X}/V\}], \sigma_i^{pk}, \sigma_i^{pb})]$$

$$S_E \left(Compute_i \left(\tilde{X} = T\right), \sigma\right) = \sigma[\sigma_i/(\sigma_i^v[\tilde{X}/\varepsilon(T, \sigma_i^v)], \sigma_i^{pk} \cup \{\tilde{X} = T\}, \sigma_i^{pb})]$$

$$S_E \left(Check_i (E), \sigma\right) = \sigma[\sigma_i/(\sigma_i^v, \sigma_i^{pk} \cup E, \sigma_i^{pb})]$$

$$\text{if } \forall Eq \in E, \varepsilon(Eq, \sigma_i^v) = True$$

$$= \sigma[\sigma_i/Error] \text{ otherwise}$$

$$S_E \left(Verif_i^{Proof} \left(Proof_j(E)\right), \sigma\right) = \sigma[\sigma_i/(\sigma_i^v, \sigma_i^{pk} \cup \{Eq | Eq \in E \text{ or}$$

$$(Attest_{j'}(E') \in E \text{ and}$$

$$Eq \in E' \text{ and}$$

$$Trust_{i,j'} \in \sigma_i^{pk})\}, \sigma_i^{pb})]$$

$$\text{if } \overline{Verif}^{Proof}((E), \sigma_i^v) = True$$

$$= \sigma[\sigma_i/Error] \text{ otherwise}$$

$$S_E \left(Verif_i^{Attest} (Attest_j(E)), \sigma\right) = \sigma[\sigma_i/(\sigma_i^v, \sigma_i^{pk} \cup \{Eq | Eq \in E \text{ and}$$

$$Trust_{i,j} \in \sigma_i^{pk}\}, \sigma_i^{pb})]$$

$$\text{if } \overline{Verif}^{Attest}((E), \sigma_i^v) = True$$

$$= \sigma[\sigma_i/Error] \text{ otherwise}$$

$$S_E \left(Spotcheck_{i,j} (X_{Ck} : V, E), \sigma\right) = \sigma[\sigma_i/(\sigma_i^v[X_{Ck}/V], \sigma_i^{pk}, \sigma_i^{pb} \cup E)]$$

$$\text{if } \forall Eq \in E,$$

$$\varepsilon(Eq[k/Ck], \sigma_i^v[X_{Ck}/V]) = True$$

$$= \sigma[\sigma_i/Error] \text{ otherwise}$$

of C_i by v, pk, and pb respectively. We assume that no event $\theta_{a'}$ with $a' > a$ involves component C_i if its state σ_i is equal to $Error$ after the occurrence of θ_a (in other words, any error in the execution of a component causes this component to stop).

The effect of Has_i and $Receive_{i,j}$ on the variable state of component C_i is the replacement of the values of the variables $\tilde{X}$ by new values $V \in Val$, which is denoted by $\sigma_i^v[\tilde{X}/V]$.

The effect of $Compute_i(\tilde{X} = T)$ is to set the variable $\tilde{X}$ to the evaluation of the value of T in the current variable state σ_i^v of C_i, which is defined by $\varepsilon(T, \sigma_i^v)$. $Spotcheck_i(X_{Ck} : V, E)$ sets the value of X_{Ck} to V. The other events do not have any effect on the variable state of C_i. The value of a variable replaced after the occurrence of an event must be $\perp$ before its occurrence[8]. We assume that it is different from $\perp$ and does not involve any $\perp$) after the event[9].

Most events also have an effect on the property states. This effect is the addition to the property states of the new knowledge or belief provided by the event. For $Compute_i\,(\tilde{X} = T)$, this new knowledge is the equality $\tilde{X} = T$; for the $Check_i$, $Verif_i$, and $Spotcheck_{i,j}$ events, the new knowledge is the properties checked or verified. In all cases except for $Spotcheck_{i,j}$ these properties are added to the pk property state because they are known to be true by component C_i; in the case of $Spotcheck_{i,j}$ the properties are added to the pb property state because they are believed by C_i: they have been checked on a sample value X_{Ck} but might still be false for some other X_k. The only guarantee provided to C_i by $Spotcheck_{i,j}$ is that C_i has always the possibility to detect an error (but he has to choose an appropriate index, that is to say an index that will reveal the error).

Functions $\overline{Verif}^{Proof}$ and $\overline{Verif}^{Attest}$ define the semantics of the corresponding verification operations. As discussed above, we do not enter into the internals of the proof and attestation verifications here and just assume that only true properties are accepted by $\overline{Verif}^{Proof}$ and only attestations provided by the authentic sender are accepted by $\overline{Verif}^{Attest}$. The distinctive feature of $Verif_i^{Attest}$ events is that they generate new knowledge only if the author of the attestation can be trusted (hence the $Trust_{i,j} \in A$ condition).

Let us note also that $Receive_{i,j}$ events do not add any new knowledge by themselves because the received properties have to be verified before they can be added to the property states.

We can now define the semantics of an architecture A as the set of the possible states produced by compatible traces.

Definition 2 (Semantics of architectures.). *The semantics of an architecture A is defined as: $\mathcal{S}(A) = \{\sigma \in State^n \mid \exists \theta \in T(A), S_T(\theta, Init^A) = \sigma\}$.*

In the following, we use $\mathcal{S}_i(A)$ to denote the subset of $\mathcal{S}(A)$ containing only states which are well defined for component C_i: $\mathcal{S}_i(A) = \{\sigma \in \mathcal{S}(A) \mid \sigma_i \neq Error\}$. The prefix ordering on traces gives rise to the following ordering on states: $\forall \sigma \in \mathcal{S}_i(A), \forall \sigma' \in \mathcal{S}_i(A), \sigma \geq_i \sigma' \Leftrightarrow \exists \theta \in T(A), \exists \theta' \in T(A), \sigma = S_T(\theta, Init^A), \sigma' = S_T(\theta', Init^A)$, and θ' is a prefix of θ.

3   Privacy Logic

Because privacy is closely connected with the notion of knowledge, epistemic logics form an ideal basis to reason about privacy properties. Epistemic logics [12] are a family of modal logics using a knowledge modality usually denoted by

---

[8] Because we consider only consistent traces. A value different from $\perp$ would mean that the variable is computed or set more than once.

[9] In other words, input values and results of computations are fully defined.

$K_i(\psi)$ to denote the fact that agent i knows the property ψ. However standard epistemic logics based on possible worlds semantics suffer from a weakness which makes them unsuitable in the context of privacy: this problem is often referred to as "logical omniscience" [17]. It stems from the fact that agents know all the logical consequences of their knowledge (because these consequences hold in all possible worlds). An undesirable outcome of logical omniscience would be that, for example, an agent knowing the hash $H(v)$ of a value v would also know v. This is obviously not the intent in a formal model of privacy where hashes are precisely used to hide the original values to the recipients. This issue is related to the fact that standard epistemic logics do not account for limitations of computational power.

Therefore it is necessary to define dedicated epistemic logics to deal with different aspects of privacy and to model the variety of notions at hand (e.g. knowledge, zero-knowledge proof, trust, etc.). In this paper, we follow the "deductive algorithmic knowledge" approach [12,28] in which the explicit knowledge of a component C_i is defined as the knowledge that this component can actually compute using his own deductive system $\rhd_i$. The deductive relation $\rhd_i$ is defined here as a relation between a set of Eq and Eq properties: $\{Eq_1, \ldots, Eq_n\} \rhd_i Eq_0$. Typically, $\rhd_i$ can be used to capture properties of the functions of the specification. For example $\{h_1 = H(x_1), h_2 = H(x_2), h_1 = h_2\} \rhd_i (x_1 = x_2)$ expresses the injectivity property of a hash function H. Another relation, Dep_i, is introduced to express that a variable can be derived from other variables. $Dep_i\left(\tilde{X}, \{\tilde{X}^1, \ldots \tilde{X}^n\}\right)$ means that a value for $\tilde{X}$ can be obtained by C_i $(\exists F, \tilde{X} = F(\tilde{X}^1, \ldots, \tilde{X}^n))$. The absence of a relation such as $Dep_i(x_k, \{y_k\})$ prevents component C_i from deriving the value of x_k from the value of y_k, capturing the hiding property of the hash application $y_k = H(x_k)$.

Table 5. Architecture logic

$$\phi ::= Has_i^{all}\left(\tilde{X}\right) \mid Has_i^{none}\left(\tilde{X}\right) \mid Has_i^{one}\left(\tilde{X}\right)$$
$$\mid K_i\left(Eq\right) \quad \mid B_i\left(Eq\right) \quad \mid \phi_1 \wedge \phi_2$$
$$Eq ::= T_1 \; Rel \; T_2 \mid Eq_1 \wedge Eq_2$$

This logic involves two modalities, denoted by K_i and B_i, which represent respectively knowledge and belief properties of a component C_i. Please note that the Eq notation (already used in the language of architectures) is overloaded, without ambiguity: it is used to denote conjunctions (rather than sets) of primitive relations in the logic. The logic can be used to express useful properties of architectures: for example $Has_i^{all}(\tilde{X})$ expresses the fact that component C_i can obtain or derive (using its deductive system $\rhd_i$) the value of $\tilde{X}_k$ for all k in $Range(X)$. $Has_i^{one}(\tilde{X})$ expresses the fact that component C_i can obtain or derive the value of X_k for at most one k in $Range(X)$. Finally, $Has_i^{none}(\tilde{X})$ is the privacy property stating that C_i does not know any X_k value. It should be noted that Has_i properties only inform on the fact that C_i can get or derive some values for the variables but they do not bring any guarantee about the correctness of these values. Such guarantees can only be ensured through integrity requirements, expressed using the $K_i(Eq)$ and $B_i(Eq)$ properties. $K_i(Eq)$ means that component C_i can establish the truthfulness of Eq while $B_i(Eq)$ expresses the fact that C_i may test this truthfulness, and therefore detect its falsehood or believe that the property is true otherwise.

We can now define the semantics of a property ϕ.

Definition 3 (Semantics of properties). *The semantics $S(\phi)$ of a property ϕ is defined in Table 6 as the set of architectures meeting ϕ.*

Table 6. Semantics of properties

$$A \in S\left(Has_i^{all}\left(\tilde{X}\right)\right) \Leftrightarrow \exists \sigma \in \mathcal{S}(A), \sigma_i^v(\tilde{X}) \text{ does not contain any } \bot$$

$$A \in S\left(Has_i^{none}\left(\tilde{X}\right)\right) \Leftrightarrow \forall \sigma \in \mathcal{S}(A), \sigma_i^v(\tilde{X}) = \bot$$

$$A \in S\left(Has_i^{one}\left(\tilde{X}\right)\right) \Leftrightarrow \forall \sigma \in \mathcal{S}(A), \sigma_i^v(\tilde{X}) = \bot \vee (\sigma_i^v(\tilde{X}) = \; < v_1, \dots, v_k > \wedge$$
$$\nexists(u, u'), u \neq u' \wedge v_u \neq \bot \wedge$$
$$v_{u'} \neq \bot)$$

$$A \in S(K_i(Eq)) \Leftrightarrow \forall \sigma' \in \mathcal{S}_i(A), \exists \sigma \in \mathcal{S}_i(A), \exists Eq', (\sigma \geq_i \sigma') \wedge (\sigma_i^{pk} \rhd_i Eq') \wedge$$
$$(Eq' \Rightarrow Eq)$$

$$A \in S(B_i(Eq)) \Leftrightarrow \forall \sigma' \in \mathcal{S}_i(A), \exists \sigma \in \mathcal{S}_i(A), \exists Eq'_1, \exists Eq'_2, (\sigma \geq_i \sigma') \wedge$$
$$(\sigma_i^{pb} \rhd_i Eq'_1) \wedge (\sigma_i^{pk} \rhd_i Eq'_2) \wedge$$
$$((Eq'_1 \wedge Eq'_2) \Rightarrow Eq)$$

$$A \in S(\phi_1 \wedge \phi_2) \Leftrightarrow A \in S(\phi_1) \wedge A \in S(\phi_2)$$

An architecture satisfies the $Has_i^{all}(\tilde{X})$ property if and only if C_i may obtain the full value of $\tilde{X}$ in at least one compatible execution trace whereas $Has_i^{none}(\tilde{X})$ holds if and only if no execution trace can lead to a state in which C_i gets a value of $\tilde{X}$ (or of any part of its content if $\tilde{X}$ is an array variable). $Has_i^{one}(\tilde{X})$ is true if and only if no execution trace can lead to a state in which C_i knows more than one of the values of the array $\tilde{X}$. The validity of $K_i(Eq)$ and $B_i(Eq)$ properties is defined with respect to correct execution traces (with respect to C_i) since an incorrect trace leads to a state in which an error has been detected by the component[10]. The condition $\sigma \geq \sigma'$ is used to discard states corresponding to incomplete traces in which the property Eq has not yet been established. As discussed above, the capacity for a component C_i to derive new knowledge or beliefs is defined by its deductive system $\rhd_i$.

In order to reason about architectures and the knowledge of the components, we introduce in Table 7 an axiomatisation of the logic presented in the previous section. The fact that an architecture A satisfies a property ϕ is denoted

---

[10] This is a usual implicit assumption in protocol verification.

Table 7. Axiomatics

$$\text{H1}\,\frac{Has_i\left(\tilde{X}\right)\in A}{A\vdash Has_i^{all}\left(\tilde{X}\right)}\qquad \text{H2}\,\frac{Receive_{i,j}\left(S,E\right)\in A\quad \tilde{X}\in\{E\}}{A\vdash Has_i^{all}\left(\tilde{X}\right)}$$

$$\text{H3}\,\frac{Compute_i\left(\tilde{X}=T\right)\in A}{A\vdash Has_i^{all}\left(\tilde{X}\right)}\qquad \text{H4}\,\frac{Spotcheck_{i,j}\left(X_k,E\right)\in A}{A\vdash Has_i^{one}\left(X\right)}$$

$$\text{H5}\,\frac{Dep_i\left(\tilde{X},\{\tilde{X}^1,\dots\tilde{X}^n\}\right)\quad \text{for all }l\in[1,n],A\vdash Has_i^{all}\left(\tilde{X}^l\right)}{A\vdash Has_i^{all}\left(\tilde{X}\right)}$$

$$\text{H6}\,\frac{\text{None of the pre-conditions of H1, H2, H3, H4, or H5 holds for }X\text{ or any }X_k}{A\vdash Has_i^{none}\left(\tilde{X}\right)}$$

$$\text{H7}\,\frac{A\vdash Has_i^{all}\left(\tilde{X}\right)}{A\vdash Has_i^{all}\left(X_k\right)}\text{ for all }k\in Range(X)\qquad \text{HNO}\,\frac{A\vdash Has_i^{none}\left(\tilde{X}\right)}{A\vdash Has_i^{one}\left(\tilde{X}\right)}$$

$$\text{H8}\,\frac{A\vdash Has_i^{none}\left(\tilde{X}\right)}{A\vdash Has_i^{none}\left(X_k\right)}\text{ for all }k\in Range(X)\qquad \text{K1}\,\frac{Compute_i\left(\tilde{X}=T\right)\in A}{A\vdash K_i(\tilde{X}=T)}$$

$$\text{K3}\,\frac{Verif_i^{Proof}\left(Proof_j(E)\right)\in A\quad Eq\in E}{A\vdash K_i(Eq)}\qquad \text{K2}\,\frac{Check_i\left(E\right)\in A\quad Eq\in E}{A\vdash K_i(Eq)}$$

$$\text{K4}\,\frac{Verif_i^{Proof}\left(Proof_j(E)\right)\in A\quad Attest_k(E')\in E\quad Trust_{i,k}\in A\quad Eq\in E'}{A\vdash K_i(Eq)}$$

$$\text{K5}\,\frac{Verif_i^{Attest}\left(Attest_j(E)\right)\in A\quad Trust_{i,j}\in A\quad Eq\in E}{A\vdash K_i(Eq)}\qquad \text{KB}\,\frac{A\vdash K_i(Eq)}{A\vdash B_i(Eq)}$$

$$\text{K}\wedge\,\frac{A\vdash K_i(Eq_1)\quad A\vdash K_i(Eq_2)}{A\vdash K_i(Eq_1\wedge Eq_2)}\qquad \text{B}\,\frac{Spotcheck_{i,j}\left(X_k,E\right)\in A\quad Eq\in E}{A\vdash B_i(Eq)}$$

$$\text{K}\triangleright\,\frac{E\triangleright_i Eq_0\quad \text{for all }Eq\in E,A\vdash K_i(Eq)}{A\vdash K_i(Eq_0)}\qquad \text{I}\wedge\,\frac{A\vdash\phi_1\quad A\vdash\phi_2}{A\vdash\phi_1\wedge\phi_2}$$

$$\text{B}\wedge\,\frac{A\vdash B_i(Eq_1)\quad A\vdash B_i(Eq_2)}{A\vdash B_i(Eq_1\wedge Eq_2)}\qquad \text{B}\triangleright\,\frac{E\triangleright_i Eq_0\quad \text{for all }Eq\in E,A\vdash B_i(Eq)}{A\vdash B_i(Eq_0)}$$

by $A\vdash\phi$. Axioms (H1-8) and (HNO) are related to properties Has_i while axioms (K1-5) and (K$\wedge$) are related to the knowledge of the components. Axioms (B), (KB), and (B$\wedge$) handle the belief case. Finally, the remaining axioms are structural axioms dealing with the conjunctive operator.

The axiomatics meets the following soundness, completeness, and decidability properties.

Property 1 (Soundness). *For all A in Γ, if $A\vdash\phi$ then $A\in S(\phi)$.*

The soundness property can be proved by considering each rule in Table 7 in turn and showing that the traces specified in Table 6 have the expected properties (or that appropriate traces can be found in the case of Has_i^{all}).

Property 2 (Completeness). *For all A in Γ, if $A \in S(\phi)$ then $A \vdash \phi$.*

Completeness can be proved by systematic inspection of the different cases in Table 4 that can make a property ϕ true in the trace semantics.

Property 3 (Decidability). *If the deductive systems $\triangleright_i$ are decidable, then the axiomatics is decidable.*

The intuition is that proofs can be stratified into proofs of Has_i^{all}, Has_i^{none}, Has_i^{one}, K_i, and B_i successively, with proofs of properties not involving the deductive systems of the components first and those involving the deductive systems of the components as the last step.

4   Smart Meter Case Study

One of the services provided by smart metering systems is the periodic billing of an amount *Fee* based on the customers consumption $Cons_t$ for periods of time t. The service $Fee = \sum_t (F(S(Cons_t)))$ (where F and S stand for pricing and metering) is expressed as $\Omega = \{Fee = \odot + (y), y_t = F(x_t), x_t = S(Cons_t)\}$. We provide the details for the provider only here but a similar approach could be used for customers or other parties.

Architecture Goals. The architecture should enable the provider P to get access to the global fee: $A \vdash Has_P^{all}(Fee)$. However, he should not be able to get access to the individual consumptions $Cons_t$ or to the intermediate variables x and y since they are the results of easily inversible functions (typically F is a mapping and S the identity): $A \vdash Has_P^{none}(Cons) \wedge Has_P^{none}(x) \wedge Has_P^{none}(y)$. Moreover, he should be convinced that the value provided for *Fee* is actually correct: $A \vdash K_P(Fee = \odot + (y) \wedge y_t = F(x_t) \wedge x_t = S(Cons_t))$.

Architecture Design. The design of an architecture meeting the above goals is described Figure 1. A strong constraint concerning the metering has to be taken into account from the start: regulators generally require the data to be metered by officially certified and tamper-resistant metrological devices M: $Has_M(Cons)$, $Compute_M(x_t = S(Cons_t))$, and $Attest_M(x_t = S(Cons_t))$.

One option for the computation of the fee is to have it performed by the meter: $Compute_M(Fee = \odot + (y))$ and $Compute_M(y_t = F(x_t))$. The result of this computation can then be sent to the provider along with the corresponding attestation and the metering attestation through a $Receive_{P,M}(\{Att\}, \{Fee\})$ primitive. Another architectural primitive $Verif_P^{Attest}(Att)$ should be added to convince the provider of the correctness of the computation (considering that the provider trusts the meter $Trust_{P,M}$).

Finally, the dependance relations have to be defined to model the computational power of the components P and M (they both have the same here for the sake of simplicity, noted Dep_i for $i \in \{P, M\}$). The relations are such that

$(Fee, \{y_t\}) \in Dep_i$, $(y_t, \{x_t\}) \in Dep_i$, $(x_t, \{y_t\}) \in Dep_i$, $(x_t, \{Const_t\}) \in Dep_i$, and $(Const_t, \{x_t\}) \in Dep_i$ (only the summation is not inversible here and we have $(y_t, \{Fee\}) \notin Dep_i$).

Application of the Axiomatics. Rules (H2) and (H6) allow us to prove respectively that the provider gets a value for the global fee since it receives it from the meter and that the consumption and the values of the intermediate variables x and y are not disclosed. Applications of rules (K5) and (K$\wedge$) prove that the correctness of the global fee is ensured thanks to the attestations and the trust relation between the provider and the meter. As expected, (H2) and (H3) prove that the meter has an access to the consumption data.

The solution chosen here for the sake of conciseness describes heavy meters performing the billing computations (which is generally not the case). Moreover, there is a direct link between the meter and the provider: the customer has to trust the meter not to disclose too much data to the provider. This issue could be solved by adding a proxy under the control of the customer which would filter the communications between the provider and the meter. Other options for smart metering such as [29] can be expressed in the same framework but space considerations prevent us from presenting them here.

5   Related Work

This paper stands at the crossroads of three different areas: engineering privacy by design, software architectures and protocols, and epistemic logics.

Several authors [16,19,22,26,32] have already pointed out the complexity of "privacy engineering" as well as the "richness of the data space"[16] calling for the development of more general and systematic methodologies for privacy by design. As far as privacy mechanisms are concerned, [19,23] points out the complexity of their implementation and the large number of options that designers have to face. To address this issue and favor the adoption of these tools, [19] proposes a number of guidelines for the design of compilers for secure computation and zero-knowledge proofs whereas [13] provides a language and a compiler to perform computations on private data by synthesising zero-knowledge protocols. In a different context (designing information systems for the cloud), [24] also proposes implementation techniques to make it easier for developers to take into account privacy and security requirements.

Software architectures have been an active research topic for several decades [31] but they are usually defined using purely graphical, informal means or within semi-formal frameworks. Dedicated languages have been proposed to specify privacy properties [3,5,21,34] but the policies expressed in these languages are usually more fine-grained than the properties considered here because they are not intended to be used at the architectural level. Similarly, process calculi such as the applied π-calculus [30] have been applied to define privacy protocols [8]. Because process calculi are general frameworks to model concurrent systems, they are more powerful than dedicated frameworks. The downside is that protocols in these languages are expressed at a lower level and the tasks of specifying a protocol and its expected properties are more complex [25,27,6]. Again, the main departure of the approach advocated in this paper with respect to this trend of work is that we reason at the level of architectures, providing ways to express properties without entering into the details of specific protocols that we assume perfect. The work presented here is a follow-up of [1] which advocates an approach based on formal models of privacy architectures. The framework introduced in [22] includes an inference system to reason about the implementation of a "detectability property" similar to the integrity property considered here. This framework makes it possible to prove that, in a given architecture, an actor "A" can detect potential errors (or frauds) in the computation of a variable "X". The logical framework presented here can be seen as a generalisation of [22] which does not include a logic for defining privacy and integrity properties.

Epistemic logics have been extensively studied [12]. A difficulty in this kind of framework in a context where hiding functions are used is the problem known as "logical omniscience". Several ways to solve this difficulty have been proposed [28,17,7]. Other works such as [15] also rely on deontic logics and focus on the expression of policies and how they relate to database security or distributed systems.

6   Directions for Further Work

The framework presented in this paper can be used to express in a formal way the main architectural choices in the design of a system and to reason about them. It also makes it possible to compare different options, based on the properties that they comply with, which is of prime importance when privacy requirements have to be reconciled with other, apparently conflicting requirements.

As stated above, the framework described here does not cover the full development cycle: ongoing work addresses the mapping from the architecture level to the protocol level to ensure that a given implementation, abstracted as an applied π-calculus protocol [30], is consistent with an architecture. Work is also ongoing to integrate this formal framework into a more user-friendly, graphical, design environment integrating a pre-defined design strategy. This strategy, which is implemented as a succession of question-answer iterations, allows the designer to find his way among all possible design options based on key decision factors such as the trust assumptions between entities. The resulting architectures can then be checked using the formal framework described here.

In this paper, we have focused on data minimisation and it should be clear that the framework presented here does not address other privacy requirements such as the purpose limitation or the deletion obligation. Indeed, privacy is a multi-faceted notion that cannot be entirely captured within a single formal framework. Another limitation of the approach is that it must be possible to define the service (or "purpose") as the result of a functional expression (e.g. the computation of a fee in electronic toll pricing or smart metering). Thus the approach does not help in situations such as social networks where the service is just the display of the data (and its access based on a given privacy policy). Last but not least, in this paper, follow a "logical" (or qualitative) approach, as opposed to a quantitative approach to privacy and we do not consider the use of auxiliary information. An avenue for further research in this area would be to study the integration of quantitative measures of privacy (such as differential privacy [10]) into the framework.

Acknowledgement. This work was partially funded by the European project PRIPARE/FP7-ICT-2013-1.5, the ANR project BIOPRIV, and the Inria Project Lab CAPPRIS.

References

1. Antignac, T., Le Métayer, D.: Privacy by design: From technologies to architectures. In: Preneel, B., Ikonomou, D. (eds.) APF 2014. LNCS, vol. 8450, pp. 1–17. Springer, Heidelberg (2014)
2. Balasch, J., Rial, A., Troncoso, C., Geuens, C.: PrETP: Privacy-Preserving electronic toll pricing. In: Proc. of the 19th USENIX Security Symp., USA, pp. 63–78 (2010)
3. Barth, A., Datta, A., Mitchell, J., Nissenbaum, H.: Privacy and contextual integrity: framework and applications. In: 2006 IEEE Symposium on Security and Privacy, pp. 15–198 (2006)
4. Bass, L., Clements, P., Kazman, R.: Software Architecture in Practice, 3rd edn. SEI series in Software Engineering. Addison-Wesley (2012)
5. Becker, M.Y., Malkis, A., Bussard, L.: A Practical Generic Privacy Language. In: Jha, S., Mathuria, A. (eds.) ICISS 2010. LNCS, vol. 6503, pp. 125–139. Springer, Heidelberg (2010)
6. Burrows, M., Abadi, M., Needham, R.: A logic of authentication. ACM Trans. Comput. Syst. 8, 18–36 (1990)
7. Cohen, M., Dam, M.: A complete axiomatization of knowledge and cryptography. In: 22nd Annual IEEE Symp. on Logic in Comp. Science, pp. 77–88 (2007)
8. Delaune, S., Kremer, S., Ryan, M.: Verifying privacy-type properties of electronic voting protocols: A taster. In: Chaum, D., Jakobsson, M., Rivest, R.L., Ryan, P.Y.A., Benaloh, J., Kutylowski, M., Adida, B. (eds.) Towards Trustworthy Elections. LNCS, vol. 6000, pp. 289–309. Springer, Heidelberg (2010)
9. Diaz, C., Kosta, E., Dekeyser, H., Kohlweiss, M., Girma, N.: Privacy preserving electronic petitions. Identity in the Information Society 1(1), 203–209 (2009)
10. Dwork, C.: Differential privacy. In: Bugliesi, M., Preneel, B., Sassone, V., Wegener, I. (eds.) ICALP 2006. LNCS, vol. 4052, pp. 1–12. Springer, Heidelberg (2006)
11. European Parliament: European parliament legislative resolution of 12 march 2014 on the proposal for a regulation of the european parliament and of the council on the protection of individuals with regard to the processing of personal data and on the free movement of such data. General Data Protection Regulation, Ordinary legislative procedure: first reading (March 2014)
12. Fagin, R., Halpern, J.Y., Moses, Y., Vardi, M.: Reasoning About Knowledge. MIT Press (2004)
13. Fournet, C., Kohlweiss, M., Danezis, G., Luo, Z.: Zql: A compiler for privacy-preserving data processing. In: Proc. of the 22Nd USENIX Conference on Security, USA, pp. 163–178 (2013)

14. Garcia, F.D., Jacobs, B.: Privacy-friendly energy-metering via homomorphic encryption. In: Cuellar, J., Lopez, J., Barthe, G., Pretschner, A. (eds.) STM 2010. LNCS, vol. 6710, pp. 226–238. Springer, Heidelberg (2011)
15. Glasgow, J., MacEwen, G., Panangaden, P.: A logic for reasoning about security. In: Proc. of the 3rd Computer Security Foundations Workshop, pp. 2–13 (1990)
16. Gürses, S., Troncoso, C., Diaz, C.: Engineering Privacy by Design. Presented at the Computers, Privacy & Data Protection Conf. (2011)
17. Halpern, J.Y., Pucella, R.: Dealing with logical omniscience. In: Proc. of the 11th Conf. on Th. Aspects of Rationality and Knowl., pp. 169–176. ACM, USA (2007)
18. de Jonge, W., Jacobs, B.: Privacy-Friendly electronic traffic pricing via commits. In: Degano, P., Guttman, J., Martinelli, F. (eds.) FAST 2008. LNCS, vol. 5491, pp. 143–161. Springer, Heidelberg (2009)
19. Kerschbaum, F.: Privacy-preserving computation. In: Preneel, B., Ikonomou, D. (eds.) APF 2012. LNCS, vol. 8319, pp. 41–54. Springer, Heidelberg (2014)
20. Krumm, J.: A survey of computational location privacy. Personal and Ubiquitous Computing 13(6), 391–399 (2009)
21. Le Métayer, D.: A Formal Privacy Management Framework. In: Degano, P., Guttman, J., Martinelli, F. (eds.) FAST 2008. LNCS, vol. 5491, pp. 162–176. Springer, Heidelberg (2009)
22. Le Métayer, D.: Privacy by design: A formal framework for the analysis of architectural choices. In: Proc. of the 3rd ACM Conference on Data and Application Security and Privacy, pp. 95–104. ACM, USA (2013)
23. Maffei, M., Pecina, K., Reinert, M.: Security and privacy by declarative design. In: IEEE 26th Computer Security Foundations Symposium, pp. 81–96 (2013)
24. Manousakis, V., Kalloniatis, C., Kavakli, E., Gritzalis, S.: Privacy in the cloud: Bridging the gap between design and implementation. In: Franch, X., Soffer, P. (eds.) CAiSE Workshops 2013. LNBIP, vol. 148, pp. 455–465. Springer, Heidelberg (2013)
25. Meadows, C.: Formal methods for cryptographic protocol analysis: emerging issues and trends. IEEE Journal on Selected Areas in Comm. 21(1), 44–54 (2003)
26. Mulligan, D.K., King, J.: Bridging the gap between privacy and design. University of Pennsylvania Journal of Constitutional Law 14(4), 989–1034 (2012)
27. Paulson, L.C.: The inductive approach to verifying cryptographic protocols. Journal of Computer Security 6(1-2), 85–128 (1998)
28. Pucella, R.: Deductive algorithmic knowledge. CoRR cs.AI/0405038 (2004)
29. Rial, A., Danezis, G.: Privacy-Preserving smart metering. Technical report MSR-TR-2010-150, Microsoft Research (2010)
30. Ryan, M.D., Smyth, B.: Applied pi calculus. In: Formal Models and Techniques for Analyzing Security Protocols. Cryptology and Information Security Series, vol. 5, pp. 112–142. IOS Press (2011)
31. Shaw, M., Clements, P.: The golden age of software architecture. IEEE Softw. 23(2), 31–39 (2006)
32. Spiekermann, S., Cranor, L.F.: Engineering privacy. IEEE Transactions on Software Engineering 35(1), 67–82 (2009)
33. Tschantz, M.C., Wing, J.M.: Formal methods for privacy. In: Cavalcanti, A., Dams, D.R. (eds.) FM 2009. LNCS, vol. 5850, pp. 1–15. Springer, Heidelberg (2009)
34. Yu, T., Li, N., Antón, A.I.: A formal semantics for P3P. In: Proc. of the 2004 Workshop on Secure Web Service, SWS 2004, pp. 1–8. ACM, USA (2004)

Monotonicity and Completeness
in Attribute-Based Access Control*

Jason Crampton[1] and Charles Morisset[2]

[1] Royal Holloway, University of London
`Jason.Crampton@rhul.ac.uk`
[2] Newcastle University
`Charles.Morisset@ncl.ac.uk`

Abstract. There have been many proposals for access control models
and authorization policy languages, which are used to inform the design of access control systems. Most, if not all, of these proposals impose
restrictions on the implementation of access control systems, thereby
limiting the type of authorization requests that can be processed or the
structure of the authorization policies that can be specified. In this paper,
we develop a formal characterization of the features of an access control
model that imposes few restrictions of this nature. Our characterization
is intended to be a generic framework for access control, from which
we may derive access control models and reason about the properties of
those models. In this paper, we consider the properties of monotonicity
and completeness, the first being particularly important for attribute-
based access control systems. XACML, an XML-based language and architecture for attribute-based access control, is neither monotonic nor
complete. Using our framework, we define attribute-based access control
models, in the style of XACML, that are, respectively, monotonic and
complete.

1 Introduction

One of the fundamental security services in modern computer systems is *access
control*, a mechanism for constraining the interaction between (authenticated)
users and protected resources. Generally, access control is enforced by a trusted
component (historically known as the *reference monitor*), which typically implements two functions: an *authorization enforcement function* (AEF) and an
authorization decision function (ADF). The AEF traps all attempts by a user to
interact with a resource (usually known as a *user request*) and transforms that
request into one or more *authorization queries* (also known as *authorization
requests*) which are forwarded to the ADF.

---

* This work was partially supported by the EPSRC/GCHQ funded project ChAISe
(EP/K006568/1) and the project "Data-Driven Model-Based Decision-Making",
part of the NSA funded Centre on Science of Security at University of Illinois at
Urbana-Champaign.

S. Mauw and C.D. Jensen (Eds.): STM 2014, LNCS 8743, pp. 33–48, 2014.

Most access control systems are policy-based. That is, an administrator specifies an authorization policy, which, in its simplest form, encodes those authorization requests that are authorized. The ADF takes an authorization query and an authorization policy as input and returns an authorization decision. For this reason, it is common to refer to the AEF and ADF as the *policy enforcement point* (PEP) and *policy decision point* (PDP), respectively; it is this terminology that we will use henceforth.

An authorization policy is merely an encoding of the access control requirements of an application using the authorization language that is understood by the PDP. It is necessary, therefore, to make a distinction between an *ideal policy* and a *realizable policy*: the former is an arbitrary function from requests to decisions; the latter is a function that can be evaluated by the PDP. Given a particular policy language, there might be some ideal policies that are not realizable, which may be a limitation of the policy language in practice. The access control system used in early versions of Unix, for example, is rather limited [1, §15.1.1]. An important consideration, therefore, when designing an access control system is the *expressivity* of the policy language.

The increasing prevalence of open, distributed, computing environments means that we may not be able to rely on a centralized authentication function to identify authorized users. This means that authorization decisions have to be made on the basis of (authenticated) user attributes (rather than user identities). In turn, this means that the structure of authorization queries needs to be rather more flexible than that used in closed, centralized environments. The draft XACML 3.0 standard, for example, uses a much "looser" query format than its predecessor XACML 2.0. However, if we have no control over the attributes that are presented to the PDP, then a malicious user (or a user who wishes to preserve the secrecy of some attributes) may be able to generate authorization decisions that are more "favorable" by withholding attributes from the PEP [2, 3]. A second important consideration, therefore, is whether authorization policies are guaranteed to be "monotonic" in the sense that providing fewer attributes in an authorization query yields a less favorable outcome (from the requester's perspective).

There is an extensive literature on languages for specifying authorization policies, most approaches proposing a new language or an extension of an existing one. The proliferation of languages led Ferraiolo and Atluri to raise the question in [4] of whether a *meta-model* for access control was needed and possible to achieve, hinting at XACML [5] and RBAC [6] as potential candidates. In response, Barker proposed a meta-model [7], which sought to identify the key components required to specify access control policies, based on a term-rewriting evaluation.

In this paper, we do not present "yet another language" for access control policies, nor do we claim to have a "unifying meta-model". We focus instead on reasoning about the properties of a language. Indeed, we advocate the idea that a language is just a tool for policy designers: just as some programming languages are better suited to particular applications, it seems unlikely that there exists a single access control model (or meta-model) that is ideal in all possible contexts. On the contrary, we believe that providing the structure to formally analyse a language might be valuable to a policy designer, in order to understand the suitability of a particular language as the basis for a specific access control system.

We conclude this section by summarizing the structure and contributions of the paper. In Sec. 2 we propose a general framework for access control, whose role is not to be used as an off-the-shelf language, but as a way to identify and reason about the key aspects of a language. In Sec. 3 we define monotonicity and completeness in the context of our framework. Then in Sec. 4 we define two attribute-based models, respectively monotonic and complete, by building on existing results from the literature on multi-valued and partial logic. The main body of the paper ends with discussions of related and future work. Results are stated without proofs; the on-line version of the paper [8] includes the proofs.

2   A Framework for Defining Access Control Models

In this section we describe the various components of our framework and introduce our formal definition of access control models and policies. Broadly speaking, we provide a generic method for designing access control models and for furnishing access control policies, which are written in the context of a model, with authorization semantics. We also introduce the notion of an ideal policy, which is an abstraction of the requirements of an organization, and relate this concept to that of an access control policy.

2.1   An Informal Overview

From an external viewpoint, an access control mechanism is a process that constrains the interactions between users and data objects. Those interactions are modeled as access requests, with the mechanism incorporating two functions: one to determine whether a request is authorized or not and one to enforce that decision. The overall process must be total, in the sense that its behavior is defined for *every* possible interaction (which may include some default behavior that is triggered when the decision function is unable to return a decision). In general, designing a particular access control mechanism for a particular set of requests is the final concrete objective of any access control framework (although we are also clearly interested in expressing general properties of the framework).

We define an access control mechanism using an *access control policy*, together with an *interpretation function* which provides the authorization semantics for a policy. Intuitively, a policy is simply a syntactical object, built from *atomic policies* and *policy connectives*. The interpretation function provides the denotational semantics of the policy, by returning a function from requests to decision, thus defining the expected behavior of the PDP. Clearly, a policy can be interpreted in different ways, and an interpretation function can interpret different policies, as long as they are built from the same atomic policies and connectives.

An *access control model* defines an *access control language*, which consists of a set of atomic polices and policy connectives, and an interpretation function.

In other words, an access control model specifies a set of access control policies and a unique way to interpret each of these policies. An *access control mechanism*, then, is an instance of an access control model if its policy belongs to the language of the model and if its interpretation function is that of the model.

2.2 The Framework

In order to provide a framework within which policies can be constructed, we introduce the notion of access control model, which is a tuple $\mathcal{M} = (Q, \mathcal{A}, \text{Ops}, \text{Dec}, [\![\cdot]\!])$, where Q is a set of *requests*, $\mathcal{A}$ a set of *atomic authorization policies*, Ops a set of *policy connectives*, Dec a set of (authorization) *decisions*, and, for each $A \in \mathcal{A}$, $[\![A]\!]$ is a total function from Q to Dec defining the *evaluation* of policy A for all requests in Q.

Each k-ary policy connective op in Ops is identified with a function op : $\text{Dec}^k \to \text{Dec}$. We construct an authorization policy P using elements of $\mathcal{A}$ and Ops. We extend the evaluation function for atomic policies to arbitrary policies: that is, $[\![P]\!] : Q \to \text{Dec}$ provides a method of evaluating requests with respect to a policy P. We say that $[\![\cdot]\!]$ defines the *authorization semantics* of the model.

The syntax by which policies are defined and the extension of the authorization semantics for atomic policies to non-atomic policies are fixed (for all models), as specified in Definition 1 below. Nevertheless, different choices for Dec, $\mathcal{A}$ and $[\![\cdot]\!]$ give rise to very different models having very different properties.

A *policy term* P is defined by a (rooted) *policy tree*, in which leaf nodes are *atomic policies* and each non-leaf node is a policy connective (we may also use the term *policy operator*). More formally we have the following definition:

Definition 1. *Let* $\mathcal{M} = (Q, \mathcal{A}, \text{Ops}, \text{Dec}, [\![\cdot]\!])$ *be a model. Then every atomic policy in* $\mathcal{A}$ *is a policy term. If* $P_1, \ldots, P_k$ *are policy terms, then for each k-ary operator* op $\in$ Ops, op$(P_1, \ldots, P_k)$ *is a policy term. For each policy term* op$(P_1, \ldots, P_k)$, *we define*

$$[\![\text{op}(P_1, \ldots, P_k)]\!](q) = \text{op}([\![P_1]\!](q), \ldots, [\![P_k]\!](q)). \qquad (1)$$

In other words, authorization policies are represented as policy trees and policies are evaluated from the bottom up by (a) evaluating atomic policies (b) combining the decisions returned for atomic policies using the relevant policy connectives.[1] We write $\mathcal{P}(\mathcal{M})$ to denote the set of policies that can be expressed within $\mathcal{M}$.

Given a set of queries Q and a set of decisions Dec, an *ideal access control policy* is a total function $\pi : Q \to \text{Dec}$.[2] We say that an ideal policy π is *realizable* by

---

[1] Strictly speaking, we should use different symbols for a policy connective and the decision operator with which it is associated. We have chosen to abuse notation in the interests of clarity, because little is gained by strict adherence to formality here.

[2] Clearly, a policy designer could define a policy extensionally, simply by associating each query with a decision. However, in practice, policies are constructed in a modular fashion, where each component defines a particular security concern and the decisions from different components are combined.

an access control model $\mathcal{M}$ if, and only if, there exists a policy term $P \in \mathcal{P}(\mathcal{M})$ such that for any query q, $\pi(q) = [\![P]\!](q)$; in the interests of simplicity we will abuse notation and write $\pi \in \mathcal{P}(\mathcal{M})$ and $\pi = (\mathcal{M}, P)$.

Figure 1 shows two policy trees each having the same atomic policies, A_1 and A_2. The figure also shows two evaluations of the tree for the same request q, where $[\![A]\!]_1(q) = 1$ and $[\![A_2]\!](q) = \bot$. The symbols 1, 0 and $\bot$ denote allow, deny and inapplicable decisions, respectively. The policy trees are evaluated using a post-order traversal, in which each leaf node is assigned a value according to the semantics defined by $[\![\cdot]\!]$ and each interior node is assigned a value by combining the values assigned to its child nodes. The policies in Figure 1 make use of three operators taken from Table 1. Both $\triangle$ and $\wedge$ are similar to the allow-overrides operator familiar from XACML (and also the two conjunction operators from Kleene's 3-valued logic) and only differ in the way in which $\bot$ is combined with 1. The $\sim$ unary operator implements a deny-by-default rule, thus $[\![P_1]\!](q) \neq [\![P_2]\!](q)$.

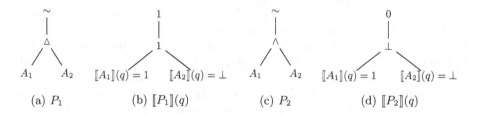

(a) P_1 (b) $[\![P_1]\!](q)$ (c) P_2 (d) $[\![P_2]\!](q)$

Fig. 1. Illustrative policy trees and their evaluation

In general, an access control model does not specify any policy in particular (unless the language is so restricted that it can only specify one policy). To some extent, an access control model (in the sense in which we use the term in this paper) is analogous to a programming language: it describes the syntax that is used to build access control policies (analogous to programs) and the semantics of the run-time mechanisms that will be used to handle input data (access control requests in this context). A realizable policy is in this case analogous to a program P written in the syntax of the model $\mathcal{M}$, that is interpreted using the authorization semantics of the model, while an ideal policy is analogous to the set of functional requirements.

Note that an ideal policy can be realized by different access control models: $\pi \in \mathcal{P}(\mathcal{M})$ and $\pi \in \mathcal{P}(\mathcal{M}')$ with $\mathcal{M} \neq \mathcal{M}'$. In other words, different access control mechanisms may be able to enforce the same security requirements. And π may be realizable by different policy terms from the same access control model: $\pi = (\mathcal{M}, P)$ and $\pi = (\mathcal{M}, P')$ with $P \neq P'$. In other words, security requirements can be enforced by the same mechanism using different policies. However, an ideal policy may not be realizable by any policy term for a given model; the extent to which a model can realize the set of ideal policies provides us with a notion of the *completeness* of a model (as we discuss in Section 3.2).

2.3 Framework Instantiation

A model provides the global structure from which access control policies can be built. A simple example of a model is the protection matrix model [9], which can be viewed as a set of triples (s, o, x), where s is a subject, o an object and x an access mode. A query is also a triple (s, o, x), and is authorized if, and only if, it belongs to the set representing the matrix. Hence, we define the set of queries Q_{AM} to be the set of all triples (s, o, x), the set of decisions $\mathsf{Dec}_{\mathsf{AM}} = \{1, 0\}$, where 1 stands for an authorized access and 0 for a denied one, the set of atomic policies $\mathcal{A}_{\mathsf{AM}} = Q_{AM} \cup \{0\}$, the set of operators $\mathsf{Ops}_{\mathsf{AM}} = \{\vee\}$, where $\vee$ is the standard boolean disjunction, and the interpretation function $[\![\cdot]\!]_{\mathsf{AM}}$ to be:

$$[\![p]\!]_{\mathsf{AM}}(q) = \begin{cases} 1 & \text{if } p = q \\ 0 & \text{otherwise.} \end{cases}$$

For instance, the policy authorizing only the accesses (s_1, o_1, x_1) and (s_2, o_2, x_2) can be defined as $(s_1, o_1, x_1) \vee (s_2, o_2, x_2)$.

Models can also consider richer sets of queries. Indeed, recent work considers the possibility that, in order to make a decision, an access control system might require more attributes than the traditional subject-object-action triple [2, 5, 10]. In order to define requests and atomic policies it is necessary to identify sets of attributes and the values that each of those attributes may take. Role-based access control, to take a simple example, defines the sets of roles, users and permissions, together with user-role and permission-role assignment relations.

We now introduce the notions of attribute vocabulary and attribute-based access control, which are intended to be as general as possible and allow for the construction of requests and policies.

Definition 2. *Let $\mathcal{N}$ denote a set of attribute names, and $\mathcal{D}$ denote a set of attribute domains. Let* $\mathsf{dom} : \mathcal{N} \to \mathcal{D}$ *be a function, where* $\mathsf{dom}(\alpha)$ *denotes the set of attribute values associated with attribute α. Then $(\mathcal{N}, \mathcal{D}, \mathsf{dom})$ defines an attribute vocabulary.*

When no confusion can occur, we will simply write $\mathcal{N}$ to denote an attribute vocabulary. A request is modeled as a set of name-value pairs of the form (α, v), where $\alpha \in \mathcal{N}$. We denote the set of requests by $\mathcal{Q}^*(\mathcal{N})$, omitting $\mathcal{N}$ when it is obvious from context. We say an attribute name-value pair (α, v) is *well-formed* if $\alpha \in \mathcal{N}$ and $v \in \mathsf{dom}(\alpha)$. We assume that a PDP can recognize (and discard) name-value pairs in a request that are not well-formed.

Attribute-based access control (ABAC) policies are modular. Hence, a policy component may be incomplete or two policy components may return contradictory decisions. Thus, it is common to see additional decisions used to denote a policy "gap" or "doubt" indicating different reasons why policy evaluation could not reach a conclusive (allow or deny) decision [11, 10]. We write $\mathsf{Three} = \{1, 0, \perp\}$, where $[\![A]\!](q) = \perp$ indicates that $[\![A]\!](q)$ is neither 0 nor 1.

In Table 1 we summarize the characteristics of some useful 3-valued operators, most of which are self-explanatory. The ? operator acts as a policy filter: $[\![p_1 ?$

Table 1. Operators over $\{1, 0, \bot\}$

d_1	d_2	$\neg d_1$	$\sim d_1$	$d_1 \wedge d_2$	$d_1 \triangle d_2$	$d_1 \vee d_2$	$d_1 \triangledown d_2$	$d_1 ? d_2$	$d_1 \bowtie d_2$	$d_1 \triangleright d_2$
1	1	0	1	1	1	1	1	1	1	1
1	0	0	1	0	0	1	1	0	$\bot$	1
1	$\bot$	0	1	$\bot$	1	1	1	$\bot$	$\bot$	1
0	1	1	0	0	0	1	1	$\bot$	$\bot$	0
0	0	1	0	0	0	0	0	$\bot$	0	0
0	$\bot$	1	0	0	0	$\bot$	0	$\bot$	$\bot$	0
$\bot$	1	$\bot$	0	$\bot$	1	1	1	$\bot$	$\bot$	1
$\bot$	0	$\bot$	0	0	0	$\bot$	0	$\bot$	$\bot$	0
$\bot$	$\bot$	$\bot$	0	$\bot$	$\bot$	$\bot$	$\bot$	$\bot$	$\bot$	$\bot$

$p_2] = [p_2]$ if $[p_1] = 1$, and evaluates to $\bot$ otherwise. The $\bowtie$ operator models policy unanimity: $p_1 \bowtie p_2$ evaluates to a conclusive decision only if both p_1 and p_2 do. In Sec. 4.3 we describe a model with a 4-valued decision set.

ABAC is designed for open distributed systems, meaning that authenticated attributes and policy components may need to be retrieved from multiple locations. Thus, some languages assume that policy evaluation may fail: it may be, for example, that a policy server or policy information point is down. PTaCL [2] relies on a three-valued logic, and considers sets of decisions in order to model indeterminacy. XACML 3.0 [5] considers a six-valued decision set, three of those decisions representing different indeterminate answers.

3   Monotonicity and Completeness

An access control model provides a policy designer with a language to construct a policy. That language may well have an impact on the policies that can be expressed and the properties of those policies. In this section we study two specific properties of access control models, monotonicity (a kind of safety property) and completeness (an expressivity property), and we present two models satisfying these properties in Section 4.

3.1   Monotonicity

Informally, a policy is monotonic whenever removing information from a request does not lead to a "better" policy decision. Such a property is of particular relevance in open systems, where users might be able to control what information they supply to the access control mechanism. A model in which all realizable policies are monotonic implies that they are not vulnerable to attribute hiding attacks [2]. That is, a malicious user gains no advantage by suppressing information when making a request.

We model information hiding using a partial ordering $\leqslant_Q$ on Q; the intuitive interpretation of $q \leqslant_Q q'$ is that q contains less information than q'. For instance, an attribute query q is less than another query q' when $q \subseteq q'$. We also need to specify what it means for a decision to "benefit" a user, and thus we assume the existence of an ordering relation $\leqslant$ on Dec; again, the intuitive interpretation of $d_1 \leqslant d_2$ is that the decision d_2 is of greater benefit than d_1.[3] For instance, we can consider the ordering $\leqslant_3$ over $\{1, 0, \bot\}$, such that $x \leqslant_3 y$ if and only if $x = y$ or $x = \bot$.

Definition 3. *Given a set of authorization queries* $(Q, \leqslant_Q)$ *and a set of decisions* $(\mathsf{Dec}, \leqslant)$, *a policy* $\phi : Q \to \mathsf{Dec}$ *is* monotonic *if, and only if, for all* $q, q' \in Q$, $q \leqslant_Q q'$ *implies* $\phi(q) \leqslant \phi(q')$. *We say that an access control model* $\mathcal{M} = (Q, \mathcal{A}, \mathsf{Dec}, \mathsf{Ops}, \llbracket \cdot \rrbracket)$ *is* monotonic *if for all* $P \in \mathcal{P}(\mathcal{M})$, $\llbracket P \rrbracket$ *is monotonic.*

Note that our definition of a monotonic policy applies equally well to an ideal policy $\pi : Q \to \mathsf{Dec}$ or a realizable policy term P with authorization semantics $\llbracket P \rrbracket : Q \to \mathsf{Dec}$. However, the notion of monotonicity is dependent on the request ordering. For instance, without further characterization, the request ordering for the access matrix could be reduced to equality, making any policy trivially monotonic. However, more complex situations can be considered by adding extra information, such as an ordering over subjects or objects.

Tschantz and Krisnamurthi have shown that XACML 2.0 is not monotonic (although they called the property "safety" rather than monotonicity) [12]. We show in Section 4.1—provided certain restrictions are imposed on the structure of requests—that it is possible to develop a monotonic, attributed-based (XACML-like) access control model, using results from partial logic [13].

3.2 Completeness

Given a model $\mathcal{M} = (Q, \mathcal{A}, \mathsf{Dec}, \mathsf{Ops}, \llbracket \cdot \rrbracket)$, any realizable policy $P \in \mathcal{P}(\mathcal{M})$ clearly corresponds to an ideal policy $\pi : Q \to \mathsf{Dec}$. However, there may exist an ideal policy π (for Q and Dec) that does not belong to $\mathcal{P}(\mathcal{M})$ and cannot, therefore, be enforced by the policy decision point. Trivially, for example, a model without any atomic policies does not realize any policies. It follows that the set of ideal policies that can be realized by a model represents an intuitive notion of expressivity. A model that can realize every ideal policy is said to be complete. More formally:

Definition 4. *An access control model* $\mathcal{M} = (Q, \mathcal{A}, \mathsf{Dec}, \mathsf{Ops}, \llbracket \cdot \rrbracket)$ *is* complete *if, and only if for any ideal policy* $\pi : Q \to \mathsf{Dec}$, $\pi \in \mathcal{P}(\mathcal{M})$.

The completeness of a model $(Q, \mathcal{A}, \mathsf{Dec}, \mathsf{Ops}, \llbracket \cdot \rrbracket)$ will depend on the authorization vocabulary, the definition of atomic policies, the set Ops and $\llbracket \cdot \rrbracket$. The access matrix model defined in Section 2.3, for example, is complete.

---

[3] Note that we consider this relation to be statically defined over decisions, and to be independent of the request.

Proposition 5. *The model* $(Q_{\mathsf{AM}}, \mathcal{A}_{\mathsf{AM}}, \mathsf{Dec}_{\mathsf{AM}}, \mathsf{Ops}_{\mathsf{AM}}, [\![\cdot]\!]_{\mathsf{AM}})$ *is complete.*

On the other hand, it is easy to show that XACML is not complete, unless we allow the inclusion of XACML conditions, which are arbitrary functions. Indeed, consider two attributes α_1 and α_2 with two respective attribute values v_1 and v_2, it is not possible to construct a policy that evaluates $q_1 = \{(\alpha_1, v_1)\}$ to Permit and $q_2 = \{(\alpha_1, v_1), (\alpha_2, v_2)\}$ to NA, intuitively because any target not applicable to q_2 cannot be applicable to q_1.

We propose an attribute-based access control model in Section 4.2 in which the representation of atomic policies can distinguish attribute name-value pairs, from which we can prove a completeness result. However, it is worth observing that, in general, if a model is both monotonic and complete, then the ordering over requests is limited to the identity relation, as illustrated above with the access matrix.

Proposition 6. *Given any model* $\mathcal{M} = ((Q, \leqslant_Q), \mathcal{A}, (\mathsf{Dec}, \leqslant), \mathsf{Ops}, [\![\cdot]\!])$, *if* $\mathcal{M}$ *is complete and monotonic and if* $|\mathsf{Dec}| > 1$, *then* $\leqslant_Q$ *is the identity relation.*

Informally, this result states that if we wish to have a (non-trivial) monotonic model then we cannot expect to have a complete model. Instead, what we should aim for is a model that realizes at least all *monotonic ideal policies*, and such a model is said to be *monotonically-complete*. In Section 4, we show how to define monotonically-complete and complete attribute-based access control models that have similar characteristics to XACML.

4   Designing Attribute-Based Access Control Models

It could be argued that the main objective of XACML is to provide a standard addressing as many practical concerns as possible, rather than a language with formal semantics. Nevertheless, the design choices can and should be analyzed with respect to the properties they entail. We do not claim here that XACML *should* be monotonic, complete, or monotonically-complete, but we show instead how, building from existing logical results, one can instantiate an access control model with these properties.

The results in this section can provide guidance to the designer of an access control system. She can choose, for example, between a system that realizes only and all monotonic policies, and a system in which all policies are realizable, but some may be non-monotonic. Clearly, the choice depends on the demands of the application and the constraints of the underlying environment. While we cannot make this choice for the policy designer, our framework can only help her make an informed decision.

If the attribute vocabulary were countably infinite (and the cardinality of the decision set is greater than 1) then the number of ideal policies would be uncountably infinite (by a standard diagonalization argument). However, the number of realizable policies can, at best, be countably infinite, by construction. Accordingly, it is only meaningful to consider completeness if we assume that the attribute vocabulary is finite (but unbounded). In practice, of course, all attribute values will be stored as variables and there will be an upper limit on the size of such variables, so the attribute vocabulary will be finite and bounded, albeit by a very large number.

4.1   ABAC$_M$: A Monotonic Monotonically-Complete Model

Recall from Definition 2 that, given a vocabulary $\mathcal{N}$, we write $\mathcal{Q}^*(\mathcal{N})$ to denote the set of requests. Note that a request may contain (well-formed) pairs $(\alpha, v_1,), \ldots, (\alpha, v_n)$ having the same attribute name and different values. One obvious example arises when α is the "role" attribute name and v_i is the identifier of a role. We define the set of atomic policies $\mathcal{A}(\mathcal{N})$ to be the set of well-formed name-value pairs. That is $\mathcal{A}(\mathcal{N}) = \{(\alpha, v) : \alpha \in \mathcal{N} \text{ and } v \in \text{dom}(\alpha)\}$. Then we define

$$[\![(\alpha, v)]\!](q) = \begin{cases} 1 & \text{if } q \ni (\alpha, v') \text{ and } v = v', \\ \bot & \text{if } q \not\ni (\alpha, v'), \\ 0 & \text{otherwise.} \end{cases}$$

Note that the above interpretation of atomic policies is by no means the only possibility. In the context of a three-value decision set, we might return 0 if $q \ni (\alpha, v')$ and $v \neq v'$, $\bot$ if $q \not\ni (\alpha, v')$ and 1 otherwise. In the context of a four-value decision set, we could return $\top$ if $q \supseteq \{(\alpha, v'), (\alpha, v)\}$, since such a request both matches and does not match the attribute value v for attribute α. We discuss these possibilities in more detail in Sec. 4.3.

The ordering on $\mathcal{Q}^*$, denoted by $\leqslant_{\mathcal{Q}}$, is simply subset inclusion. We define the ordering $\leqslant_3$ on Three, where $x \leqslant_3 y$ if and only if $x = y$ or $x = \bot$. It is worth observing that if a request contains at most one value for each attribute, then each atomic policy is monotonic. More formally, if we define the set of queries $\mathcal{Q}^? = \{q \subseteq \mathcal{A}(\mathcal{N}) \mid \forall \alpha \; (\alpha, v) \in q \wedge (\alpha, v') \in q \Rightarrow v = v'\}$, we can prove the following proposition.

Proposition 7. *For all requests $q, q' \in \mathcal{Q}^?$ such that $q \leqslant_{\mathcal{Q}} q'$ and for all atomic policies $(\alpha, v) \in \mathcal{A}(\mathcal{N})$, we have $[\![(\alpha, v)]\!](q) \leqslant_3 [\![(\alpha, v)]\!](q')$.*

We will see in the following section that we can define a complete ABAC model that accepts requests from $\mathcal{Q}^*$, but we can no longer ensure monotonicity. We now define a monotonic and monotonically-complete attribute-based access control (ABAC) model.

Definition 8. ABAC$_M$ *is defined to be* $(\mathcal{Q}^?, \mathcal{A}(\mathcal{N}), \text{Three}, \{\neg, \wedge, \vee, \between, ?\}, [\![\cdot]\!])$.

ABAC$_M$ is not merely of academic interest because it incorporates a number of features that are similar to XACML. In particular, we can

- construct targets from conjunctions and disjunctions of atomic policies;
- use the operators $\wedge$ and $\vee$ to model deny-overrides and allow-overrides policy-combining algorithms;

- construct (XACML) rules, policies and policy sets using policies of the form $p_1 ? p_2$, since $[\![p_1 ? p_2]\!] = [\![p_2]\!]$ if $[\![p_1]\!] = 1$ (corresponding to "matching" a request to "target" p_1 and then evaluating policy p_2).

The correspondence between $\mathsf{ABAC_M}$ and XACML cannot be exact, given that XACML is not monotonic. The main difference lies in the way in which $\wedge$ and $\vee$ handle the $\perp$ decision. The operators $\wedge$ and $\vee$ are what Crampton and Huth called intersection operators [14], whereas the policy-combining algorithms in XACML are union operators. Informally, an intersection operator requires both operands to have conclusive decisions, while a union operator ignores inconclusive decisions. Thus, for example, $1 \wedge \perp = \perp$, whereas the XACML deny-overrides algorithm would return 1 given the same arguments.

A practical consequence of the design goals of $\mathsf{ABAC_M}$ is that the $\perp$ decision will be returned more often than for analogous policies in XACML (or other non-monotonic languages). In practice, the policy enforcement point will have to either (a) ask the requester to supply additional attributes in the request; or (b) deny all requests that are not explicitly allowed.

Theorem 9. $\mathsf{ABAC_M}$ *is monotonic and monotonically complete.*

The proof of this result and other results in this section can be found in the on-line version [8]. Theorem 9 demonstrates that all access control policies built and evaluated using $\mathsf{ABAC_M}$ are monotonic, and that all monotonic ideal policies can be realized by a policy in $\mathsf{ABAC_M}$. Hence, if policy monotonicity is an important feature for a system designer, then $\mathsf{ABAC_M}$ provides that guarantee. However, $\mathsf{ABAC_M}$ is not complete, since some (non-monotonic) ideal policies cannot be built from it. We propose in the following section a complete model.

4.2 $\mathsf{ABAC_C}$: A Complete Model

In some situations, one might want to define non-monotonic policies or we might want to consider a query set in which the same attribute can have different values within a given query. In such situations, we consider the model $\mathsf{ABAC_C}$ which, in addition to being complete, is defined over the set of queries $\mathcal{Q}^*$.

Definition 10. $\mathsf{ABAC_C}$ *is defined to be* $(\mathcal{Q}^*, \mathcal{A}(\mathcal{N}), \mathsf{Three}, \{\neg, \sim, \vee\}, [\![\cdot]\!])$.

Theorem 11. $\mathsf{ABAC_C}$ *is complete.*

It is trivial to see that by considering $\mathcal{Q}^*$, we lose the monotonicity with respect to the inclusion ordering $\leqslant_\mathcal{Q}$. In particular, for $v, v' \in \mathsf{dom}(\alpha)$ with $v \neq v'$, we have $\{(\alpha, v')\} \leqslant_\mathcal{Q} \{(\alpha, v), (\alpha, v')\}$, but $0 = [\![(\alpha, v)]\!](\{(\alpha, v')\}) \not\leqslant [\![(\alpha, v)]\!](\{(\alpha, v), (\alpha, v')\}) = 1$.

The function $[\![\cdot]\!]$ is monotonic for atomic policies and requests in $\mathcal{Q}^*$ if we adopt the ordering $\perp < 0 < 1$. This means that omitting attributes can cause the evaluation of an atomic policy to change from 1 to 0 or $\perp$, or from 0 to $\perp$. While this seems to be reasonable, when combined with operators such as

$\triangle$, omitting attributes can cause the evaluation of a policy to change from 0 to 1. (Thus a user may be able to construct a request $q \subseteq q'$ that is allowed when q' is not. Any non-monotonic language, such as XACML, incorporates this vulnerability.)

4.3   ABAC with Explicit Conflict

The above choice to evaluate an atomic policy (α, v) to 1 if both (α, v) and (α, v') belongs to the query with $v \neq v'$ and $v, v' \in \mathsf{dom}(\alpha)$ could be regarded as being logically inconsistent in the sense that the request also contains a non-matching value. One could equally well argue, for example, that the request should evaluate to 0.

In order to cope with such situations, we might, therefore, choose to work with the 4-valued logic $\mathsf{Four} = \{1, 0, \bot, \top\}$, using $\top$ to denote conflicting information (in contrast to $\bot$ which signifies lack of information). We introduce the ordering $\leqslant_4$, where $d_1 \leqslant_4 d_2$ if, and only if, $d_1 = \bot$, $d_1 = d_2$ or $d_2 = \top$, and we define

$$
[\![(\alpha, v)]\!](q) = \begin{cases} \top & \text{if } q \ni (\alpha, v), (\alpha, v') \text{ such that } v, v' \in \mathsf{dom}(\alpha) \text{ and } v' \neq v, \\ 1 & \text{if } q \ni (\alpha, v) \text{ and } q \not\ni (\alpha, v') \text{ such that } v' \neq v, \\ 0 & \text{if } q \not\ni (\alpha, v) \text{ and } q \ni (\alpha, v') \text{ such that } v' \neq v, \\ \bot & \text{otherwise.} \end{cases}
$$

The definition of the policy operators ∇ and $\triangle$ can be extended to unary operators on Four, where

$$
\nabla d = \begin{cases} 1 & \text{if } d = \top, \\ d & \text{otherwise;} \end{cases} \qquad \triangle d = \begin{cases} 0 & \text{if } d = \top, \\ d & \text{otherwise.} \end{cases}
$$

Then the policy $\nabla(\alpha, v)$ allows a request q whenever q contains a matching attribute, while the policy $\triangle(\alpha, v)$ denies a request q whenever q contains a non-matching attribute value. Although the notion of conflicting policy decision has already been studied [11], to the best of our knowledge, this is the first time this notion of conflict has been used to evaluate targets. Intuitively, a conflict indicates that the request provides too much information for this particular policy. It is worth observing that atomic policies are monotonic with respect to the ordering $\leqslant_4$, i.e., for all requests q and q' such that $q \leqslant_{\varrho^*} q'$ and for all atomic policies (α, v), we have:

$$
[\![(\alpha, v)]\!](q) \leqslant_4 [\![(\alpha, v)]\!](q').
$$

A possible way to extend the operators defined in Table 1 is to consider the value $\top$ as absorbing: for any operator $\oplus : \mathsf{Three}^k \to \mathsf{Three}$, we define the operator $\hat{\oplus} : \mathsf{Four}^k \to \mathsf{Four}$ as follows:

$$
\hat{\oplus}(d_1, \ldots, d_k) = \begin{cases} \top & \text{if } d_i = \top \text{ for some } i \in [1, k], \\ \oplus(d_1, \ldots, d_k) & \text{otherwise.} \end{cases}
$$

Clearly, given an operator $\oplus$ defined over Three, if $\oplus$ is monotonic according to $\leqslant_3$, then $\hat{\oplus}$ is also monotonic with respect to $\leqslant_4$. It follows that we can still safely use the operators generated by the operators $\neg$, $\wedge$, $\vee$ and $\times$, and we can deduce that any realizable policy is also monotonic. However, we lose the result of monotonic completeness, and we can no longer ensure that any monotonic operator can be generated from this set of operators. Obtaining such a result requires a deeper study of four-valued logic, and we leave it for future work.

5   Related Work

Much of the work on specification of access control languages can be traced back to the early work of Woo and Lam, which considered the possibility that different policy components might evaluate to different authorization decisions [15]. More recent work has considered larger sets of policy decisions or more complex policy operators (or both), and propose a formal representation of the corresponding metamodel [16, 17, 11, 14, 18, 2, 19–23, 5, 24]. The "metamodels" in the literature are really attempts to fix an authorization vocabulary, by identifying the sets and relations that will be used to define access control policies.

In contrast, our framework makes very few assumptions about access control models and policies that are written in the context of a model. In this, our framework most closely resembles the work of Tschantz and Krishnamurthi [12], which considered a number of properties of a policy language, including determinism, totality, safety and monotonicity.

The notion of a monotonic operator (as defined by [12]) is somewhat different from ours. This is in part because a different ordering on the set of decisions Three is used and because monotonicity is concerned with the inclusion of sub-policies and the effect this has on policy evaluation. This contrasts with our approach, where we are concerned with whether the exclusion of information from a request can influence the decision returned. (In fact, our concept of monotonicity is closer to the notion of safety defined in [12]: if a request q is "lower" than q', then the decision returned for q is "lower" than that of q'.) We would express their notion of monotonicity in the following way: a policy operator $\oplus$ is monotonic (in the context of model $\mathcal{M}$) if for all $p_1, \ldots, p_t \in \mathcal{P}(\mathcal{M})$ and all $q \in \mathcal{Q}$, if $\oplus(p_1 \ldots, p_t)(q) \in \{1, 0\}$, then $\oplus(p_1, \ldots, p_i, p', p_{i+1}, p_t)(q) \neq \perp$ for any i and any policy $p' \in \mathcal{P}(\mathcal{M})$. Moreover, our framework is concerned with arbitrary authorization vocabularies and queries, unlike that of Tschantz and Krishnamurthi, which focused on the standard subject-object-action request format. The only assumption we make is that all policies can be represented using a tree-like structure and that policy decisions can be computed from the values assigned to leaf nodes and the interpretation of the operators at each non-leaf node.

In addition, we define the notion of *completeness* of a model, which is concerned with the expressivity of the policy operators. There exists prior work on comparing the expressive power of different access control models or the extent to which one model is able to simulate another [25–27]. In this paper, we show how our framework enables us to establish whether a model based on a particular set of atomic policies, decision set and policy connectives is complete. We can, therefore, compare the completeness of two different models by, for example, fixing an authorization vocabulary and comparing the completeness of models that differ in one or more of the models' components (that is, ones that differ in the set of connectives, decision sets, atomic policies and authorization semantics). While this is similar in spirit to earlier work, this is not the primary aim of this paper, although it would certainly be a fertile area for future research.

6   Concluding Remarks

We have presented a generic framework for specifying access control controls, within which a large variety of access control models arise as special cases, and which allows us to reason about the global properties of such systems. A major strength of our approach is that we do not provide "yet another access control language". The framework is not intended to provide an off-the-shelf policy language or PDP (unlike XACML, for example), nor is it intended to be an access control model (in the style of RBAC96, say). Rather, we try to model all aspects of an access control system at an abstract level and to provide a framework that can be instantiated in many different ways, depending on the choices made for request attributes, atomic policies, policy decisions and policy evaluation functions. In doing so we are able to identify (i) how and why an access control system may fail to be sufficiently expressive (completeness), and (ii) how and why having an expressive access control system may lead to vulnerabilities (monotonicity).

There are many opportunities for future work. The notions of monotonicity and completeness are examples of general properties of an access control model that we can characterize formally within our framework. We have already noted that there are at least two alternative semantics for atomic policies having the form (α, v) for a three-valued decision set and even more alternatives for a four-valued decision set. It would be interesting to see how these alternative semantics affect monotonicity and completeness. We would like to study the composition of access control models, and under what circumstances composition preserves monotonicity and completeness. Further properties that are of interest include policy equivalence, policy ordering (where, informally, one policy P_1 is "more restrictive" than P_2 if it denies every request that is denied by P_2), which may allow us to define what it means for a realizable policy to be "optimal" with respect to an (unrealizable) ideal policy. Moreover, our definition of monotonicity is dependent on the ordering on the set of decisions. Monotonicity, in the context of the ordering $0 < \perp < 1$, for example, is a stronger property than the one we have considered in this paper. Again, it would be interesting to investigate the appropriateness of different forms of monotonicity. Furthermore, although XACML is proven not to be monotonic, it is not known under which conditions it can be monotonically-complete, and if additional operators are needed to prove this property, which is also likely to depend on the decision orderings considered.

In this paper, we have assumed that there exists an ideal policy and that such a policy is fixed. Generally, however, a system evolves over time, and an access control policy will need to be updated to cope with changes to that system that affect the users, resources, or context. Thus it may be more realistic to specify an initial ideal policy, which might be extremely simple, and the access control policy that best approximates it, and then define rules by which the access control policy may evolve. With this in mind, it makes sense to regard the access control policy (or components thereof) as a protected object. Security is then defined in terms of properties that "reachable" access control policies must satisfy. Typical examples of such properties are "liveness" and "safety" [28]. Including administrative policies within our framework and investigating properties such as liveness and safety will be an important aspect of our future work in this area.

References

1. Bishop, M.: Computer Security: Art and Science. Addison-Wesley (2002)
2. Crampton, J., Morisset, C.: PTaCL: A language for attribute-based access control in open systems. In: Degano, P., Guttman, J.D. (eds.) Principles of Security and Trust. LNCS, vol. 7215, pp. 390–409. Springer, Heidelberg (2012)
3. Griesmayer, A., Morisset, C.: Automated certification of authorisation policy resistance. In: Crampton, J., Jajodia, S., Mayes, K. (eds.) ESORICS 2013. LNCS, vol. 8134, pp. 574–591. Springer, Heidelberg (2013)
4. Ferraiolo, D., Atluri, V.: A meta model for access control: why is it needed and is it even possible to achieve? In: Proceedings of the 13th ACM Symposium on Access Control Models and Technologies, pp. 153–154. ACM (2008)
5. eXtensible Access Control Markup Language (XACML) Version 3.0, OASIS, committee Specification 01 (2010)
6. Ferraiolo, D.F., Kuhn, D.R.: Role-based access control. In: Proceedings of the 15th National Computer Security Conference, pp. 554–563 (1992)
7. Barker, S.: The next 700 access control models or a unifying meta-model? In: Carminati, B., Joshi, J. (eds.) SACMAT, pp. 187–196. ACM (2009)
8. Crampton, J., Morisset, C.: Towards a generic formal framework for access control systems. CoRR, vol. abs/1204.2342 (2012)
9. Harrison, M., Ruzzo, W., Ullman, J.: Protection in operating systems. Communications of the ACM 19(8), 461–471 (1976)
10. Rao, P., Lin, D., Bertino, E., Li, N., Lobo, J.: An algebra for fine-grained integration of XACML policies. In: Carminati, B., Joshi, J. (eds.) SACMAT, pp. 63–72. ACM (2009)
11. Bruns, G., Huth, M.: Access control via Belnap logic: Intuitive, expressive, and analyzable policy composition. ACM Transactions on Information and System Security 14(1), 9 (2011)
12. Tschantz, M.C., Krishnamurthi, S.: Towards reasonability properties for access-control policy languages. In: Ferraiolo, D.F., Ray, I. (eds.) SACMAT, pp. 160–169. ACM (2006)
13. Blamey, S.: Partial Logic. In: Handbook of Philosophical Logic, vol. 5, pp. 261–353. Kluwer Academic Publishers (2002)
14. Crampton, J., Huth, M.: An authorization framework resilient to policy evaluation failures. In: Gritzalis, D., Preneel, B., Theoharidou, M. (eds.) ESORICS 2010. LNCS, vol. 6345, pp. 472–487. Springer, Heidelberg (2010)
15. Woo, T.Y.C., Lam, S.S.: Authorizations in distributed systems: A new approach. Journal of Computer Security 2(2-3), 107–136 (1993)

16. Bertino, E., Catania, B., Ferrari, E., Perlasca, P.: A logical framework for reasoning about access control models. ACM Transactions on Information and System Security 6(1), 71–127 (2003)
17. Bonatti, P., De Capitani Di Vimercati, S., Samarati, P.: An algebra for composing access control policies. ACM Transactions on Information and System Security 5(1), 1–35 (2002)
18. Crampton, J., Huth, M.: A framework for the modular specification and orchestration of authorization policies. In: Aura, T., Järvinen, K., Nyberg, K. (eds.) NordSec 2010. LNCS, vol. 7127, pp. 155–170. Springer, Heidelberg (2012)
19. Damianou, N., Dulay, N., Lupu, E.C., Sloman, M.: The Ponder policy specification language. In: Sloman, M., Lobo, J., Lupu, E.C. (eds.) POLICY 2001. LNCS, vol. 1995, pp. 18–38. Springer, Heidelberg (2001)
20. Jajodia, S., Samarati, P., Sapino, M.L., Subrahmanian, V.S.: Flexible support for multiple access control policies. ACM Transactions on Database Systems 26(2), 214–260 (2001)
21. Li, N., Wang, Q., Qardaji, W.H., Bertino, E., Rao, P., Lobo, J., Lin, D.: Access control policy combining: theory meets practice. In: Carminati, B., Joshi, J. (eds.) SACMAT, pp. 135–144. ACM (2009)
22. Ni, Q., Bertino, E., Lobo, J.: D-algebra for composing access control policy decisions. In: Li, W., Susilo, W., Tupakula, U.K., Safavi-Naini, R., Varadharajan, V. (eds.) ASIACCS, pp. 298–309. ACM (2009)
23. eXtensible Access Control Markup Language (XACML) Version 2.0, OASIS, committee Specification (2005)
24. Wijesekera, D., Jajodia, S.: A propositional policy algebra for access control. ACM Transactions on Information and System Security 6(2), 235–286 (2003)
25. Habib, L., Jaume, M., Morisset, C.: A formal comparison of the Bell & LaPadula and RBAC models. In: Rak, M., Abraham, A., Casola, V. (eds.) IAS, pp. 3–8. IEEE Computer Society (2008)
26. Osborn, S., Sandhu, R., Munawer, Q.: Configuring role-based access control to enforce mandatory and discretionary access control policies. ACM Transactions on Information and System Security 3(2), 85–106 (2000)
27. Tripunitara, M.V., Li, N.: A theory for comparing the expressive power of access control models. Journal of Computer Security 15(2), 231–272 (2007)
28. Schneider, F.B.: Enforceable security policies. ACM Trans. Inf. Syst. Secur. 3(1), 30–50 (2000)
29. Carminati, B., Joshi, J. (eds.): Proceedings of the 14th ACM Symposium on Access Control Models and Technologies, SACMAT 2009, Stresa, Italy, June 3-5. ACM (2009)

Caching and Auditing in the RPPM Model

Jason Crampton and James Sellwood

Royal Holloway University of London,
Egham, United Kingdom
jason.crampton@rhul.ac.uk, james.sellwood.2010@live.rhul.ac.uk
https://www.royalholloway.ac.uk/isg/home.aspx

Abstract. Crampton and Sellwood recently introduced a variant of relationship-based access control based on the concepts of relationships, paths and principal matching, to which we will refer as the RPPM model. In this paper, we show that the RPPM model can be extended to provide support for caching of authorization decisions and enforcement of separation of duty policies. We show that these extensions are natural and powerful. Indeed, caching provides far greater advantages in RPPM than it does in most other access control models and we are able to support a wide range of separation of duty policies.

Keywords: access control, path condition, relationship, principal matching, authorization, caching, auditing, separation of duty, Chinese Wall.

1 Introduction

Whilst the majority of computer systems employ some form of role-based access control model, social networking sites have made use of the relationships between individuals as a means of determining access to resources. Recent work on relationship-based access control models has attempted to further develop this concept but has frequently remained focused on the relationships that exist between individuals [4, 10]. Crampton and Sellwood define a more general model for access control utilising relationships between entities, where those entities can represent any physical or logical component of a system [8]. These entities and their (inter-)relationships are described by a multigraph, called the *system graph*. Authorization requests in the RPPM model are processed by first determining a list of matching principals. This list of principals is identified using principal-matching rules and the system graph. Once a list of matched principals is determined, the specific action in the request is authorized or denied based on authorization rules defined for those principals and the object.

The RPPM model provides the necessary foundations for general purpose relationship-based access control systems, but there are a number of simple enhancements which would greatly increase its utility and efficiency. The evaluation of path conditions can be complex in system graphs containing many nodes of high degree. Support for caching of previously matched principals would significantly reduce the processing necessary during the evaluation of an authorization request. The introduction of caching support is, therefore, our first enhancement.

S. Mauw and C.D. Jensen (Eds.): STM 2014, LNCS 8743, pp. 49–64, 2014.

Our second enhancement adds support for request evaluation audit records to be kept, such that future authorization requests may be evaluated both on the current relationships within the system graph but also using historical information about past actions by subjects. Such mechanisms allow us to support constraints such as separation of duty and Chinese Wall policies and lay a foundation for future work on workflow authorization using the model.

The rest of this paper is arranged with background information on the RPPM model provided in Section 2 and then the two enhancements described individually in Sections 3 (caching) and 4 (audit records). We discuss related work in Section 5 and draw conclusions of our contributions and identify future work in Section 6. Space constraints mean that proofs are not included in the paper; the full version of the paper is available on the Web [7].

2   The RPPM Model

The RPPM model, described in detail in [8], employs a system graph to capture the entities of a system and their (inter-)relationships. The entities (physical or logical system components) are nodes within the system graph whilst the relationships are labelled edges. The system graph's 'shape' is constrained by a system model, which identifies the types of entities and relationship which are supported. It does so by defining a permissible relationship graph whose nodes are the possible types of entities in the system graph and whose labelled edges indicate the relationships which *may* exist in the system graph between entities of the connected types.

Definition 1. *A system model comprises a set of types T, a set of relationship labels R, a set of symmetric relationship labels $S \subseteq R$ and a permissible relationship graph $G_{PR} = (V_{PR}, E_{PR})$, where $V_{PR} = T$ and $E_{PR} \subseteq T \times T \times R$.*

Definition 2. *Given a system model (T, R, S, G_{PR}), a system instance is defined by a system graph $G = (V, E)$ where V is the set of entities and $E \subseteq V \times V \times R$. Making use of a mapping function $\tau : V \to T$ which maps an entity to its type, we say G is well-formed if for each entity v in V, $\tau(v) \in T$, and for every edge $(v, v', r) \in E$, $(\tau(v), \tau(v'), r) \in E_{PR}$.*

Within the RPPM model, authorization requests have the form $q = (s, o, a)$, where a subject s requests authorization to perform action a on target object o. The authorization policy is abstracted away from subjects by the use of security principals. These principals are matched to requests through the satisfaction of path conditions using edges in the system graph, where a path condition π represents a sequence of relations with specific labels from the set R.

Definition 3. *Given a set of relationships R, we define a path condition recursively:*

- *$\diamond$ is a path condition;*
- *r is a path condition, for all $r \in R$;*
- *if π and π' are path conditions, then $\pi \, ; \pi'$, π^+ and $\overline{\pi}$ are path conditions.*

A path condition of the form r or r̄, where r ∈ R, is said to be an edge condition.

Informally, $\pi ; \pi'$ represents the concatenation of two path conditions; π^+ represents one or more occurrences, in sequence, of π; and $\overline{\pi}$ represents π reversed; $\diamond$ defines an "empty" path condition.

Definition 4. *Given a set of relationships R, we define a* simple path condition *recursively:*

- $\diamond$, *r and r̄, where r ∈ R, are simple path conditions;*
- *if $\pi \neq \diamond$ and $\pi' \neq \diamond$ are simple path conditions, then $\pi ; \pi'$ and π^+ are simple path conditions.*

A path condition can describe highly complex and variable-length paths within the system graph. However, Crampton and Sellwood proved that every path condition can be reduced to an equivalent simple path condition [8, §2.2], thereby simplifying the design of the principal-matching algorithm.

Definition 5. *Given a system graph $G = (V, E)$ and $u, v \in V$, we write $G, u, v \models \pi$ to denote that G, u and v satisfy path condition π. Formally, for all G, u, v, π, π':*

- $G, u, v \models \diamond$ *iff $v = u$;*
- $G, u, v \models r$ *iff $(u, v, r) \in E$;*
- $G, u, v \models \pi ; \pi'$ *iff there exists $w \in V$ such that $G, u, w \models \pi$ and $G, w, v \models \pi'$;*
- $G, u, v \models \pi^+$ *iff $G, u, v \models \pi$ or $G, u, v \models \pi ; \pi^+$;*
- $G, u, v \models \overline{\pi}$ *iff $G, v, u \models \pi$.*

Definition 6. *Let P be a set of authorization principals. A* principal-matching rule *is a pair (π, p), where π is a path condition and $p \in P$ is the associated principal. A list of principal-matching rules is a* principal-matching policy.

In the context of a principal-matching rule, a path condition is called the *principal-matching condition*.

The request and system graph are evaluated against the principal-matching policy utilising a *principal-matching strategy* (PMS) to determine the list of matched principals for the request. The PMS specifies how principal-matching rules should be evaluated, for example whether the first matching principal applies (in the case of the FirstMatch PMS) or whether all matching principals apply (AllMatch). A *default* principal-matching rule $(\top, p')$ may, optionally, be employed as the last rule in the policy and will automatically result in its principal p' being matched whenever the rule is evaluated.

A system graph G, two nodes u and v in G, a principal-matching policy ρ, and a principal-matching strategy σ determines a list of principals MP associated with the pair (u, v). We evaluate each principal-matching rule (π, p) in turn and add p to the list of matched principals if and only if $G, u, v \models \pi$. We then apply the principal-matching strategy to the list of matched principals to obtain MP. (Obviously, optimizations are possible for certain principal-matching strategies.) We write $G, u, v \xrightarrow{\rho, \sigma} MP$ to denote this computation.

Once determined, the list of matched principals is used to identify relevant authorization rules in the authorization policy.

Definition 7. *An authorization rule has the form (p, o, a, b), where p is a principal, o is an object, a is an action and $b \in \{0, 1\}$, where $b = 0$ denies the action and $b = 1$ grants the action. In order to ease authorization policy specification we allow for the use of $\star$ instead of o, to represent all objects, or instead of a, to represent all actions. These global authorization rules, therefore, have the form $(p, \star, a, b)$, $(p, o, \star, b)$ or $(p, \star, \star, b)$. An authorization policy is a list of authorization rules.*

The matching of principals to authorization rules yields a list of authorization decisions, which is reduced to be single decision using a *conflict resolution strategy* (CRS). The CRS is used in much the same way as a rule-combining or policy-combining algorithm is used in XACML. It may specify that particular outcomes are prioritised, such as (AllowOverride or DenyOverride), or that the first conclusive decision should be used (FirstMatch).

To summarise, given a request (s, o, a), where s and o are nodes in the system graph and a is an action, we first compute the list of matched principals $G, s, o \xrightarrow{\rho, \sigma} MP$. We then use MP and the authorization policy to determine which actions are granted and denied for those principals and apply the CRS to determine a final decision. In this paper, we assume the use of the AllMatch PMS and DenyOverride CRS throughout.

3 Caching

The most complex part of evaluating an authorization request in the RPPM model is the principal matching stage [8, §3]. This process attempts to satisfy path conditions within principal-matching rules using paths between the subject and the object of the request. It is important to note that the requested action is immaterial during this processing stage (only becoming relevant when the authorization rules are considered). The list of matched principals for a subject-object pair remains static until a change is made to the system graph or certain associated policy components. Even then, not all of the possible changes would impact the matched principals between a particular subject and object.

We introduce the concept of *caching edges* and make use of the relative stability of matched principals in order to reduce the processing required for future authorization requests. We first redefine the system graph to support these new edges. In particular, when we evaluate a request (s, o, a) that results in a list of matched principals MP, we add an edge (s, o, MP) to the system graph, directed from s to o and labelled with MP.

Informally, a caching edge (s, o, MP) directly links s to o and identifies the matching principals MP relevant to requests of the form (s, o, a). The processing of subsequent authorization requests can skip the principal matching stage and use MP in conjunction with the authorization rules to evaluate a request of the form (s, o, a).

To illustrate, consider the simple system graph G_1, shown in Figure 1a, and the following principal-matching and authorization policies

$$\rho = [(r_1, p_1), (r_2, p_2), (r_3, p_3), (r_1 ; r_3, p_4), (r_2 ; r_3, p_5)]$$
$$PA = [(p_5, \star, a_1, 1), (p_5, \star, a_2, 0)].$$

If an authorization request $q_1 = (v_2, v_4, a_1)$ is made, then $G_1, v_2, v_4 \xrightarrow{\rho, \sigma} [p_5]$, because the only principal-matching condition from the policy which can be satisfied between v_2 and v_4 in G_1 is $r_2 ; r_3$. Then the authorization rule $(p_5, \star, a_1, 1)$ applies and the set of possible decisions $PD = \{1\}$; thus the request is authorized. At this stage we may add a caching edge $(v_2, v_4, [p_5])$ to produce the system graph shown in Figure 1b. We use the convention that caching edges have a diamond-shaped arrow head.

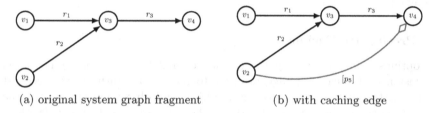

(a) original system graph fragment   (b) with caching edge

Fig. 1. Adding a caching edge

If an authorization request $q_2 = (v_2, v_4, a_2)$ is subsequently made, the caching edge $(v_2, v_4, [p_5])$ allows us to evaluate the request without re-evaluating the principal-matching policy; the authorization rule $(p_5, \star, a_2, 0)$ subsequently results in request q_2 being denied ($PD = \{0\}$).

To consider the scale of the potential benefit of caching edges, we review the experimental data reported by Crampton and Sellwood for numbers of nodes visited (n) and edges considered (e) during sample request evaluations (see Table 1 and [8, §3.3]). With support for caching edges, if the subject-object pairs participating in any of these requests were to be involved in subsequent requests the processing would instead be limited to locating the appropriate caching edge. It should be clear that when considering requests which may require upwards of 50 edge evaluations (in a small example system graph), replacing this with a single caching edge lookup could dramatically improve evaluation performance.

In the worst case, the number of caching edges directed out of a node is $O(|V|)$, where V is the set of nodes in the system graph. However, there are strategies that can be used to both prevent the system graph realizing the worst case and to reduce the impact of large numbers of caching edges. To maintain an acceptable number of caching edges, we could, for example, use some form of cache purging. We can also distinguish between relationship edges and caching edges using some flag on the edges and index the caching edges to dramatically decrease the time taken to search the set of caching edges. Employing these

Table 1. Experiment results from [8, §3.3]

Path condition	Request	n	e	Match Found
π_1	q_1	5	19	Yes
π_1	q_2	7	24	Yes
π_2	q_3	4	15	Yes
π_3	q_4	17	58	Yes
π_3	q_5	7	24	No

techniques should enable the benefits of caching edges to be realised without incurring unacceptable costs during identification of the relevant caching edge. Further experimental work is required to determine how best to make use of caching edges.

3.1 Preemptive Caching

Any optimisation provided by the caching of matched principals relies upon the existence of a caching edge in order to reduce the authorization request processing; the first request between a subject and object must, therefore, be processed normally in order to determine the list of matched principals which will label the caching edge. If this initial evaluation were only performed when an authorization request were submitted, then the benefit of caching edges would be limited to repeated subject-object interactions alone.

However, many authorization systems will experience periods of time when no authorization requests are being evaluated. The nature of many computing tasks is such that authorization is required sporadically amongst longer periods of computation by clients of the authorization system and idle time for the authorization system itself. These periods of reduced load on the authorization system can be employed for the purpose of *preemptive caching*.

Thus for pairs of nodes (u, v) in the system graph, we may compute $G, u, v \xrightarrow{\rho, \sigma} MP$ and insert a caching edge (u, v, MP). The fact that a request's action is not employed during the principal matching process means that to perform this further optimization an authorization system solely requires a subject and object between whom the matched principals are to be identified. There are numerous potential strategies for determining which subject-object pairs should be considered for preemptive caching. Here we describe two simple and natural strategies.

Subject-Focused. Subject-focused preemptive caching assumes that subjects who have recently made authorization requests are *active* and so will likely make further requests. The authorization system, therefore, prioritises determining the list of matched principals between the most recently active subjects and a set of target objects. The set of target objects could be selected at random or may be systematically chosen using an appropriate mechanism for the system defined in the system graph. This might involve the target objects being *popular*, *significant* or those whose access may be particularly *time-sensitive*. We envisage that the interpretation of these concepts may be system specific, as may their relative worth.

As preemptive caching builds the number of caching edges within the system graph the number of subjects and objects under consideration could be expanded to provide greater coverage of the potential future requests.

Object-Focused. In certain applications, there will be resources that will be used by most users, such as certain database tables. Thus, it may make sense to construct caching edges for all active users for certain resources.

No matter the strategy, preemptive caching makes use of available processing time in order to perform the most complex part of authorization request evaluation: principal matching. Any requests that are made utilising a subject-object pair which have already been evaluated by preemptive caching will be able to make use of the caching edge already established, even if that request were the first received for that pair. Once determined, caching edges resulting from preemptive caching are no different from those established as a result of request evaluation.

3.2 Cache Management

A change to any of the following components of the model could modify the list of matched principals for a subject and object:

- the system graph;
- the principal-matching policy;
- the principal-matching strategy.

Such changes, therefore, may affect the correctness of caching edges. (The obvious exception is a change to the system graph resulting from the addition or deletion of a caching edge.) The most crude management technique for handling such changes involves removing all caching edges from the system graph whenever one of the above changes occurs.

In certain specific scenarios it may be possible for a system to identify a scope of impact for a particular change and thus apply a more refined management technique. For example, if a change to the principal-matching policy removes all rules which are used to match a certain principal (and nothing more), then it would be sufficient for only caching edges labelled with a list including that principal to be purged. Whilst such a refinement may further optimise the operations performed by the authorization system, its applicability will depend upon the configuration of the authorization system in its entirety.

We have already noted that it may make sense to purge the cache in order to limit the number of caching edges in the system graph. Again, there are several possible purging strategies. One would be simply to set a maximum threshold for the number of caching edges in the system graph. A second, perhaps more useful, strategy would be to set a maximum threshold for the out-degree (measured in terms of caching edges) for any node in the graph. We may also "retire" caching edges: any edge that hasn't been used as part of a request evaluation for some time period will be purged. And we could employ mixed strategies, which might depend on the application and the nature of the system graph.

4   Audit Records

Currently, the RPPM model's authorization request processing is "memoryless" with respect to previous requests and their respective outcomes. Various scenarios and security policy principles make use of historical data. Reputation systems and history-based access control (HBAC) systems [1, 9, 15], for example, rely on knowledge of previous interactions and requests in order to correctly make authorization decisions. The Chinese Wall [3] and non-static separation of duty principles [12, 16] also rely on knowledge of previous actions to enforce their constraints.

We introduce the concept of *audit edges*, through which we track the outcomes of authorization requests for subsequent use in policy evaluation. Audit edges come in two flavours: those which directly record the decision of a previous authorization request (authorized and denied *decision audit edges*) and those which, more generally, record an entity's interest in other entities based on its authorized requests (active and blocked *interest audit edges*). It should be noted that whilst we make direct use of audit edges for policy evaluation, they also have value in a system purely as an audit record. We extend the set of relationships and further redefine the system graph to support these new edges. Specifically, in the case of decision audit edges:

- for each action a, we define two relationships $a^{\oplus}$ and $a^{\ominus}$ and include the sets $\{a^{\oplus} : a \in A\}$ and $\{a^{\ominus} : a \in A\}$ in the set of relationships;
- if the decision for request (u, o, a) is allow, then we add the edge $(u, o, a^{\oplus})$ into the system graph;
- if the decision for request (u, o, a) is deny, then we add the edge $(u, o, a^{\ominus})$ into the system graph.

Both authorized and denied decision audit edges are inserted, automatically, into the system graph after request evaluation completes. If such an edge does not already exist, a decision audit edge is added between the subject and object of the evaluated request, indicating its result.

The addition of interest audit edges also occurs automatically after request evaluation completes. For such edges, the subject is the source node of the interest edge (as for decision audit edges); however, the destination node may not be the object of the request. Interest audit edges are discussed in more detail in Section 4.2.

4.1   Enforcing Separation of Duty

Separation of duty requires that certain combinations of actions are performed by a number of distinct individuals so as to reduce the likelihood of abuse of a system. In its simplest form, separation of duty constraints require two individuals to each perform one of a pair of distinct actions so that a single individual cannot abuse the system. A common application environment for such constraints is that of a finance system, where, for example, the individual authorized to add new suppliers should not be the same individual who is authorized to approve the payment of invoices to suppliers. If a single individual were able to perform both of these actions they could set themselves up as a supplier within the finance system and then approve for payment any invoices they submitted as that supplier. We define a mechanism here through which n individuals can be required to perform n actions on an object. Before doing so, we explain a simplified version of the mechanism for the case $n = 3$.

Let us consider the system graph G_2 (see Figure 2a), the principal-matching policy $\rho = [(r, p)]$ and the authorization policy $PA = [(p, o, \star, 1)]$. With these policies and without audit edges, if individual u_1 makes the request $q_1 = (u_1, o, a_1)$ this will be authorized by matching principal p, as will subsequent requests $q_2 = (u_1, o, a_2)$ and $q_3 = (u_1, o, a_3)$. A similar result would have occurred if these requests had been submitted with u_2 or u_3 as the subject.

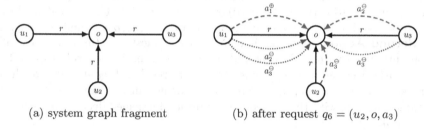

(a) system graph fragment   (b) after request $q_6 = (u_2, o, a_3)$

Fig. 2. Adding decision audit edges

A basic implementation of separation of duty can be employed by introducing a new principal p_{seen} which matches if a user has performed any action on the object. We change the principal-matching and authorization policies to

$$[(a_1^\oplus, p_{seen}), (a_2^\oplus, p_{seen}), (a_3^\oplus, p_{seen}), (r, p)] \quad \text{and} \quad [(p_{seen}, o, \star, 0), (p, o, \star, 1)]$$

respectively[1]. Using this combination of policies means that any user who has performed an action on object o is prevented from performing another action as all actions are denied to the principal p_{seen}.

Whilst this basic implementation fulfils the requirement that no user may perform more than one action on the object, we may wish to specify more refined separation of duty policies within the system. The basic implementation has several limitations which RPPM's policies are flexible and powerful enough to resolve. Specifically, all actions within the system are included in the separation of duty constraint due to the use of an authorization rule for all actions

---

[1] We assume the use of the AllMatch PMS and the DenyOverride CRS, but we could equally employ the FirstMatch PMS with any CRS as long as we ensure that the constraint principal-matching rules are added before any existing rules.

$(p_{seen}, o, \star, 0)$. Additionally, having performed an action on o a user is unable to repeat the action performed, as well as being unable to perform any other action.

If we wish to enforce a more flexible separation of duty constraint on a subset of actions $\{a_1, a_2, a_3\} \subseteq A$ such that distinct individuals are required to perform each action, we can modify the principal-matching policy to $\rho = [(a_1^{\oplus}, p_1), (a_2^{\oplus}, p_2), (a_3^{\oplus}, p_3), (r, p)]$ and the authorization policy to:

$$PA = [(p_1, o, a_2, 0), (p_1, o, a_3, 0), \ (p_2, o, a_1, 0), (p_2, o, a_3, 0),$$
$$(p_3, o, a_1, 0), (p_3, o, a_2, 0), \ (p, o, \star, 1)]$$

The First Action. Revisiting our example for G_2, an initial request $q_1 = (u_1, o, a_1)$ will, once again, be authorized (with $MP = [p]$) but will, this time, result in the addition of an authorized decision audit edge $(u_1, o, a_1^{\oplus})$. If u_1 then makes a request $q_2 = (u_1, o, a_2)$ this will be denied as $MP = [p_1, p]$ and the authorization rule $(p_1, o, a_2, 0)$ indicates a deny which overrides the authorization from the rule $(p, o, \star, 1)$. Similarly if u_1 makes a request $q_3 = (u_1, o, a_3)$ this will be denied as once again $MP = [p_1, p]$ and the deny authorization rule $(p_1, o, a_3, 0)$ overrides $(p, o, \star, 1)$. These two denied requests would result in denied decision audit edges $(u_1, o, a_2^{\ominus})$ and $(u_1, o, a_3^{\ominus})$.

The Second Action. However, if u_3 makes the request $q_4 = (u_3, o, a_2)$ this will be authorized with $MP = [p]$ and use of the authorization rule $(p, o, \star, 1)$; the authorized decision audit edge $(u_3, o, a_2^{\oplus})$ results. If u_3 attempts to then make request $q_5 = (u_3, o, a_3)$ this will be denied in the same manner that request q_3 was, with the subsequent addition of a denied decision audit edge $(u_3, o, a_3^{\ominus})$.

The Last Action. As a_1 was performed by u_1 and a_2 was performed by u_3 it remains, for successful operation, for u_2 to make request $q_6 = (u_2, o, a_3)$. This request will be authorized with $MP = [p]$ and the use of the authorization rule $(p, o, \star, 1)$, resulting in the authorized decision audit edge $(u_2, o, a_3^{\oplus})$. The system graph that results after all of these requests have been made is as shown in Figure 2b.

More generally, suppose we have a principal-matching policy ρ and an authorization policy PA. If we require that the actions $\{a_1, \ldots, a_n\}$ should each be performed by different users (and the same action may be repeated), we add the rules

$$(a_1^{\oplus}, p_1), \ldots, (a_n^{\oplus}, p_n)$$

to ρ and let the new policy be ρ'. And for each principal p_i, we add the set of rules

$$\{(p_i, o, a_j, 0) : 1 \leq j \leq n, j \neq i\}.$$

to PA denoting the new policy PA'. We then have the following result

Proposition 1. *Given an RPPM separation of duty policy, as described above, for any user u the request (u, o, a) is allowed if the request is authorized by ρ' and PA' and no request of the form (u, o, a'), where $a' \neq a$, has been previously authorized; the request is denied otherwise.*

4.2   Enforcing Chinese Walls

The Chinese Wall principle may be used to control access to information in order to prevent any conflicts of interest arising. The standard use case concerns a consultancy that provides services to multiple clients, some of whom are competitors. It is important that a consultant does not access documents of company A if she has previously accessed documents of a competitor of A.

To support the Chinese Wall policy, systems classify data using conflict of interest classes [3], indicating groups of competitor entities. Requests to access a company's resources within a conflict of interest class will only be authorized if no previous request was authorized accessing resources from another company in that conflict of interest class.

Unlike the general approach for separation of duty, a general approach for Chinese Wall requires fewer policy changes but does rely on a particular basic layout of system graph. This layout is such that the users who will be making requests are connected (directly or indirectly) to the companies (which may or may not be competitors of each other). These companies are then connected to their respective data entities, which will be the targets of users' requests. This arrangement is depicted, conceptually, in Figure 3a, with the path condition π_1 representing the chain of relationships between users and companies and π_2 between the data entities and the companies.[2] In other words, the path from an authorized user to a company will contain the same labels (and will match the path condition π_1), irrespective of the specific identities of the user and companies. Similarly, the path from a data object to its owner company will contain the same labels (and match the path condition π_2). Thus, the principal that is authorized to access companies' data objects would be matched using the path condition π_1 ; $\overline{\pi_2}$.

To support the Chinese Wall constraint, the basic layout is supplemented by conflict of interest classes, to which companies are connected directly by the member (m) relationship (see Figure 3a). We assume here that membership of conflict of interest classes is determined when the system graph is initially populated and remains fixed through the lifetime of the system. When users are authorized (or denied) access to particular data entities, authorized (or denied) decision audit edges will result for these requests as shown in Figure 3b. We additionally introduce interest audit edges into the system graph which are added between users and companies (see Figure 3b). Active interest audit edges are labelled with $i^\oplus$, blocked interest audit edges are labelled with $i^\ominus$. We, therefore, extend the set of relationships to include the set $\{i^\oplus, i^\ominus\}$, thus allowing the system graph to support these new edges. Graphically, we represent active interest audit edges with a filled circle head, whilst blocked interest audit edges have a filled square head.

Informally, when a subject's request to access a company's data is authorized, an active interest audit edge is added (if it doesn't already exist) between the

---

[2] It should be noted that Figure 3 does not show system graphs; it shows high-level representations of the 'shape' of a system graph.

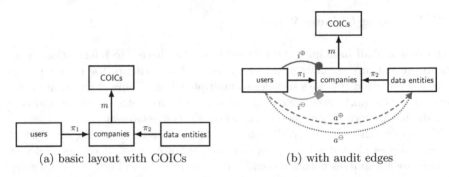

(a) basic layout with COICs   (b) with audit edges

Fig. 3. Chinese Wall Generalisation

subject and the company whose data was accessed. (We will also add an authorized decision audit edge between the subject and the data entity if it does not already exist.) Additionally, blocked interest audit edges are added (if they don't already exist) between the subject and all other companies who are members of the conflict of interest class to which the first company is a member. Interest audit edges are not added after denied authorization requests.

For a concrete example, consider the system graph G_4 shown in Figure 4a, where a member of staff u_1 works for an employer e_1. This employer supplies numerous clients (c_1, c_2 and c_3) which have data in the form of files (f_1, f_2, f_3 and f_4). In this example users are connected to companies by $\pi_1 = w \; ; \; s$ whilst data entities are connected to companies by $\pi_2 = d$.

If we assume the existence of a principal-matching policy $\rho = [(w \; ; \; s \; ; \; \overline{d}, p)]$ and authorization policy $PA = [(p, \star, \mathsf{read}, 1)]$, then u_1 would be authorized to read all files. However, the clients are members of conflict of interest classes (i_1 and i_2) with clients c_1 and c_2 being competitors in i_1. Accordingly, we modify the principal-matching and authorization policies as follows:

$$\rho_{cw} = [(i^\ominus \; ; \; \overline{d}, p_{cw}), (w \; ; \; s \; ; \; \overline{d}, p)] \quad \text{and} \quad PA_{cw} = [(p_{cw}, \star, \star, 0), (p, \star, \mathsf{read}, 1)].$$

We now consider four different types of request that can arise. Figure 4b shows the graph G_4 after all four requests have been made.

Initial Declaration of Interest. The request $q_1 = (u_1, f_1, \mathsf{read})$ to read data belonging to client c_1 in the graph G_4 will be authorized: the first principal-matching rule is not matched but the second one is. Thus $MP = [p]$ and the request is authorized, resulting in an authorized decision audit edge $(u_1, f_1, \mathsf{read}^\oplus)$ being added to the graph along with the interest edges $(u_1, c_1, i^\oplus)$ and $(u_1, c_2, i^\ominus)$.

Continued Interest. If u_1 makes a second request $q_2 = (u_1, f_4, \mathsf{read})$ for data of client c_1 this will also be authorized. The first principal-matching rule cannot be matched, as before, and the second can with principal p, once again, being authorized to read all objects. The authorized decision audit edge $(u_1, f_4, \mathsf{read}^\oplus)$ will be added to the graph but no new interest edges are added as the required edges already exist.

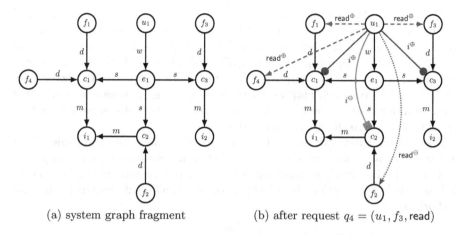

(a) system graph fragment   (b) after request $q_4 = (u_1, f_3, \text{read})$

Fig. 4. Enforcing the Chinese Wall policy in RPPM

Conflict of Interest Request. If u_1 requests data for a competing client c_2 using a third request $q_3 = (u_1, f_2, \text{read})$, this will be denied. This time, the principal-matching rule $(i^\ominus ; \overline{d}, p_{cw})$ is matched and p_{cw} is denied all actions on all objects. A denial audit edge $(u_1, f_2, \text{read}^\ominus)$ is added to the graph.

New Declaration of Interest Which Doesn't Conflict. Lastly u_1 makes a request $q_4 = (u_1, f_3, \text{read})$ for data of a third client c_3 who does not conflict with c_1 (with membership in a different conflict of interest class). As with the first two requests, this request will be authorized using the second principal-matching rule and matched principal p. An authorized decision audit edge $(u_1, f_3, \text{read}^\oplus)$ is then added to the graph along with the active interest edge $(u_1, c_3, i^\oplus)$. No blocked interest edges are added as there are no companies other than c_3 who are members of conflict of interest class i_2.

More generally, suppose we have a principal-matching policy ρ. In order to enforce the Chinese Wall constraint using this basic layout we add a new principal-matching rule $(i^\ominus ; \pi_2, p_{cw})$ to ρ to produce a new policy ρ_{cw}. The p_{cw} principal is denied all actions on all data entities through the inclusion of an authorization rule $(p_{cw}, \star, \star, 0)$ into the existing authorization policy PA, producing a new authorization policy PA_{cw}.[3]

Proposition 2. *Given an RPPM Chinese Wall constraint, as described above, for any user u the request (u, o, a) is allowed if the request is authorized by ρ_{cw} and PA_{cw} and the user u does not have an active interest in any company c' which is a member of the same conflict of interest class as the company $c \neq c'$ responsible for o. In all other cases the request is denied.*

---

[3] Once again, whilst we use the AllMatch PMS and the DenyOverride CRS we could equally employ the FirstMatch PMS with any CRS as long as we ensure that the constraint principal-matching rules are added before any existing rules.

The basic model described above is consistent with that used by Brewer and Nash, where there is a simple and fixed relationship between users and companies (path condition π_1) and between data objects and companies (path condition π_2). However, this approach is unnecessarily restrictive (and was chosen for ease of exposition), in that we may wish to define more complex authorization requirements between such entities. In practice, there is no reason why multiple path conditions cannot be used between users, objects and companies, each of which is mapped to the appropriate principal.

For example, given two paths of relations between users and companies ($w\,;s$ and $w\,;p\,;s$) and two paths of relations between data entities and companies (d and $f\,;d$) the principal-matching policy from our running example is modified to include both options for blocking paths and all combinations for normal authorization.

$$\rho_{cw_2} = [(i^\ominus\,;\overline{d},p_{cw_2}),(i^\ominus\,;\overline{d}\,;\overline{f},p_{cw_2}),$$
$$(w\,;s\,;\overline{d},p),(w\,;s\,;\overline{d}\,;\overline{f},p),(w\,;p\,;s\,;\overline{d},p),(w\,;p\,;s\,;\overline{d}\,;\overline{f},p)]$$

5   Related Work

Relationship-based access control is becoming an increasingly important alternative approach to specifying and enforcing authorization policies. A number of models have been proposed in recent years [4–6, 8, 10, 18], but most have focused on access control in social networks [4–6, 10, 18]. In this paper, we extend the RPPM model of Crampton and Sellwood [8] by introducing additional types of edges to support efficient request evaluation and history-based access control policies.

History-based access control, where an authorization decision is dependent (in part) on the outcome of previous requests, has been widely studied since Brewer and Nash's seminal paper on the Chinese Wall policy [3]. The enforcement mechanism for this policy is based on a history matrix, which records what requests have previously been allowed. It is very natural to record such information as audit edges in the system graph and to use these edges to define and enforce history-based policies. Fong et al. recently proposed a relationship-based model that incorporated temporal operators, enabling them to specify and enforce history-based policies [11]. This work extended Fong's ReBAC model, developed in the context of social networks, and is thus unsuitable for the more generic access control applications for which the RPPM model was designed. In particular, there is no obvious way in which it can support Chinese wall policies.

There has been some interest in recent years in reusing, recycling or caching authorization decisions at policy enforcement points in order to avoid recomputing decisions [2, 13, 14, 17]. In principle, these techniques are particularly valuable in large-scale, distributed systems, providing faster decisions, and the potential to recover from failures in the communication infrastructure or failure of one of the components, in the (distributed) authorization system. However, many of the techniques are of limited value because the correlation between access control decisions and the structure of access control policies is typically rather low. In contrast, caching in the RPPM model has the potential to substantially speed up decision-making because a cached edge is of real value as it enables the decision-making apparatus to sidestep the expensive step of principal matching and proceed directly to evaluating the authorization policy. Moreover, a cached edge applies to multiple requests, irrespective of whether the request has previously been evaluated, unlike many, if not all, proposals in the literature.

6   Conclusion

The RPPM model fuses ideas from relationship-based access control (by using a labelled graph), role-based access control (in its use of principals to simplify policy specification) and Unix (by mapping a user-object relationship to a principal before determining whether a request is authorized). This unique blend of features make it suitable for large-scale applications in which the relationships between users are a crucial factor in specifying authorization rules.

In addition to these advantages, the RPPM model is particularly suitable for recording information that may be generated in the process of making authorization decisions. In this paper, we focus on two new types of edges. Caching edges introduce shortcuts in the system graph indicating the principals associated with a user-object pair. Such edges can introduce substantial efficiencies to the evaluation of decisions. Audit edges allow for the enforcement of history-based policies, including separation of duty and Chinese wall policies.

The introduction of audit edges lays the foundation for future work supporting workflow tasks within the RPPM model. This work may, additionally, require the model to be further extended with the introduction of stateful entities.

References

1. Abadi, M., Fournet, C.: Access control based on execution history. In: NDSS. The Internet Society (2003)
2. Borders, K., Zhao, X., Prakash, A.: CPOL: high-performance policy evaluation. In: Atluri, V., Meadows, C., Juels, A. (eds.) ACM Conference on Computer and Communications Security, pp. 147–157. ACM (2005)
3. Brewer, D.F.C., Nash, M.J.: The Chinese Wall security policy. In: IEEE Symposium on Security and Privacy, pp. 206–214. IEEE Computer Society (1989)
4. Carminati, B., Ferrari, E., Perego, A.: Enforcing access control in web-based social networks. ACM Trans. Inf. Syst. Secur. 13(1) (2009)
5. Cheng, Y., Park, J., Sandhu, R.S.: Relationship-based access control for online social networks: Beyond user-to-user relationships. In: SocialCom/PASSAT, pp. 646–655. IEEE (2012)
6. Cheng, Y., Park, J., Sandhu, R.: A user-to-user relationship-based access control model for online social networks. In: Cuppens-Boulahia, N., Cuppens, F., Garcia-Alfaro, J. (eds.) DBSec 2012. LNCS, vol. 7371, pp. 8–24. Springer, Heidelberg (2012)
7. Crampton, J., Sellwood, J.: Caching and auditing in the RPPM model. CoRR abs/1407.7841 (2014)

8. Crampton, J., Sellwood, J.: Path conditions and principal matching: a new approach to access control. In: Osborn, S.L., Tripunitara, M.V., Molloy, I. (eds.) SACMAT, pp. 187–198. ACM (2014)
9. Edjlali, G., Acharya, A., Chaudhary, V.: History-based access control for mobile code. In: Vitek, J., Jensen, C.D. (eds.) Secure Internet Programming. LNCS, vol. 1603, pp. 413–431. Springer, Heidelberg (1999)
10. Fong, P.W.L.: Relationship-based access control: protection model and policy language. In: Sandhu, R.S., Bertino, E. (eds.) CODASPY, pp. 191–202. ACM (2011)
11. Fong, P.W.L., Mehregan, P., Krishnan, R.: Relational abstraction in community-based secure collaboration. In: Sadeghi, A.R., Gligor, V.D., Yung, M. (eds.) ACM Conference on Computer and Communications Security, pp. 585–598. ACM (2013)
12. Gligor, V.D., Gavrila, S.I., Ferraiolo, D.F.: On the formal definition of separation-of-duty policies and their composition. In: IEEE Symposium on Security and Privacy, pp. 172–183. IEEE Computer Society (1998)
13. Kohler, M., Brucker, A.D., Schaad, A.: Proactive caching: Generating caching heuristics for business process environments. In: CSE (3), pp. 297–304. IEEE Computer Society (2009)
14. Kohler, M., Fies, R.: Proactive caching - a framework for performance optimized access control evaluations. In: POLICY, pp. 92–94. IEEE Computer Society (2009)
15. Krukow, K., Nielsen, M., Sassone, V.: A logical framework for history-based access control and reputation systems. Journal of Computer Security 16(1), 63–101 (2008)
16. Simon, R.T., Zurko, M.E.: Separation of duty in role-based environments. In: CSFW, pp. 183–194. IEEE Computer Society (1997)
17. Wei, Q., Crampton, J., Beznosov, K., Ripeanu, M.: Authorization recycling in hierarchical rbac systems. ACM Trans. Inf. Syst. Secur. 14(1), 3 (2011)
18. Zhang, R., Artale, A., Giunchiglia, F., Crispo, B.: Using description logics in relation based access control. In: Grau, B.C., Horrocks, I., Motik, B., Sattler, U. (eds.) Description Logics. CEUR Workshop Proceedings, vol. 477, CEUR-WS.org (2009)

BlueWallet: The Secure Bitcoin Wallet

Tobias Bamert[1], Christian Decker[1], Roger Wattenhofer[1], and Samuel Welten[2]

[1] OpenSystems AG, ETH Zurich, Switzerland
[2] BitSplitters GmbH
tbamert@ee.ethz.ch, cdecker@tik.ee.ethz.ch,
wattenhofer@ethz.ch, welten@bitsplitters.com

Abstract. With the increasing popularity of Bitcoin, a digital decentralized currency and payment system, the number of malicious third parties attempting to steal bitcoins has grown substantially. Attackers have stolen bitcoins worth millions of dollars from victims by using malware to gain access to the private keys stored on the victims' computers or smart phones. In order to protect the Bitcoin private keys, we propose the use of a hardware token for the authorization of transactions. We created a proof-of-concept Bitcoin hardware token: BlueWallet. The device communicates using Bluetooth Low Energy and is able to securely sign Bitcoin transactions. The device can also be used as an electronic wallet in combination with a point of sale and serves as an alternative to cash and credit cards.

Keywords: Bitcoin, Transaction, Security, Wallet, Public/Private Key, Authorization.

1 Introduction

The digital currency and payment system Bitcoin has become more popular in recent years. As the price of a bitcoin increased to more than 1200 USD in 2013, the number of Bitcoin users and investors increased dramatically.[1] Unlike other payment systems, Bitcoin is not controlled by a central authority. Instead, it is operated by a decentralized authority, the Bitcoin network. This peer-to-peer network collectively handles the creation and transfer of funds using public-key cryptography. As a digital payment system, Bitcoin enables global and secure transactions with low transaction fees.

With its growth in popularity, Bitcoin has also attracted malicious third parties trying to steal other users' bitcoins. In Bitcoin transactions, users receive bitcoins to their Bitcoin *addresses*. To spend the funds associated to a Bitcoin address, control of the corresponding *private key* is needed. Losing access to a private key is equivalent to losing the bitcoins associated to the Bitcoin address. Even though the Bitcoin system itself is protected by strong cryptography, attackers have stolen bitcoins worth millions of dollars by gaining access to the

---

[1] We use *Bitcoin* to describe the system and *bitcoin* when we talk about the currency.

S. Mauw and C.D. Jensen (Eds.): STM 2014, LNCS 8743, pp. 65–80, 2014.
© Springer International Publishing Switzerland 2014

private keys of the victims. The private keys are generally stored on the computers or mobile phones of the users, where they could be exposed to malware and spyware attacks. A study by Litke and Stewart [1] shows that the amount of cryptocurrency-stealing malware has increased with the popularity of Bitcoin.

Whenever the private key is stored on a device connected to the Internet, there is a potential for theft. Our solution is to use a dedicated hardware token to store the private key needed to sign and thus authorize transactions: *BlueWallet*. This hardware token is used in combination with a device that is connected to the Bitcoin network, like the user's computer. The computer can prepare a Bitcoin transaction, but it cannot sign it. The user can use BlueWallet to review the transaction and sign it. Then, the computer can broadcast the signed transaction to the Bitcoin network. The securely stored private key never leaves the device and is only unlocked if the user correctly enters her PIN.

The hardware token delegates the creation of transactions to another entity and allows independent review of transaction details before signing. It can therefore also be used as an electronic wallet: in combination with a point of sale (POS) connected to the Bitcoin network, the device can be used to directly make Bitcoin payments. BlueWallet offers a mobile and fast solution to securing the user's bitcoins, while at the same time serving as an alternative to cash and credit cards.

2   Bitcoin

Bitcoin is an entirely digital, decentralized currency. The Bitcoin specification was introduced in 2008 by Satoshi Nakamoto [2] and a proof-of-concept client was created in 2009. Bitcoin enables instant global payments. There is no central financial authority like in traditional payment systems. Instead, the whole Bitcoin network acts as the financial authority, using cryptography to control the transfer and creation of money.

2.1   Transactions

In the Bitcoin network, a transaction describes the transfer of a specific amount of bitcoins from one individual to another. Every single Bitcoin transaction is recorded in a public ledger called the *blockchain*. A Bitcoin transaction is a digitally signed data structure that is broadcast in the Bitcoin network [3]. It consists of one ore more *inputs* and one or more *outputs*. Inputs are references to previous transactions and specify the addresses which own the bitcoins that are going to be transferred. Outputs specify the addresses that are going to receive the bitcoins, as well as the amount of bitcoins being transferred.

Each Bitcoin address is associated with a private key that is required to spend the funds assigned to the address. The Bitcoin address is derived from the public key corresponding to the private key. The user signs transactions accessing the funds of the Bitcoin address with her private key and the peers in the network verify the transaction using her public key.

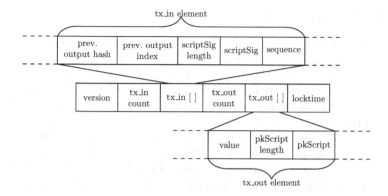

Fig. 1. Transaction packet with different fields

To understand how Bitcoin transactions are signed and verified, it is vital to know how raw bitcoin transactions look like. Figure 1 gives an overview of the transaction structure as defined in the protocol specification:

- **version:** The transaction data format version, a four byte field, with default value 1.
- **tx_in[ ]:** A list of transaction inputs with **tx_in count** elements.
- **tx_out[ ]:** List of the transaction outputs with **tx_out count** elements.
- **locktime:** The block number or timestamp at which the transaction is locked. By default set to 0, meaning the transaction is immediately locked.

Each *tx_out* output element contains a destination address and the amount of bitcoins that are transferred to this address:

- **value:** Eight byte field holding the transaction value transferred to this output.
- **pkScript:** Script of length **pkScript length** containing the destination address for the bitcoins transferred to this output.

A *tx_in* element comprises a reference to a previous transaction's output and a script containing the signature needed to claim this output:

- **prev. output hash:** 32-byte hash of the previous transaction which is referenced in the input.
- **prev. output index:** Four byte index specifying which output of the referenced previous transaction is used as an input.
- **scriptSig:** Script of length **scriptSig length** containing the signature needed to claim the referenced output and the public key matching the address owning that output.
- **sequence:** Sequence number allowing replacement of transactions.

The *previous output hash* combined with *previous output index* points to a *pkScript* of the referenced previous transaction. This way, the address owning the bitcoins used for the input is determined.

2.2 Bitcoin Cryptography

Bitcoin uses digital signatures to ensure that bitcoins can only be spent by their owner. Ownership of bitcoins is determined by the Bitcoin addresses. The owner of a Bitcoin address holds the private key associated with this address. When creating a transaction to transfer bitcoins from this address, the owner has to prove that she has the right to do so by providing a signature created with the matching private key. As we have seen, a transaction can have multiple inputs. For a transaction to be valid, the owner must provide a valid signature for each input, thus proving that she has the rights to transfer all of the funds.

The Bitcoin protocol prescribes the use of the Elliptic Curve Digital Signature Algorithm (ECDSA) in order to sign and verify transactions. This class of cryptographic signature algorithms uses algebraic operations on elliptic curves over finite fields. The public key is derived by multiplying the base point of the curve by the private key. The base point of the curve is defined by the curve parameters. Bitcoin uses the secp256k1 curve defined in the standards for efficient cryptography [4]. The security of ECDSA depends on the fact that even though the base point and the public key are public knowledge, it is infeasible to derive the private key from this information.

The primitives provided by ECDSA are *sign()* and *verify()*. The first can be used to calculate a signature S given a message M and the signer's private key p_a, while the latter allows to verify an existing signature given the message and the public key q_a of the signer.

$$S = sign(p_a, M)$$
$$verify(q_a, S, M) = \{true, false\}$$

In Bitcoin, the transaction without any signatures in the inputs is used as the message, hence the signature establishes authenticity and integrity, i.e., the transaction cannot be changed without invalidating the signature attached to the inputs:

$$S = sign(p_a, M) \wedge M' \neq M \rightarrow verify(q_a, S, M') = false$$

In order to create secure ECDSA signatures, a random parameter k is necessary. It is important to select a different k for each signature that is created with the same private key. Otherwise, the private key can be obtained through mathematical backtracking. For example, Sony's implementation of elliptic curve cryptography on their gaming console *Play Station 3* failed to do so, resulting in a compromised private key and full access to the system [5].

3   BlueWallet

The main purpose of BlueWallet is to sign Bitcoin transactions and thus authorize the transfer of bitcoins. In Bitcoin, transactions are usually created by the owner of the transferred bitcoins. It is however possible for another entity to prepare an unsigned transaction that tries to spend these bitcoins. While any entity may create such a transaction, only the owner of the bitcoins can provide the signatures needed to authorize the transaction.

By delegating the preparation of the unsigned transaction to another entity, BlueWallet does not have to be connected to the Bitcoin network. This allows us to build a device with a low power consumption and with small memory requirements. The user's private key needed to sign a transaction is safely stored on BlueWallet. The private key never leaves BlueWallet and is only unlocked if the user correctly enters her PIN.

There are two applications for BlueWallet. Firstly, it can be used in combination with the user's home computer or smart phone, similar to e-banking solutions. The user can create a Bitcoin transaction on a device which is connected to the Bitcoin network and use BlueWallet to sign it. The private key needed to access the user's funds is no longer stored on her personal computer or smart phone, which is compromised more easily.

The second application is fundamentally different from the first. The transaction is created by an untrusted third party and BlueWallet acts as an electronic wallet. An example of this third party could be the POS in a store, a restaurant or any other place where one would normally pay with cash, debit or credit card. Since the transaction is created by an untrusted party, additional security measures have to be implemented in BlueWallet to minimize the risk incurred by the user. In addition to the signing ability of BlueWallet, the user may review and authorize the transaction independently from the POS and BlueWallet has to ensure that only the authorized bitcoins are transferred.

We will subsequently focus on the second application since it is more challenging. If BlueWallet manages to meet all the necessary requirements for the use with an untrusted POS, it can be used in conjunction with a computer or smart phone owned by the user.

3.1 Creating a Transaction

Assuming a customer in a shop intends to make a payment to the POS using BlueWallet. The POS is connected to the Bitcoin network and will be tasked with the creation of the unsigned payment transaction. In order for the POS to create the transaction, it first needs to learn the customer's address. This is the address whose corresponding private key is stored in the BlueWallet. The POS therefore contacts the BlueWallet and retrieves the address.

Once the POS has the customer's address it scans its local copy of the transaction history for outputs that may be claimed by the address, i.e., earlier transactions that funded the address. The POS will then create a transaction incrementally selecting the found outputs until the desired amount is covered and adding inputs referencing them in the payment transaction. Table 1 shows an example of an unsigned transaction in the same format as it would be transferred from the POS to the BlueWallet. Two outputs are added to the transaction, one transferring the payment amount to the POS, destined to the POS' address (*tx_out[1]*), and the other totaling the remaining bitcoins that are sent back to

Table 1. The complete unsigned transaction as prepared by the POS

version		01 00 00 00
tx_in count		01
tx_in[0]	prev. output hash	13 cb 3b 56 7d ef 7f fa dc aa 69 de 20 cb 19 09 00 29 02 8b 05 d8 a9 73 d1 5d b5 cf 43 37 a5 a1
	prev. output index	00 00 00 00
	scriptSig length	00
	scriptSig	<empty>
	sequence	ff ff ff ff
tx_out count		02
tx_out[0]	value	c0 2a 99 1c 00 00 00 00
	pkScript length	19
	pkScript	76 a9 14 29 4f db f5 26 0a be 18 48 9b 48 07 f7 ba f0 62 07 70 c3 b7 88 ac
tx_out[1]	value	80 96 98 00 00 00 00 00
	pkScript length	19
	pkScript	76 a9 14 8e e6 7a 65 55 28 b6 1d e2 29 f4 5f c0 16 a0 0f 08 f3 cc 32 88 ac
locktime		00 00 00 00

the address of the BlueWallet (*tx_out[0]*). Should the POS be unable to locate enough outputs to claim the desired amount, it will return an error and abort the transaction creation.

The transaction will be completed by adding the default values for the locktime (0 to lock the transaction immediately) and the sequence in the inputs (0xffffffff to disallow replacement). It should be noted that the signature fields scriptSig length and scriptSig are set to an empty string with length 0.

Once the unsigned transaction is created, the POS will contact the BlueWallet and transfer the previous transactions as well as the newly created unsigned transaction.

3.2 Unsigned Transaction Verification

The lack a connection to the Bitcoin poses some unique problems to the system when verifying the correctness of a transaction created by untrusted the POS.

Once an output has been referenced in a confirmed transaction it is marked as claimed and cannot be claimed again. This means that the entire value associated with an output is always spent in the claiming transaction. This is why Bitcoin transactions usually have at least two outputs. One for the address to which a certain amount of bitcoins shall be transferred, and one returning the remaining funds as a new output.

The inputs in a transaction do not state their associated value. A Bitcoin Core client retrieves the value associated with an input by looking up the corresponding output, but this information is not available to BlueWallet. Since the wallet cannot know how many of our bitcoins are going to be transferred, it would have to rely on the POS to return the correct amount of bitcoins back to our address.

In order to solve this problem the POS is required to also send us all of the prior transactions that are referenced in the inputs of the current transactions. By looking at the outputs of the prior transactions, BlueWallet can determine the sum of all inputs, i.e., how many bitcoins we are going to transfer. BlueWallet compares this sum to the total value of all the outputs. The value of the bitcoins returned to us should be the sum of all our inputs minus the amount of bitcoins transferred to the POS minus an acceptable transaction fee.

Given the previous transactions we can verify the amounts being transferred. However, BlueWallet, has no way to verify that the previous transactions the POS sent were confirmed by the Bitcoin network. In order to verify the claim that the sent previous transactions are indeed the origin of the bitcoins being transferred BlueWallet calculates the hashes all the received prior transactions. These hashes are compared to the *previous output hashes* in the inputs of the current transaction. If all the hashes match, we know that the POS sent unmodified prior transactions. Even one single byte-change in a prior transaction would lead to a completely different hash, and thus a rejection of the current transaction.

But what if the POS changed the *previous output hashes* in the current transaction in order to match the hashes of forged previous transactions? In that case, BlueWallet accepts the current transaction. The Bitcoin network, however, would reject the transaction, since the modified *previous output hashes* do not reference existing prior transactions. In the end, the POS would not receive any bitcoins at all. This is a strong incentive for the POS to send us the correct prior transactions and to return the correct amount of bitcoins to our address.

3.3   Signing Transactions

Creating the required signatures to authorize a transaction is a rather involved process. To sign a transaction, the owner of the transferred bitcoins has to create a valid signature for every one of the inputs. To create a valid signature for an input, the following steps have to be taken.

First, BlueWallet creates a temporary copy of the unsigned transaction, which is needed to generate the signature. This temporary copy is then modified. The *scriptSig* of the input we want to create the signature for has to be filled with the *pkScript* of the referenced output we want to claim. Remember, the input references a previous transaction's output and this output contains a *pkScript*. This *pkScript* includes the Bitcoin address which owns the output.

Since the output of the previous transaction is owned by the BlueWallet's Bitcoin address, this is a *pkScript* containing our Bitcoin address. The *pkScript* is exactly the same for all outputs owned by our address. In this case, we already encountered it in Table 1. It is included in the transaction change output, since this output will also be owned by our address.

In order to create the signature for the input, BlueWallet replaces *scriptSig* of *tx_in[0]* in Table 1 with the *pkScript* containing our Bitcoin address, and updates *scriptSig length*.

Before BlueWallet can create the signature, it will have to append a so called *hash type* field to the copy of the unsigned transaction. The default value of this

Table 2. The complete signed transaction created by BlueWallet

version		01 00 00 00
tx_in count		01
tx_in[0]	prev. output hash	13 cb 3b 56 7d ef 7f fa dc aa 69 de 20 cb 19 09 00 29 02 8b 05 d8 a9 73 d1 5d b5 cf 43 37 a5 a1
	prev. output index	00 00 00 00
	scriptSig length	6b
	scriptSig	48 30 45 02 21 00 b7 28 96 62 40 49 55 c0 87 50 57 2f 8b 6a f4 f4 cf 69 60 c7 67 78 17 64 fd 53 6e f1 99 d0 d8 50 02 20 27 22 90 02 e4 42 a6 1e 8d 98 2a 09 22 57 8f fb 8a cc aa d6 6e 13 d6 e4 80 88 03 6f 71 88 e4 76 01 21 02 84 db aa 32 5f 58 f1 4f 3c 95 c9 55 78 ff 0a 57 10 25 05 eb b8 4c 28 a5 19 f4 f0 e5 07 f8 f4 da
	sequence	ff ff ff ff
tx_out count		02
tx_out[0]	value	c0 2a 99 1c 00 00 00 00
	pkScript length	19
	pkScript	76 a9 14 29 4f db f5 26 0a be 18 48 9b 48 07 f7 ba f0 62 07 70 c3 b7 88 ac
tx_out[1]	value	80 96 98 00 00 00 00 00
	pkScript length	19
	pkScript	76 a9 14 8e e6 7a 65 55 28 b6 1d e2 29 f4 5f c0 16 a0 0f 08 f3 cc 32 88 ac
locktime		00 00 00 00

four byte field is 1. This *hash type* is called *SIGHASH_ALL* and indicates that all the outputs are signed. Therefore, each output can only be claimed by its rightful owner. There are also other hash types, but they are not relevant to our use-case.

The modified copy of the unsigned transaction is now double-SHA256 hashed, and the resulting hash is signed with the private key corresponding to our Bitcoin address. The result is a DER-encoded signature [6]. To this signature a one-byte *hash type* has to be added. As the name suggests *scriptSig* is a script that wraps the DER-encoded signature. It starts with a byte indicating the length of the DER-encoded signature including the hashtype-byte. This is followed by the signature and the hashtype-byte itself. Next comes one byte containing the length of the public key. Finally, the public key is added. The final *scriptSig* is shown in the first input in Table 2.

In case the transaction has more than one input, a signature has to be created for every single input. This is done one signature at a time. For every signature a copy of the unsigned transaction is created and only the *scriptSig* of the input we want to create the signature for is temporarily filled with the corresponding *pkScript*. The other inputs are left as is, with empty *scriptSig*.

The valid signed transaction is then created by adding the *scriptSig* generated with the modified copy of the unsigned transaction to the original unsigned transaction shown in Table 1. The empty *scriptSig* field is replaced by the newly generated *scriptSig*, and the *scriptSig length* field is updated accordingly. The complete signed transaction as created by BlueWallet is illustrated in Table 2.

3.4   Verifying Transactions

Once all signatures have been added to the transaction, it is sent back to the POS, which will then verify the transaction's validity.

The POS has to check that its address and the correct value is still listed in the outputs of the signed transaction it received from the BlueWallet. To verify a Bitcoin transaction, its signatures have to be verified. The necessary steps to verify a signature are similar to the steps taken to create a signature. From the signed transaction a transaction equal to the modified copy of the unsigned transaction has to be created. This transaction is then also double-SHA256 hashed, which will lead to the hash that was originally used to create the signature. Using a cryptographic verification algorithm and the public key from the signed transaction, it can now be determined, whether the signature was created from this hash.

If the transaction is not valid, the POS is not going to receive any bitcoins, since the transaction would be rejected by the Bitcoin network. In case the transaction is invalid, the POS aborts the payment process.

If the transaction is found to be valid, the POS releases it into the Bitcoin network. The transaction is verified by other peers and eventually confirmed by the Bitcoin network. A transaction is confirmed when it ends up in the blockchain, the public ledger of the Bitcoin network. This process may take between 10 and 40 minutes. Since waiting this long to complete the payment process is neither in the interest of the POS nor the customer, the POS will have to accept so-called fast payments [7]. Here, the POS does not wait for confirmation by the Bitcoin network. It accepts payments as soon as it sees the transaction being forwarded in the network. Fast payments build upon trusting a transaction to be eventually confirmed by the network. But this might not always be the case.

By accepting fast payments the POS becomes susceptible to double-spend attempts. A double-spend attempt is an attack where the attacker tries to acquire a good or service from a merchant without paying for it. From the POS' view, we could be such an attacker. Our double-spend attempt would include the following steps. Upon receiving the unsigned transaction by the POS, we create a second transaction using the same previous outputs as inputs. The second transaction may transfer the bitcoins to another address, which could be our own. We then sign the original transaction and send it to the POS. If we manage to release the second transaction into the Bitcoin network at the same time, it will be verified by peers in the network and could later be confirmed by the Bitcoin network. Since outputs can only be spent once, the transaction that is supposed to pay the POS will then eventually be rejected by the network. By then, we would have long left the store with the goods.

In order to prevent such double-spend attacks, the POS constantly monitors the Bitcoin network for other transactions spending the outputs chosen for the payment transaction. Furthermore, to secure fast payments the POS could implement the techniques described by [8]. The POS is always connected to a large amount of other peers in the network. For a fast payment transaction to be accepted, a certain percentage of the connected peers must have seen the transaction after a couple of seconds.

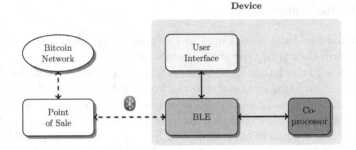

Fig. 2. System overview with contributing components

4   Implementation

In this section, we illustrate how we created a prototype of BlueWallet with the previously mentioned capabilities.

Figure 2 illustrates the POS scenario and shows the main components of Blue-Wallet. For communication with the POS BlueWallet incorporates a Bluetooth Low Energy (BLE) module. Compared to classic Bluetooth it provides a considerably reduced power consumption. To process and sign transactions quickly and to improve security, BlueWallet features a co-processor. This co-processor consumes more power than the other parts of the system and therefore immediately enters the stand-by mode whenever it is not used.

4.1   BlueWallet Prototype

The user interface of BlueWallet consists of an OLED display and four buttons. The display is used to show relevant information to the user, the buttons are required for user input. The four buttons are placed next to the four corners of the display. On the right side of the display, we have an *OK* button, used to confirm user input and transactions and a *CANCEL* button, used to cancel user input and reject transactions. On the left side of the display, there is an *UP* and a *DOWN* button, used for selection purposes and for choosing the digits when entering the PIN code.

The Bluetooth Low Energy module is a Bluegiga BLE113 with integrated microcontroller and Bluetooth radio. The BLE113 is the heart of BlueWallet. It is capable of communicating over Bluetooth Low Energy with the POS, interfaces with the microcontroller needed for cryptographic calculations, reacts to user input and controls the display.

The integrated microcontroller in the BLE113 is a 8-bit CC2541 by Texas Instruments. It is a power-optimized chip for BLE applications. The BlueWallet application running on the CC2541 chip is the major building block of our device and implements the state machine, which handles the different states of BlueWallet. It was developed using the BLE software development platform by Texas Instruments.

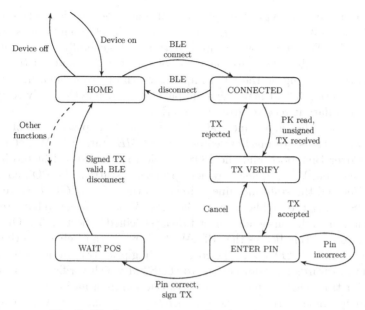

Fig. 3. The important states for the payment process

For data communication with the POS, BlueWallet uses the Generic Attribute (GATT) layer of the BLE protocol stack. Using a *GATT profile* BlueWallet is able to provide access to GATT *characteristics*. These characteristics contain values that can be written and read by a connected device, depending on the characteristics' properties.

In order to sign transactions, BlueWallet requires more computational resources than the CC2541 could provide. Initial tests with an implementation of ECDSA on this power-saving chip resulted in run-times for a single signature of over 90 seconds, which might be acceptable for non time critical scenarios such as e-Banking, but not for the POS scenario.

Thus, BlueWallet features an STM32F205RE co-processor (STM), a 32-bit microcontroller by STMicroelectronics, that is used for all cryptographic operations. It provides approximately two orders of magnitude speedup, verifying and signing transactions with one input in under a second.

Moreover, by separating the cryptographic domain from the Bluetooth domain, we can improve the overall security of BlueWallet. By only storing the PIN-encrypted private key needed for signature generation on the STM, we can make sure that even if the Bluetooth connection is compromised the private key is not. Eventually we will use a tamper resistant cryptoprocessor, so that even physical access to BlueWallet would not give access to the encrypted private key. At the time of writing no such processor exists due to the choice of the secp256k1 curve in the Bitcoin protocol.

The BLE113 and the STM communicate over UART via a direct connection. In addition, the BLE113 has the ability to wake up the STM from standby mode. This is necessary because the STM has a significantly higher power consumption when in run mode. The typical supply current when the chip is clocked at 120 MHz lies between 33 and 61 mA. In standby mode the chip only draws around 4 µA. Since BlueWallet is powered by a battery, we generally want to use as little power as possible and thus make use of the standby mode of the STM. The application running on the STM implements the Bitcoin signature scheme described in Section 3.3. It acts like a simple state machine that only reacts to commands and data it receives from the BLE113.

Figure 3 shows the important states for the payment process. Upon starting BlueWallet, the state machine enters the *HOME* state. BlueWallet is now advertising over Bluetooth and the POS is able to establish a Bluetooth Low Energy connection. When a new payment process is started, the POS connects to BlueWallet and the state machine switches to the *CONNECTED* state.

The POS reads the public key of the BlueWallet's owner (characteristic 0xfff1) and builds the unsigned transaction as specified in Section 3.1. Once the *device state* (0xfff5) indicates that BlueWallet is ready to receive data the POS sends the unsigned (0xfff3) and the corresponding prior transactions (0xfff7). The BLE113 forwards the transactions to the STM which verifies the unsigned and the prior transactions and sends the transaction information back.

The state machine switches to the *TX VERIFY* state and BlueWallet displays the transaction information to the user. In addition to the automatic verification of the unsigned transaction that is done by the STM, the user has to manually confirm the correctness of the transaction. Looking at the display, she can verify the address she is going to transfer bitcoins to, the amount of bitcoins that are transferred and also check the transaction fee.

If the transaction information is correct, the user accepts the transaction and the state machine switches to the *ENTER PIN* state. Each transaction has to be authorized by the owner of BlueWallet with her PIN. This ensures that, even when BlueWallet is lost or stolen, a third party is unable to make payments.

Upon entering the PIN, the BLE113 instructs the STM to sign the transaction. The STM signs the unsigned transaction with the user's private key and returns the signed transaction. The BLE113's state machine switches to the *WAIT POS* state. Now that the signed transaction is ready, which is again signaled by the device state characteristic, the POS reads the signed transaction (0xfff2) and uses the user's public key to verify it. If everything is in order, the POS informs BlueWallet that the payment has been accepted by writing the *POS state* (0xfff6) characteristic and closes the Bluetooth connection. This causes the state machine to return to the *HOME* state.

For the BlueWallet prototype we created a printed circuit board (PCB) which physically supports and connects all the components. The size of the PCB is restricted by the size of our final device. There are several constraints for the size of the device: the display needs to be large enough to accommodate the necessary information and the buttons should be easily reachable, yet BlueWallet should be small enough to be carried around by the user. The PCB for the prototype has a size of 65 x 30 mm. The buttons and the display are placed on the top of the PCB, whereas the two microcontrollers and most of the other electrical components are located on the bottom of the PCB.

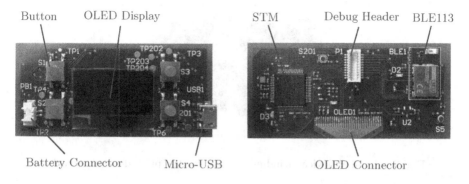

Fig. 4. The top and bottom views of the PCB

To determine how much current BlueWallet would draw at most, we summed up the maximum supply currents of the two microcontrollers and the OLED display. The OLED display has a maximum operating current of 28.9 mA, the BLE113 needs 18.2mA and the STM 61mA at most [9,10,11]. This results in a total maximum supply current needed for BlueWallet of 108.1mA. Therefore, we chose a lithium polymer battery with a capacity of 110mAh to power BlueWallet. This way, BlueWallet will at least run one hour before having to be charged again. A payment process does generally not take longer than 30 seconds. Thus, a user can complete around 100 payment processes before having to charge BlueWallet again. It should be noted that we looked at the maximum operating current of each component. Generally, each component should draw less current resulting in an even longer battery life.

Eventually, the battery will be discharged. To provide the user with a simple way of recharging the battery, we added a micro-USB connector and a battery charger circuit to BlueWallet.

For the prototype, we chose a multi-layer PCB with four layers. It consists of the top and the bottom layer which will hold the electrical components, a power plane, and a ground plane. Components can be connected to these planes using through-hole vias.

The bottom layer of the PCB with the components in place is shown in Figure 4. It should be noted that even though the display is located on the top layer of the PCB, the pads to connect the display are placed on the bottom layer. The display's pins are located on a flexible flat cable. The cable is soldered to the pads on the bottom layer of the PCB and then bent around the edge of the PCB. As a result, the display will come to rest on the top layer of the PCB.

On the top layer illustrated in Figure 4, there are only a few electrical components. Soldered to the top layer are the four buttons, the micro-USB port needed for charging the battery and a 2-pin connector for the battery.

Evaluating the prototype, we found that it takes approximately 1.5 seconds to send the unsigned transaction and one previous transaction to BlueWallet. Upon receiving the transaction details, they are displayed almost instantly by BlueWallet. A thorough review of the transaction details can be done in about 10 seconds. The time it takes to enter the PIN code depends on the length

Fig. 5. The final device including the case for the printed circuit board

of the PIN code, but generally does not take longer than 10 seconds. The co-processor signs a transaction in less than one second. Then, it again takes around 1.5 seconds to return the signed transaction to the POS. A complete payment process at a POS should therefore take around 20 seconds.

4.2 Point of Sale

To test the BlueWallet in the POS scenario, we implemented the POS on a computer using a CSR 4.0 USB dongle to for Bluetooth Low Energy communication. To establish a connection with the Bitcoin network, our POS uses *bitcoind*, a variant of the reference client. The bitcoind client provides a JSON-RPC API. Our POS application makes use of this RPC interface and is also able to access the Bluetooth Low Energy functions of the USB dongle.

When the POS has established the connection to BlueWallet and read our Bitcoin address, it uses bitcoind to look up the balance of the address and find possible outputs of previous transactions associated to this address that can be used as inputs for the new transaction. With this information it creates the new unsigned transaction. Furthermore, for each input the POS has to send the complete previous transaction to BlueWallet. The POS serializes the previous transactions as illustrated in Figure 6. The total number of previous transactions is followed by the first previous transaction. If there is more than one input in the unsigned transaction, the POS adds the additional previous transactions as well. This data is written to the *prior transaction* characteristic of BlueWallet. Then, the POS sends the unsigned transaction to BlueWallet.

To know when BlueWallet has signed the transaction, the POS subscribes to the *device state* characteristic. The POS will be notified by BlueWallet when the

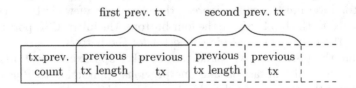

Fig. 6. Previous transactions serialized by the point of sale

characteristic changes its value. If the value indicates that the transaction has been signed, the POS reads the *signed transaction* characteristic. Then, again using bitcoind, the POS verifies the correctness of the signed transaction and sends it to the Bitcoin network.

5 Related Work

The security of using Bitcoins for fast payment scenarios, like using Bitcoin at a point of sale, where payment confirmation is required immediately, was first analyzed by Karame et al. [7]. The use of Bitcoin at a point of sale using near field communication to exchange payment information with a smart phone was examined by Bronleewe [12]. A proof of concept for a point of sale scenario implementing and expanding upon fast payment security was developed by Bamert et al. [8].

The increase of malware attacks on Bitcoin clients resulting in compromised private keys and theft of bitcoins is discussed by Barber et al. [13]. An analysis of German and US law with regards to theft of bitcoins was conducted by Boehm et al. [14]. They found that traditional criminal law is not well equipped to handle the theft of virtual goods. These findings show that it is vital to protect private keys. Litke and Stewart describe the best practices for storing private keys, including hardware tokens [15]. The benefits of hardware tokens supporting public-key cryptography with regards to e-banking are discussed by Hiltgen [16].

An approach to public-key cryptography called elliptic curve cryptography was proposed independently by Koblitz and Miller [17,18]. Elliptic curve cryptography is the foundation for the Elliptic Curve Digital Signature Algorithm (ECDSA) which is used by the Bitcoin protocol to sign transactions and is described in detail by Johnson and Menezes [19]. A review of ECDSA in practice to reveal vulnerabilities was done by Bos et al. [20]. They found that repeated per-message signature secrets led to compromised private keys of Bitcoin users.

The benefits of Bluetooth Low Energy when it comes to low energy devices are described by Gomez et al. [21]. Kamath and Lindh measure Bluetooth Low Energy power consumption of a CC2541 chip by Texas Instruments [22].

6 Conclusion

BlueWallet can be used to sign and authorize transactions that are created by the user's computer or smart phone. Using Bluetooth Low Energy to communicate with the entity creating the unsigned transaction we were able to build a device that features a low power consumption and thus is well equipped to be used on the go. Furthermore, by delegating the creation of the unsigned transaction to another entity BlueWallet can directly be used as an electronic wallet in combination with a point of sale. Implementing several security precautions, BlueWallet makes sure that transactions created by an untrusted point of sale can be used to make Bitcoin payments in a store. We found that signing Bitcoin transactions with BlueWallet is secure and fast. A user can simply pay with

Bitcoin by reviewing the transaction information on the screen of BlueWallet and entering her PIN code. Therefore, our electronic wallet is a viable alternative to card based payment methods and cash.

References

1. Litke, P., Stewart, J.: Cryptocurrency-stealing malware landscape (2014) (retrieved March 2014)
2. Nakamoto, S.: Bitcoin: A peer-to-peer electronic cash system (2008), http://bitcoin.org/bitcoin.pdf (retrieved March 2014)
3. Decker, C., Wattenhofer, R.: Information propagation in the bitcoin network. In: Peer-to-Peer Computing (P2P) (2013)
4. Standards for Efficient Cryptography (SEC): SEC 2: Recommended elliptic curve domain parameters. Technical report, Certicom Research (2000)
5. Jonathan Fildes: PS3 ECDSA security failure, http://www.bbc.co.uk/news/technology-12116051 (retrieved March 2014)
6. Dubuisson, O.: ASN. 1: communication between heterogeneous systems. Morgan Kaufmann (2001)
7. Karame, G., Androulaki, E., Capkun, S.: Two bitcoins at the price of one? double-spending attacks on fast payments in Bitcoin. IACR Cryptology ePrint Archive (2012)
8. Bamert, T., Decker, C., Elsen, L., Wattenhofer, R., Welten, S.: Have a Snack, Pay with Bitcoins. In: 13th IEEE International Conference on Peer-to-Peer Computing (P2P), Trento, Italy (2013)
9. Univision Technology Inc.: UG-2864HSWEG01 datasheet, SAS1-9046-B (2009) (retrieved March 2014)
10. Bluegiga: BLE113 datasheet v1.2 (2013) (retrieved March 2014)
11. STMicroelectronics: STM32F205xx STM32F207xx datasheet, Doc ID 15818 Rev 9 (2012) (retrieved March 2014)
12. Bronleewe, D.A.: Bitcoin NFC. Technical report, University of Texas (2011)
13. Barber, S., Boyen, X., Shi, E., Uzun, E.: Bitter to better — how to make bitcoin a better currency. In: Keromytis, A.D. (ed.) FC 2012. LNCS, vol. 7397, pp. 399–414. Springer, Heidelberg (2012)
14. Boehm, F., Pesch, P.: Bitcoin: A First Legal Analysis - with Reference to German and American Law. In: Workshop on Bitcoin Research (2014)
15. Litke, P., Stewart, J.: Enterprise best practices for cryptocurrency adoption (2014) (retrieved March 2014)
16. Hiltgen, A., Kramp, T., Weigold, T.: Secure internet banking authentication. Security & Privacy (2006)
17. Koblitz, N.: Elliptic curve cryptosystems. Mathematics of Computation (1987)
18. Miller, V.S.: Use of elliptic curves in cryptography. In: Williams, H.C. (ed.) CRYPTO 1985. LNCS, vol. 218, pp. 417–426. Springer, Heidelberg (1986)
19. Johnson, D., Menezes, A., Vanstone, S.: The elliptic curve digital signature algorithm (ECDSA). International Journal of Information Security (2001)
20. Bos, J.W., Halderman, J.A., Heninger, N., Moore, J., Naehrig, M., Wustrow, E.: Elliptic curve cryptography in practice. Microsoft Research (November 2013)
21. Gomez, C., Oller, J., Paradells, J.: Overview and evaluation of Bluetooth Low Energy: An emerging low-power wireless technology. Sensors (2012)
22. Kamath, S., Lindh, J.: Measuring Bluetooth Low Energy power consumption. Texas instruments application note AN092, Dallas (2010)

Ensuring Secure Non-interference of Programs by Game Semantics

Aleksandar S. Dimovski

IT University of Copenhagen, 2300 Copenhagen S, Denmark
adim@itu.dk

Abstract. Non-interference is a security property which states that improper information leakages due to direct and indirect flows have not occurred through executing programs. In this paper we investigate a game semantics based formulation of non-interference that allows to perform a security analysis of closed and open procedural programs. We show that such formulation is amenable to automated verification techniques. The practicality of this method is illustrated by several examples, which also emphasize its advantage compared to known operational methods for reasoning about open programs.

1 Introduction

We address the problem of ensuring secure information flow of programs, which contain two kinds of global variables labeled as: "high security" (secert) and "low-security" (public). Our aim is to prove that a program will not leak sensitive information about its high-security inputs to an external observer (attacker) who can see its low-security outputs. Thus we need to ensure that low-security outputs in all computations of the program do not depend on sensitive high-security inputs. This is also known as *non-interference* property [15], because it states that secret data may not interfere with public data. We can show that the non-interference property holds for a program if no difference in low-security outputs can be observed between any two computations (executions) of the program that differ only on their high-security inputs.

In this paper we propose a game semantics based approach to verify the non-interference property of closed and open programs. Game semantics [1] is a kind of denotational semantics which provides syntax-independent fully abstract (sound and complete) models for a variety of programming languages. This means that the obtained models are sound and complete with respect to observational equivalence of programs, and thus they represent the most accurate models we can find for a programming language. Compared to operational semantics several features of game (denotational) semantics make it very promising for automatic verification of security properties. First, it provides models for any open program fragments, i.e. programs with undefined identifiers such as calls to library functions. This allows us to reason about open programs, which is very difficult to do by using the known operational semantics based techniques. Second, the interpretation of programs is compositional, i.e. it is defined

S. Mauw and C.D. Jensen (Eds.): STM 2014, LNCS 8743, pp. 81–96, 2014.

by induction on the program structure, which means that the game semantics model of a larger program is obtained from the models of its constituting subprograms, using a notion of composition. This is essential for achieving modular analysis, which is necessity for scalability when the method is applied to larger programs. Third, game semantics takes into account only extensional properties (what the program computes) of programs. Thus, programs are modeled by how they observationally interact with their environment, and the details of local-state manipulation are hidden, which results in small models with a maximum level of abstraction. This feature of game semantics is very important for efficient establishing of non-interference, since the non-interference also abstracts away from implementation details of a program and focusses on its visible input-output behaviour. Finally, game semantics models have been given certain kinds of concrete automata and process-theoretic representations, and in this way they provide direct support for automatic verification (by model checking) and program analysis of several interesting programming language fragments [9,6]. Here we present another application of algorithmic game semantics for automatically verifying security properties of programs.

In this work we provide characterizations of non-interference based on the idea of self-composition [2], and on the observation that game semantics is consistent and computationally adequate w.r.t. the operational semantics. In this way the problem of verifying non-interference is reduced to the verification of safety properties of programs. This will enable the use of existing game semantics based verification tools for checking non-interference. If the property does not hold, the tool reports a counter-example trace witnessing insecure computations of the given program.

1.1 Related Work

The most common ways in which secret information can be leaked to an external observer are direct and indirect leakages, which are described by the non-interference property. There are also other ways to leak secret information within programs using mechanisms, known as *covert channels* [15], whose primary task is not information transfer. Timing and termination leaks are examples of such covert channels. Here a program can leak sensitive information through its timing (resp., termination) behaviour, where an external attacker can observe the total running time (resp., termination) of programs.

The first attempts to verify security properties were by Denning in [4]. His work on program certification represents an efficient form of static program analysis that can be used to ensure secure information flows. However, this method offers only intuitive arguments for its correctness, and no formal proof is given.

Recently, a new formal approach has been developed to ensure security properties of programs by using security-type systems [11]. In this approach, for every program component are defined security types, which contain information about their types and security levels. Programs that are well-typed under these type systems satisfy certain security properties. Type systems for enforcing non-interference of programs have been proposed by Volpano and Smith in [16], and subsequently they have been extended to detect also covert timing channels in [17]. The main drawback of this approach is its imprecision, since many secure programs are not typable and so are rejected. For example, in the case of non-interference the secure program: $l := h$; $l := 0$, where l and h are low- and high-security variables respectively, is not typable because there is an insecure direct flow in its subprogram $l := h$. One way to address this problem is to use static (information-flow and control-flow) analysis [3]. However, this approach is still imprecise due to the over-approximation and rejects many secure programs.

Semantics based models, that formalize security in terms of program behavior, appear to be essential for allowing more precise security analysis of programs. Security properties can be naturally expressed in terms of end-to-end program behaviour and, thus, become suitable for reasoning by semantic models of programs. For example, in [12,14] programming-language semantics has been used to rigorously specify and verify the non-interference property.

Game semantics was also previously used for information-flow analysis [13], but based on approximate representations of game semantics models. This was considered only as a possible application of the broader approach to develop program analysis by abstract interpretation in the setting of game semantics. However, this approach did not result in any practical implementations.

2 The Language

Idealized Algol (IA) [1] is a call-by-name λ-calculus extended with imperative features and locally-scoped variables. The data types D are finite integers and booleans ($D ::= \text{int}_n = \{0, \ldots, n-1\} \mid \text{bool} = \{tt, ff\}$). The base types B are expressions, commands, and variables ($B ::= \exp D \mid \text{com} \mid \text{var}D$). In this paper we work with the second-order fragment of IA, denoted as IA_2, where function types T are restricted to have arguments of base types ($T ::= B \mid B \to T$).

Well-typed terms are given by typing judgements of the form $\Gamma \vdash M : T$, where $\Gamma = x_1 : T_1, \ldots, x_k : T_k$ is a type *context* consisting of a finite number of typed free identifiers. Typing rules are standard [1], but the general application rule is broken up into the linear application and the contraction rule[1].

$$\frac{\Gamma \vdash M : B \to T \qquad \Delta \vdash N : B}{\Gamma, \Delta \vdash MN : T} \qquad \frac{\Gamma, x_1 : T, x_2 : T \vdash M : T'}{\Gamma, x : T \vdash M[x/x_1, x/x_2] : T'}$$

We use these two rules to have control over multiple occurrences of free identifiers in terms during typing. The language also contains a set of constants and constructs: i : expint_n ($0 \leq i < n$), tt, ff : expbool, skip : com, diverge : com, op : $\exp D \to \exp D \to \exp D'$, ; : $\text{com} \to B \to B$, if : $\text{expbool} \to B \to B \to B$, while : $\text{expbool} \to \text{com} \to \text{com}$, := : $\text{var}D \to \exp D \to \text{com}$, ! : $\text{var}D \to \exp D$, new_D : $(\text{var}D \to \text{com}) \to \text{com}$, mkvar_D : $(\exp D \to \text{com}) \to \exp D \to \text{var}D$. Each construct represents a different programming feature, which can also be given in the more traditional form. For example, sequential composition ; $(M, N) \equiv$

---

[1] $M[N/x]$ denotes the capture-free substitution of N for x in M.

M ; N, branching if$(M, N_1, N_2) \equiv$ if M then N_1 else N_2, assignment $:= (M, N) \equiv$ $M := N$, de-referencing [2] $!(M) \equiv M$, etc. We say that a term M is closed if $\vdash M : T$ is derivable. Any input/output operation in a term is done through global variables (i.e. free identifiers of type var$D$). So an input is read by de-referencing a global variable, while an output is written by an assignment to a global variable.

A type context is called var-*context* if all identifiers in it have type var$D$. Given a var-context Γ, we define a Γ-state s as a (partial) function assigning data values to the variables in Γ. We write $St(\Gamma)$ for the set of all such states. Let s be a Γ-state and s$'$ be a Γ'-state such that all variables in Γ and Γ' are distinct. Then, s $\otimes$ s$'$ is a $\{\Gamma, \Gamma'\}$-state, such that s $\otimes$ s$'(x)$ is equal either to s(x) if $x \in \Gamma$, or to s$'(x)$ if $x \in \Gamma'$. The *canonical forms* of the language are defined by $V ::= x \mid v \mid \lambda x.M \mid$ skip $\mid$ mkvar$_D MN$, where x ranges over identifiers and v ranges over data values of D.

The *operational semantics* is defined by a big-step reduction relation: $\Gamma \vdash M, s \Longrightarrow V, s'$, where Γ is a var-context, and s, s$'$ represent Γ-states before and after evaluating the (well-typed) term $\Gamma \vdash M : T$ to a canonical form V. Reduction rules are standard (see [1] for details). Since the language is deterministic, every term can be reduced to at most one canonical form.

Given a term $\Gamma \vdash M :$ com, where Γ is a var-context, we say that M *terminates* in state s, written $M, s \Downarrow$, if $\Gamma \vdash M, s \Longrightarrow$ skip, s$'$ for some state s$'$. If M is a closed term then we abbreviate the relation $M, \emptyset \Downarrow$ with $M \Downarrow$. We define a *program context* $C[-] \in Ctxt(\Gamma, T)$ to be a term with (several occurrences of) a hole in it, such that if $\Gamma \vdash M : T$ is derivable then $\vdash C[M] :$ com. We say that a term $\Gamma \vdash M : T$ is an *approximate* of a term $\Gamma \vdash N : T$, denoted by $\Gamma \vdash M \precsim N$, if and only if for all program contexts $C[-] \in Ctxt(\Gamma, T)$, if $C[M] \Downarrow$ then $C[N] \Downarrow$. If two terms approximate each other they are considered *observationally-equivalent*, denoted by $\Gamma \vdash M \cong N$.

Let $\Gamma, \Delta \vdash M : T$ be a term where Γ is a *var*-context and Δ is an arbitrary context. Such terms are called *split terms*, and we denote them as $\Gamma \mid \Delta \vdash M : T$. If Δ is empty, then these terms are called *semi-closed*. The semi-closed terms have only some global variables, and the operational semantics is defined only for them. In the following we fix a context $\Gamma_1 = l :$ var$D, h :$ varD', where l represents a low-security (public) variable and h represents a high-security (secret) variable. We say that h is *non-interfering* with l in $\Gamma_1 \mid - \vdash M :$ com if the same values for l and different values for h in a state prior to evaluation of the term M always result in a state after the evaluation of M where values for l are the same.

Definition 1. *A variable h is* non-interfering *with l in $\Gamma_1 \mid - \vdash M :$ com if*

$$\forall s_1, s_2 \in St(\Gamma_1). \ s_1(l) = s_2(l) \wedge s_1(h) \neq s_2(h) \wedge$$
$$\Gamma_1 \vdash M, s_1 \Longrightarrow \text{skip}, s_1' \wedge \Gamma_1 \vdash M, s_2 \Longrightarrow \text{skip}, s_2' \quad (1)$$
$$\Rightarrow s_1'(l) = s_2'(l)$$

---

[2] De-referencing is made explicit in the syntax. Thus, $!M$ is a term of type exp$D$ denoting the contents of a term M of type var$D$.

As it was argued in [2], the formula (1), where two evaluations (computations) of the same term are considered, can be replaced by an equivalent formula, where we consider only one evaluation of the sequential composition of the given term with another its copy, such that the global variables are suitably renamed in the latter. So sequential composition enables us to place these two evaluations one after the other. Let $\Gamma_1 \vdash M : \mathsf{com}$ be a term, we define $\Gamma_1' = l' : \mathsf{var}D, h' : \mathsf{var}D'$, and $M' = M[l'/l, h'/h]$. We will use these definitions for Γ_1' and M' in the rest of the paper. The following can be shown: $\Gamma_1 \vdash M, s_1 \implies \mathsf{skip}, s_1' \wedge \Gamma_1' \vdash M', s_2 \implies \mathsf{skip}, s_2'$ iff $\Gamma_1, \Gamma_1' \vdash M; M', s_1 \otimes s_2 \implies \mathsf{skip}, s_1' \otimes s_2'$. In this way, we provide an alternative definition to formula (1) as follows. We say that a variable h is *non-interfering* with l in a semi-closed term $\Gamma_1 \mid - \vdash M : \mathsf{com}$ if

$$\forall\, s_1 \in St(\Gamma_1), s_2 \in St(\Gamma_1').\ s_1(l) = s_2(l') \wedge s_1(h) \neq s_2(h') \wedge$$
$$\Gamma_1, \Gamma_1' \vdash M; M', s_1 \otimes s_2 \implies \mathsf{skip}, s_1' \otimes s_2' \qquad (2)$$
$$\Rightarrow s_1'(l) = s_2'(l')$$

It is easy to show that (1) and (2) are equivalent.

Definition 2. *We say that a variable h is* non-interfering *with l in a split (open) term $\Gamma_1 \mid \Delta \vdash M : \mathsf{com}$, where $\Delta = x_1 : T_1, \ldots, x_k : T_k$, if for all program contexts $C[-] \in Ctxt(\Gamma, T)$ that do not contain any occurrences of variables h and l, we have that h is non-interfering with l in $\Gamma_1 \mid - \vdash C[M] : \mathsf{com}$.*

Finally, we say that a term is *secure* if all global high-security variables are non-interfering with any of its global low-security variables.

3   Game Semantics

The game semantics model for IA$_2$ can be represented by regular languages [9], which we sketch below. In game semantics, a kind of game is played by two participants: the Player, who represents the term being modeled, and the Opponent, who represents the context (environment) in which the term is used. The two alternate to make *moves*, which can be either a question (a demand for information) or an answer (a supply of information). Types are interpreted as *arenas* in which games are played, computations as *plays* of a game, and terms as *strategies* (sets of plays) for a game. In the regular-language representation, arenas (types) are expressed as *alphabets of moves*, plays (computations) as *words*, and strategies (terms) as *regular-languages* over alphabets of moves.

Each type T is interpreted by an alphabet of moves $\mathcal{A}_{[\![T]\!]}$, which can be partitioned into two subsets of *questions* $Q_{[\![T]\!]}$ and *answers* $A_{[\![T]\!]}$.

$$Q_{[\![\exp D]\!]} = \{q\} \qquad A_{[\![\exp D]\!]} = D$$
$$Q_{[\![\mathsf{com}]\!]} = \{run\} \qquad A_{[\![\mathsf{com}]\!]} = \{done\}$$
$$Q_{[\![\mathsf{var}D]\!]} = \{read, write(a) \mid a \in D\} \qquad A_{[\![\mathsf{var}D]\!]} = D \cup \{ok\}$$

For function types, we have $\mathcal{A}_{[\![B_1^1 \to \ldots \to B_k^k \to B]\!]} = \sum_{1 \leq i \leq k} \mathcal{A}_{[\![B_i]\!]}^i + \mathcal{A}_{[\![B]\!]}$, where $+$ means a disjoint union of alphabets. We will use superscript tags to keep record from which type of the disjoint union each move originates. Each move in an alphabet represents an observable action that a term of the corresponding type can perform. So for expressions, we have a question move q to request the value of the expression, and possible responses are taken from the data type D. For commands, there is a question move *run* to initiate a command, and an answer move *done* to signal successful termination of a command. For variables, we have moves for writing to the variable: *write(a)*, which is acknowledged by the move *ok*, and for reading from the variable: a question move *read*, and answers are from D.

Terms in β-normal form are interpreted by regular languages specified by *extended regular expressions R*. They are defined inductively over finite alphabets $\mathcal{A}$ using the following operations: the empty language $\emptyset$, the empty word ε, the elements of the alphabet $a \in \mathcal{A}$, concatenation $R \cdot S$, Kleene star R^*, union $R + S$, intersection $R \cap S$, restriction $R \upharpoonright_{\mathcal{A}'} (\mathcal{A}' \subseteq \mathcal{A})$ which removes from words of R all letters from $\mathcal{A}'$, substitution $R[S/w]$ which replaces all occurrences of the subword w in words of R by words of S, composition $R \, {}_9^o \, S$ which is defined below, and shuffle $R \bowtie S$ which generates the set of all possible interleavings $w_1 \bowtie w_2$ for any words w_1 of R and w_2 of S. Composition of regular expressions R defined over alphabet $\mathcal{A}^1 + \mathcal{B}^2$ and S over $\mathcal{B}^2 + \mathcal{C}^3$ is given as follows:

$$R \, {}_9^o{}_{\mathcal{B}^2} \, S = \{w[s^1/a^2 \cdot b^2] \mid w \in S, a^2 \cdot s^1 \cdot b^2 \in R\}$$

where R is a set of words of the form $a^2 \cdot s^1 \cdot b^2$, such that $a^2, b^2 \in \mathcal{B}^2$ and s contains only letters from $\mathcal{A}^1$. So the composition is defined over $\mathcal{A}^1 + \mathcal{C}^3$, and all letters of $\mathcal{B}^2$ are removed. It is a standard result that any extended regular expression obtained from the operations above denotes a regular language [9, pp. 11–12], which can be recognized by a finite automaton.

A term $\Gamma \vdash M : T$ is interpreted by a regular expression $[\![\Gamma \vdash M : T]\!]$ defined over the alphabet

$$\mathcal{A}_{[\![\Gamma \vdash T]\!]} = \Big(\sum_{x:T' \in \Gamma} \mathcal{A}^x_{[\![T']\!]} \Big) + \mathcal{A}_{[\![T]\!]}$$

where all moves corresponding to types of free identifiers are tagged with the names of those free identifiers. Every word in $[\![\Gamma \vdash M : T]\!]$ corresponds to a complete play in the strategy for $\Gamma \vdash M : T$, and it represents the observable effects of a completed computation of the term.

Free identifiers are interpreted by the so-called copy-cat (identity) strategies, which contain all possible computations that terms of that type can have. In this way they provide the most general context in which an open term can be used. The general definition is:

$$[\![\Gamma, x : B_1^{x,1} \to \dots B_k^{x,k} \to B^x \vdash x : B_1^1 \to \dots B_k^k \to B]\!] =$$
$$\sum_{q \in Q_{[\![B]\!]}} q \cdot q^x \cdot \Big(\sum_{1 \leq i \leq k} \Big(\sum_{q_1 \in Q_{[\![B_i]\!]}} q_1^{x,i} \cdot q_1^i \cdot \sum_{a_1 \in A_{[\![B_i]\!]}} a_1^i \cdot a_1^{x,i} \Big) \Big)^* \cdot \sum_{a \in A_{[\![B]\!]}} a^x \cdot a$$

So if a first-order non-local function x is called, it may evaluate any of its arguments, zero or more times, in an arbitrary order and then it can return any

allowable answer from $A_{\llbracket B \rrbracket}$ as a result. For example, $\llbracket \Gamma, x : \exp D \vdash x : \exp D \rrbracket =$
$q \cdot q^x \cdot \sum_{n \in D} n^x \cdot n$. Here Opponent starts any play (word) by asking what is the
value of this expression with the move q, and Player responds by asking what is
the value of the non-local expression x with the move q^x. Then Opponent can
provide an arbitrary value n from D for x, which will be copied by Player as
answer to the first question q.

For the linear application, we have $\llbracket \Gamma, \Delta \vdash M\,N : T \rrbracket = \llbracket \Delta \vdash N : B^1 \rrbracket \, {}_9^\circ A^1_{\llbracket B \rrbracket}$
$\llbracket \Gamma \vdash M : B^1 \to T \rrbracket$. The contraction $\llbracket \Gamma, x : T^x \vdash M[x/x_1, x/x_2] : T' \rrbracket$ is obtained
from $\llbracket \Gamma, x_1 : T^{x_1}, x_2 : T^{x_2} \vdash M : T' \rrbracket$, such that the moves associated with x_1
and x_2 are de-tagged so that they represent actions associated with x.

To represent local variables, we first need to define a (storage) 'cell' strategy
cell_v which imposes the good variable behaviour on the local variable. So cell_v
responds to each $write(n)$ with ok, and plays the most recently written value in
response to $read$, or if no value has been written yet then answers the $read$ with
the initial value v. Then we have:

$$\mathsf{cell}_v = (read \cdot v)^* \cdot \left(\sum_{n \in D} write(n) \cdot ok \cdot (read \cdot n)^* \right)^*$$

$$\llbracket \Gamma \vdash \mathsf{new}_D\, x := v \text{ in } M : B \rrbracket = \left(\llbracket \Gamma, x : \mathsf{var}D \vdash M \rrbracket \cap (\mathsf{cell}_v^x \bowtie A^*_{\llbracket \Gamma \vdash B \rrbracket}) \right) \restriction_{A^x_{\llbracket \mathsf{var}D \rrbracket}}$$

Note that all actions associated with x are hidden away in the final model for
new, since x is a local variable and so not visible outside of the term.

Language constants and constructs are interpreted as follows:

$$\llbracket v : \exp D \rrbracket = \{q \cdot v\} \qquad \llbracket \mathsf{skip} : \mathsf{com} \rrbracket = \{run \cdot done\} \qquad \llbracket \mathsf{diverge} : \mathsf{com} \rrbracket = \emptyset$$
$$\llbracket \mathsf{op} : \exp D^1 \times \exp D^2 \to \exp D' \rrbracket = q \cdot q^1 \cdot \sum_{m \in D} m^1 \cdot q^2 \cdot \sum_{n \in D} n^2 \cdot (m \text{ op } n)$$
$$\llbracket ; : \mathsf{com}^1 \to \mathsf{com}^2 \to \mathsf{com} \rrbracket = run \cdot run^1 \cdot done^1 \cdot run^2 \cdot done^2 \cdot done$$
$$\llbracket \mathsf{if} : \mathsf{expbool}^1 \to \mathsf{com}^2 \to \mathsf{com}^3 \to \mathsf{com} \rrbracket = run \cdot q^1 \cdot tt^1 \cdot run^2 \cdot done^2 \cdot done+$$
$$run \cdot q^1 \cdot ff^1 \cdot run^3 \cdot done^3 \cdot done$$
$$\llbracket \mathsf{while} : \mathsf{expbool}^1 \to \mathsf{com}^2 \to \mathsf{com} \rrbracket = run \cdot (q^1 \cdot tt^1 \cdot run^2 \cdot done^2)^* \cdot q^1 \cdot ff^1 \cdot done$$
$$\llbracket :=: \mathsf{var}D^1 \to \exp D^2 \to \mathsf{com} \rrbracket = \sum_{n \in D} run \cdot q^2 \cdot n^2 \cdot write(n)^1 \cdot ok^1 \cdot done$$
$$\llbracket ! : \mathsf{var}D^1 \to \exp D \rrbracket = \sum_{n \in D} q \cdot read^1 \cdot n^1 \cdot n$$

We can see that any constant v is modeled by a word where the initial question
q is answered by the value of that constant, whereas the "do-nothing" command
skip is modeled by a word where Player immediately responds to the initial
question run with $done$. The regular expression for any arithmetic-logic operation
op asks for values of the arguments with moves q^1 and q^2, and after obtaining
them by m and n responds to the initial question q by the value $(m \text{ op } n)$.

Example 1. Consider the term:

$$n : \exp \mathrm{int}_2{}^n, c : \mathsf{com}^c \vdash \mathsf{new}_{\mathrm{int}_2}\, x := 0 \text{ in if } (!x = n) \text{ then } c \text{ else skip} : \mathsf{com}$$

The model of this term is: $run \cdot q^n \cdot (0^n \cdot run^c \cdot done^c + 1^n) \cdot done$.

In the model are represented observable interactions of the term with its environment, so we can see only the moves associated with the non-local identifiers n

and c as well as with the top-level type com. When the term (Player) asks for the value of n with the move q^n, the environment (Opponent) provides an answer which can be 0 or 1, because the data type of n is $int_2 = \{0, 1\}$. If the value 0 is provided for n, then since x has also initial value 0 the command c is executed by moves run^c and $done^c$. Otherwise, if 1 is provided for n, the term terminates without running c. Note that all moves associated with the local variable x are not visible in the final model.   □

3.1   Formal Properties

We first show how this model is related with the operational semantics. In order to do this, the state needs to be represented explicitly in the model. A Γ-state s, where $\Gamma = x_1 : \mathsf{var}D_1, \ldots, x_k : \mathsf{var}D_k$, is interpreted by the following strategy:

$$[\![s : \mathsf{var}D_1^{x_1} \times \ldots \times \mathsf{var}D_k^{x_k}]\!] = \mathsf{cell}_{\mathsf{s}(x_1)}^{x_1} \bowtie \ldots \bowtie \mathsf{cell}_{\mathsf{s}(x_k)}^{x_k}$$

So $[\![s]\!]$ is defined over the alphabet $\mathcal{A}_{[\![\mathsf{var}D_1]\!]}^{x_1} + \ldots + \mathcal{A}_{[\![\mathsf{var}D_k]\!]}^{x_k}$, and words in $[\![s]\!]$ are such that projections onto x_i-component are the same as those of suitable initialized $\mathsf{cell}_{\mathsf{s}(x_i)}$ strategies. The interpretation of $\Gamma \vdash M : \mathsf{com}$ at state s is:

$$[\![\Gamma \vdash M]\!] \circ [\![s]\!] = \left([\![\Gamma \vdash M]\!] \cap ([\![s]\!] \bowtie \mathcal{A}_{[\![\mathsf{com}]\!]}^*) \right) \restriction_{\mathcal{A}_{[\![\Gamma]\!]}}$$

which is defined over the alphabet $\mathcal{A}_{[\![\mathsf{com}]\!]}$. This interpretation can be studied more closely by considering the words in which moves associated with Γ are not hidden. Such words are called *interaction sequences*. For any interaction sequence $run \cdot t \cdot done$ from $[\![\Gamma \vdash M]\!] \circ [\![s]\!]$, where t is an even-length word over $\mathcal{A}_{[\![\Gamma]\!]}$, we say that it leaves the state s' if the last write moves in each x_i-component are such that x_i is set to the value s'(x_i). For example, let s = $(x \mapsto 1, y \mapsto 2)$, then the interaction sequence, $run \cdot write(5)^y \cdot ok^y \cdot read^x \cdot 1^x \cdot done$, leaves the state s' = $(x \mapsto 1, y \mapsto 5)$. The following results are proved in [1] for the full IA, but they also hold for the fragment we use here.

Lemma 1. *If $\Gamma \vdash M : \{\mathsf{com}, \mathsf{expD}\}$ and $\Gamma \vdash M, s \implies V, s'$, then for each interaction sequence $i \cdot t$ from $[\![\Gamma \vdash V]\!] \circ [\![s']\!]$ (i is an initial move) we have some interaction $i \cdot t' \cdot t$ from $[\![\Gamma \vdash M]\!] \circ [\![s]\!]$ such that t' is a word over $\mathcal{A}_{[\![\Gamma]\!]}$ which leaves the state s'. Moreover, every interaction sequence from $[\![\Gamma \vdash M]\!] \circ [\![s]\!]$ is of this form.*

Theorem 1 (Consistency). *If $\Gamma \vdash M, s \implies V, s'$ then $[\![\Gamma \vdash M]\!] \circ [\![s]\!] = [\![\Gamma \vdash V]\!] \circ [\![s']\!]$.*

Theorem 2 (Computational Adequacy). *If $[\![\Gamma \vdash M]\!] \circ [\![s]\!] = run \cdot done$ then $\Gamma \vdash M, s \implies \mathsf{skip}, s'$.*

Theorem 3 (Full Abstraction). *$\Gamma \vdash M \cong N$ iff $[\![\Gamma \vdash M]\!] = [\![\Gamma \vdash N]\!]$.*

Suppose that there is a special free identifier abort of type com^{abort} in Γ. We say that a term $\Gamma \vdash M$ is *safe* iff $\Gamma \vdash M[\mathsf{skip}/\mathsf{abort}] \sqsubseteq M[\mathsf{diverge}/\mathsf{abort}]$; otherwise we say that a term is *unsafe*. Since the game-semantics model is fully abstract, the following can be shown (see also [5]).

Lemma 2. *A term* $\Gamma \vdash M$ *is safe iff* $[\![\Gamma \vdash M]\!]$ *does not contain any play with moves from* $A_{[\![\mathsf{com}]\!]}^{abort}$, *which we call unsafe plays.*

For example, $[\![\mathsf{abort} : \mathsf{com}^{abort} \vdash \mathsf{skip} \,; \mathsf{abort} : \mathsf{com}]\!] = run \cdot run^{abort} \cdot done^{abort} \cdot done$, so this term is unsafe.

4   Checking Non-interference

We first describe how the game semantics model can be used to check the non-interference property of a semi-closed term.

Theorem 4. *Let* $\Gamma_1 \mid - \vdash M : \mathsf{com}$ *be a semi-closed term. We have that* [3] [4]

$$
[\![k : \mathsf{exp}D, k' : \mathsf{exp}D', \mathsf{abort} : \mathsf{com} \vdash \mathsf{new}_D \ l := k \ \text{in} \ \mathsf{new}_{D'} \ h := k' \ \text{in}
$$
$$
\mathsf{new}_D \ l' := !l \ \text{in} \ \mathsf{new}_{D'} \ h' := k' \ \text{in} \qquad (3)
$$
$$
M; \ M'; \ \text{if} \ (!l \neq !l') \ \text{then} \ \mathsf{abort} : \mathsf{com}]\!]
$$

contains no unsafe plays Iff *h is non-interfering with l in $\Gamma_1 \mid - \vdash M : \mathsf{com}$ as defined by (2).*

Proof. Let us assume that the term in (3) is safe. Let $\Delta = k : \mathsf{exp}D, k' : \mathsf{exp}D'$, then we have:

$$
[\![\Delta, \mathsf{abort} : \mathsf{com} \vdash \mathsf{new}_D \ l := k \ \text{in} \ \mathsf{new}_{D'} \ h := k' \ \text{in} \ \mathsf{new}_D \ l' := !l \ \text{in} \ \mathsf{new}_{D'} \ h' := k' \ \text{in}
$$
$$
M; \ M'; \ \text{if} \ (!l \neq !l') \ \text{then} \ \mathsf{abort}]\!] =
$$
$$
[\![\Gamma_1, \Gamma_1', \mathsf{abort} : \mathsf{com} \vdash M; \ M'; \ \text{if} \ (!l \neq !l') \ \text{then} \ \mathsf{abort}]\!] \circ [\![s_1 \otimes s_2]\!]
$$

where $s_1 = (l \mapsto v_1, h \mapsto v_2)$ and $s_2 = (l' \mapsto v_1, h' \mapsto v_2')$, for arbitrary values $v_1 \in D$, $v_2, v_2' \in D'$. By assumption $[\![\Gamma_1, \Gamma_1', \mathsf{abort} : \mathsf{com} \vdash M; \ M'; \ \text{if} \ (!l \neq !l') \ \text{then} \ \mathsf{abort}]\!] \circ [\![s_1 \otimes s_2]\!]$ is safe, so any of its interaction sequences leaves the state $s_1' \otimes s_2'$, such that $s_1'(l) = s_2'(l')$. Otherwise, we would have unsafe plays. The last if statement does not change the state, because it does not contain write moves. So by Theorem 2 and Lemma 1 it follows that the fact (2) holds.

For the opposite direction, we assume that the fact (2) holds. Let consider $[\![\Gamma_1, \Gamma_1', \mathsf{abort} : \mathsf{com} \vdash M; \ M']\!] \circ [\![s_1 \otimes s_2]\!]$, where $s_1 = (l \mapsto v_1, h \mapsto v_2)$ and $s_2 = (l' \mapsto v_1, h' \mapsto v_2')$, for arbitrary values $v_1 \in D$, $v_2, v_2' \in D'$. By Theorem 1 and Lemma 1, any interaction sequence in $[\![\Gamma_1, \Gamma_1', \mathsf{abort} : \mathsf{com} \vdash M; \ M']\!] \circ [\![s_1 \otimes s_2]\!]$ leaves the state $s_1' \otimes s_2'$, such that $s_1'(l) = s_2'(l')$. Therefore the last if statement in $[\![\Gamma_1, \Gamma_1', \mathsf{abort} : \mathsf{com} \vdash M; \ M'; \ \text{if} \ (!l \neq !l') \ \text{then} \ \mathsf{abort}]\!] \circ [\![s_1 \otimes s_2]\!]$ is evaluated in the state $s_1' \otimes s_2'$, and so its condition always evaluates to false, which implies that this model has no unsafe plays. Thus, the term in (3) is safe. $\qquad \square$

---

[3] We use the free identifier k in (3) to initialize the variables l and l' to an arbitrary value from D which is the same for both l and l', while k' is used to initialize the variables h and h' to arbitrary (possibly different) values from D'.

[4] After declaring local variables in the term in (3), we can add the command: if $(!h = !h')$ then diverge, in order to eliminate from the model all redundant computations for which initial values of h and h' are the same.

We can verify the non-interference property of a semi-closed term by checking safety of the term extended as in the formula (3). If its model is safe, then the term does satisfy the non-interference property; otherwise a counter-example (unsafe play) is reported, which shows how high-security information can be leaked by the term.

Example 2. Consider the term from the Introduction section:

$$l, h : \text{var int}_2 \vdash l := !h : \text{com}$$

To verify that h is non-interfering with l, we need to check the safety of the following term obtained by (3):

$$k, k' : \text{expint}_2, \text{abort} : \text{com} \vdash \text{new}_{int_2}\ l := k \text{ in new}_{int_2}\ h := k' \text{ in}$$
$$\text{new}_{int_2}\ l' := !l \text{ in new}_{int_2}\ h' := k' \text{ in}$$
$$l := !h;\ l' := !h';\ \text{if } (!l \neq !l') \text{ then abort} : \text{com}$$

The game semantics model of this term contains all possible observable interactions of the term with its environment, which contains non-local identifiers k, k', and abort. The model is represented by the following regular expression:

$$run \cdot q^k \cdot (0^k + 1^k) \cdot q^{k'} \cdot \left(0^{k'} \cdot q^{k'} \cdot 0^{k'} + 1^{k'} \cdot q^{k'} \cdot 1^{k'} + \right.$$
$$\left. (0^{k'} \cdot q^{k'} \cdot 1^{k'} + 1^{k'} \cdot q^{k'} \cdot 0^{k'}) \cdot run^{abort} \cdot done^{abort}\right) \cdot done$$

where the value for k read from the environment is used to initialize l and l', and the two values read for k' are used to initialize h and h' respectively.

We can see that this model contains four unsafe plays corresponding to all possible combinations of initial values (from $int_2 = \{0, 1\}$) for l, h, l', and h', such that the values for l and l' are the same and the values for h and h' are different. For example, an unsafe play is:

$$run \cdot q^k \cdot 0^k \cdot q^{k'} \cdot 0^{k'} \cdot q^{k'} \cdot 1^{k'} \cdot run^{abort} \cdot done^{abort} \cdot done$$

corresponding to two computations of the given term with initial values of h: 0 and 1 respectively, which will have two different final values for l. The interaction sequence corresponding to this unsafe play, where all interactions with local variables l, h, l', and h' are not hidden, is the following:

$$run \cdot q^k \cdot 0^k \cdot write(0)^l \cdot ok^l \cdot q^{k'} \cdot 0^{k'} \cdot write(0)^h \cdot ok^h \cdot read^l \cdot 0^l \cdot write(0)^{l'} \cdot ok^{l'} \cdot$$
$$q^{k'} \cdot 1^{k'} \cdot write(1)^{h'} \cdot ok^{h'} \cdot read^h \cdot 0^h \cdot write(0)^l \cdot ok^l \cdot read^{h'} \cdot 1^{h'} \cdot$$
$$write(1)^{l'} \cdot ok^{l'} \cdot read^l \cdot 0^l \cdot read^{l'} \cdot 1^{l'} \cdot run^{abort} \cdot done^{abort} \cdot done$$

It becomes apparent from this interaction sequence that the different initial values for h and h' are propagated as final values for l and l' respectively, which in effect causes the abort to be executed.

Let us check the security of the term:

$$l, h : \text{var int}_2 \vdash l := !h;\ l := 0 : \text{com}$$

The model of the term extended by using (3) is given by:

$$run \cdot q^k \cdot (0^k + 1^k) \cdot q^{k'} \cdot (0^{k'} + 1^{k'}) \cdot q^{k'} \cdot (0^{k'} + 1^{k'}) \cdot done$$

This model contains no unsafe plays, and so we can conclude that the corresponding term is secure.   □

To verify non-interference and security of a split (open) term $\Gamma_1 \mid \Delta \vdash M$: com, where $\Delta = x_1 : T_1, \ldots, x_k : T_k$, we need to check the state after evaluating

$$\Gamma_1, \Gamma_1' \vdash C[M]; C[M'], s_1 \otimes s_2 \tag{4}$$

for all contexts $C[-]$ that do not contain any occurrences of variables from Γ_1 and Γ_1', and for all states $s_1 \in St(\Gamma_1)$, $s_2 \in St(\Gamma_1')$, such that $s_1(l) = s_2(l')$. We can decompose the term $C[M]$ as follows:

$$C[M] = \left(\lambda u : T_1 \times \ldots \times T_k \to com . C[u] \right) \left(\lambda x_1 : T_1 . \ldots . \lambda x_k : T_k . M \right)$$

and its game semantics is: $\llbracket \Gamma_1 \vdash C[M] \rrbracket = \llbracket \Gamma_1, \Delta \vdash M \rrbracket \mathbin{\mathring{\mathmr{}}} \llbracket u \vdash C[u] \rrbracket$. Since variables from Γ_1 and Γ_1' do not occur in $C[-]$, the state $s_1 \otimes s_2$ in the term in (4) can be changed only when terms M or M' are evaluated in the context $C[-]$. As for the case of semi-closed terms, we can check the values of l and l' in the state left after evaluating the term $M; M'$. But now terms M and M' are run in the same context $C[-]$, so we are interested in examining only those behaviors of $M; M'$ in which free identifiers from Δ behave uniformly in M and M'. If we remove these additional constraints, we obtain an *over-approximated model* $\llbracket \Gamma_1, \Gamma_1', \Delta \vdash M; M' \rrbracket$ in which M and M' are run in possibly different contexts, i.e. all identifiers from Δ can behave freely in both M and M'.

Theorem 5. *Let $\Gamma_1 \mid \Delta \vdash M$: com be a split (open) term, and $\Delta = x_1 : T_1, \ldots, x_k : T_k$. If the model*

$$\llbracket k : \exp D, k' : \exp D', abort : com, \Delta \vdash \mathsf{new}_D\, l := k \text{ in } \mathsf{new}_{D'}\, h := k' \text{ in}$$
$$\mathsf{new}_D\, l' := {!}l \text{ in } \mathsf{new}_{D'}\, h' := k' \text{ in} \tag{5}$$
$$M;\, M';\, \text{if } ({!}l \neq {!}l') \text{ then abort} : com \rrbracket$$

contains no unsafe plays, Then h is non-interfering with l in $\Gamma_1 \mid \Delta \vdash M$: com.

Note that if an unsafe play is found in (5), it does not follow that M is insecure, i.e. the found counter-example may be spurious introduced due to the over-approximation in (5). This is the case, since free identifiers of type T are modeled by copy-cat strategies, which contain all possible behaviours of terms of type T. So by using game semantics we generate the most general context for the term $M; M'$ in (5), but we would like the obtained context for M to be the same for M', because we use the term $M; M'$ only to compare two different computations of the same term M.

Example 3. Consider the term:

$$l, h : \mathsf{varint}_2, f : com^{f,1} \to com^f \vdash f(l := 1) : com$$

where f is a non-local call-by-name function. The model for this term is:

$$run \cdot run^f \cdot (run^{f,1} \cdot write(1)^l \cdot ok^l \cdot done^{f,1})^* \cdot done^f \cdot done$$

It represents all possible computations of the term, i.e. f may evaluate its argument, zero or more times, and then the term terminates successfully. Notice that moves tagged with f represent the actions of calling and returning from the function f, while moves tagged with $f, 1$ are the actions caused by evaluating the first argument of f. We can see that whenever f calls its argument, the value 1 is written into l.

We can check that the model corresponding to the extended term obtained by (5) contains the unsafe play:

$$run \cdot q^k \cdot 0^k \cdot q^{k'} \cdot 1^{k'} \cdot q^{k'} \cdot 0^{k'} \cdot run^f \cdot run^{f,1} \cdot done^{f,1} \cdot done^f \cdot$$
$$run^f \cdot done^f \cdot run^{abort} \cdot done^{abort} \cdot done$$

It shows two computations with the initial value of l set to 0, where the first one corresponds to evaluating f which calls its argument once, and the second corresponds to evaluating f which does not call its argument at all. Both will have two different final values for l: 1 and 0 respectively. But this represents a spurious counter-example, since f does not behave uniformly in the two computations, i.e. it calls its argument in the first but not in the second computation. □

In order to address the above problem, we define an *under-approximation* of the required model, which is a regular language and can be used for deciding insecurity of split terms. Suppose that $\Gamma_1 \mid \Delta \vdash M$ is derived without using the contraction rule for Δ, i.e. any identifier from Δ occurs at most once in M. We define a model which runs M and M' in the same context as follows:

$$[\![\Gamma_1, \Gamma_1' \mid \Delta \vdash M; M']\!]^m = [\![\Gamma_1, \Gamma_1' \mid \Delta \vdash M; M']\!] \cap$$
$$(\mathsf{delta}_{T_1,m}^{x_1} \bowtie \ldots \bowtie \mathsf{delta}_{T_k,m}^{x_k} \bowtie \mathcal{A}_{[\![\Gamma_1,\Gamma_1'\vdash com]\!]}^*) \qquad (6)$$

where $m \geq 0$ denotes the number of times that identifiers from Δ of first-order function type may evaluate their arguments, and $\mathsf{delta}_{T,m}$ runs an arbitrary behaviour of type T zero, once, or two times. It is defined inductively on types T as follows.

$$\mathsf{delta}_{\exp D,m} = \epsilon + q \cdot \textstyle\sum_{n \in D} n \cdot (\epsilon + q \cdot n)$$
$$\mathsf{delta}_{com,m} = \epsilon + run \cdot done \cdot (\epsilon + run \cdot done)$$
$$\mathsf{delta}_{var D,m} = \epsilon + (read \cdot \textstyle\sum_{n \in D} n \cdot (\epsilon + read \cdot n)) +$$
$$(\textstyle\sum_{n \in D} write(n) \cdot ok \cdot (\epsilon + write(n) \cdot ok))$$

for any $m \geq 0$. In the case of first-order function types T, in order $\mathsf{delta}_{T,m}$ to be a regular language, we have to limit the number of times its arguments can be evaluated. For simplicity, we will only give the definition for $com \to com$ whose argument can be evaluated at most m times.

$$\mathsf{delta}_{com^1 \to com,m} = \epsilon + run \cdot \sum_{r=0}^{m} (run^1 \cdot done^1)^r \cdot done \cdot (\epsilon + run \cdot (run^1 \cdot done^1)^r \cdot done)$$

If $T = B_1 \rightarrow \ldots \rightarrow B_k \rightarrow B$, i.e. it has k arguments, we have to remember not only how many times arguments are evaluated in the first call, but also the exact order in which arguments are evaluated.

Let some identifier from Δ occur more than once in M. Let $\Gamma_1 \mid \Delta_1 \vdash M_1$ be derived without using the contraction for Δ_1, such that $\Gamma_1 \mid \Delta \vdash M$ is obtained from it by applying one or more times the contraction rule for identifiers from Δ. In this case, $[\![\Gamma_1, \Gamma_1' \mid \Delta \vdash M; M']\!]^m$ is generated by first computing $[\![\Gamma_1, \Gamma_1' \mid \Delta_1 \vdash M_1; M_1']\!]^m$ as described above, and then by suitable tagging all moves associated with several occurrences of the same identifier from Δ. So we have that $[\![\Gamma_1, \Gamma_1', \Delta \vdash M; M']\!]^m$, for any $m \geq 0$, is an under-approximation of the required model where M and M' are run in the same context. Thus, we can use it to check (in)security of split terms.

Theorem 6. *Let $\Gamma_1 \mid \Delta \vdash M$ be a split (open) term, and $\Delta = x_1 : T_1, \ldots, x_k : T_k$. If the model*

$$[\![k : \exp D, k' : \exp D', \mathsf{abort} : \mathsf{com}, \Delta \vdash \mathsf{new}_D \, l := k \text{ in } \mathsf{new}_{D'} \, h := k' \text{ in}$$
$$\mathsf{new}_D \, l' := \, !l \text{ in } \mathsf{new}_{D'} \, h' := k' \text{ in} \qquad (7)$$
$$M; \, M'; \, \mathsf{if} \, (!l \neq !l') \, \mathsf{then} \, \mathsf{abort} : \mathsf{com}]\!]^m$$

is unsafe (contains unsafe plays), Then $\Gamma_1 \mid \Delta \vdash M$ does not satisfy the non-interference property between l and h.

In the above definition of $\mathsf{delta}_{T,m}$ we allow an arbitrary behavior of type T to be played zero, once, or two times, since it is possible that a term does not evaluate an occurrence of a free identifier. In our case, this means that it is possible an occurrence of a free identifier from Δ to be evaluated only by M, or only by M', or by none of them.

Example 4. Consider the term:

$$\Gamma_1 \mid z, w : \exp \mathsf{int}_2 \vdash \mathsf{if} \, (!h > 0) \, \mathsf{then} \, l := z \, \mathsf{else} \, l := w : \mathsf{com}$$

This term is not secure, and the counter-example witnessing this contains one computation where l is updated by z, and another one where l is updated by w. So this counter-example will be captured by the model defined in (7), only if $\mathsf{delta}_{T,m}$ is defined as above, i.e. it may run exactly once a behaviour of T. □

We can combine results in Theorems 5 and 6 to obtain a procedure for verifying the non-interference between l and h in $\Gamma_1 \mid \Delta \vdash M$ as follows. First, we generate the model in (7) for some $m > 0$ and check its safety. If an unsafe play is found, then it witnesses that the non-interference property is not satisfied. Otherwise, if the model in (7) is safe, we generate the model in (5) and check its safety. If no unsafe plays are found, then h is non-interfering with l in M.

5   Applications

The game semantics model presented here can be also given concrete representation by using the CSP process algebra [6]. The verification tool in [6] automatically converts an IA term into a CSP process that represents its game semantics.

Safety of terms is then verified by calls to the FDR tool, which is a model checker for the CSP process algebra. In the input syntax, we use simple type annotations to indicate what finite sets of integers will be used to model free identifiers and local variables of type integer. An operation between values of types int_{n_1} and int_{n_2} produces a value of type $int_{max\{n_1,n_2\}}$. The operation is performed modulo $max\{n_1, n_2\}$. The tool in [6] was used to practically check the security of the following terms.

We first analyse an introductory (semi-closed) term M_1:

$$l, h : \mathsf{varint_3} \vdash \mathsf{new_{int_3}}\ x := 0\ \mathsf{in}\ \mathsf{new_{int_3}}\ y :=!h\ \mathsf{in}$$
$$\mathsf{while}\ (!x <!y)\ \mathsf{do}\ x :=!x + 1;$$
$$\mathsf{if}\ (!x > 0)\ \mathsf{then}\ l := 1 : \mathsf{com}$$

whose model is given by: $run \cdot read^h \cdot \left(0^h + (1^h + 2^h)\right) \cdot write(1)^l \cdot ok^l) \cdot done$.

We can see that if the value of h read from the environment is 0 then the guards of while and if commands are both false causing the term to terminate immediately. Otherwise, if the value of h is 1 or 2, then the body of while where x is increased will be run once or two times respectively, which makes the guard of if command to evaluate to true and subsequently the value 1 is written into l.

If the term M_1 is extended by using formula (3), we obtain a counter-example (unsafe play) corresponding to two computations with initial values of l set to 0 and the initial value of h set to 0 in the first and to 1 (or 2) in the second computation.

Let us consider the term M_2 defined as:

$$l, h : \mathsf{varint_2}, f : \mathsf{com}^{f,1} \to \mathsf{com}^f \vdash f(\mathsf{if}\ (!h \neq 0)\ \mathsf{then}\ l := 1) : \mathsf{com}$$

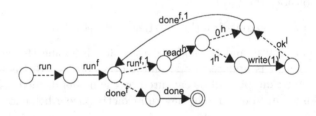

Fig. 1. The model for M_2

The model representing this term is shown in Fig. 1. When f calls its argument, the term asks for the value of h by $read^h$. If the value provided from the environment is different from 0, the value 1 is written into l.

Insecurity of this term can be established by checking safety of the extended term obtained by the formula (7) for any $m \geq 1$. For example, if $m = 1$ the following genuine unsafe play is found:

$$run \cdot q^k \cdot 0^k \cdot q^{k'} \cdot 1^{k'} \cdot q^{k'} \cdot 0^{k'} \cdot run^f \cdot run^{f,1} \cdot done^{f,1} \cdot done^f \cdot$$
$$run^f \cdot run^{f,1} \cdot done^{f,1} \cdot done^f \cdot run^{abort} \cdot done^{abort} \cdot done$$

This unsafe play corresponds to one computation where l is set to 0, h is set to 1, and the argument of f is evaluated once; and another computation where initial values of l and h are both 0, and f also calls its argument once. The final value of l will be 1 in the first case and 0 in the second.

Consider the term M_3 which implements the linear-search algorithm:

$$l, h : \mathsf{varint}_2, x[k] : \mathsf{varint}_2 \vdash$$
$$\mathsf{new}_{int_{k+1}}\ i := 0 \text{ in } \mathsf{new}_{int_2}\ y := !h \text{ in}$$
$$\mathsf{new}_{bool}\ present := f\!\!f \text{ in}$$
$$\mathsf{while}\ (i < k)\ \mathsf{do}\ \{\ \mathsf{if}\ (!x[i] = !y) \text{ then } present := tt;\ \ i := !i + 1;\ \}$$
$$\mathsf{if}\ (\neg !present) \text{ then } l := 1\ : \mathsf{com}$$

The meta variable $k > 0$ represents the array size. The term first copies the input value of h into a local variable y. The linear-search algorithm is then used to find whether the value stored in y is in the array x. If the the value is not found, l is updated to 1.

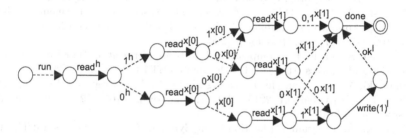

Fig. 2. The model for M_3 with $k=2$

In Fig. 2 is shown the model for this term with $k = 2$. If the value read from the environment for h is not present in any element of the array x, then the value 1 is written into l. Otherwise, the term terminates without writing into l. We can analyse this term with different values of k and different finite sets of integers used to model global variables l, h, and the array x, by generating the model in (7) for $m = 0$. We obtain that this term is insecure, with a counter-example corresponding to two computations, such that initial values of h are different, the initial value of l is 0, and the search succeeds in the one and fails in the other computation, thus they are leaving two different final values for l.

6   Conclusion

We presented a game semantics based approach for verifying security properties of closed and open sequential programs. The applicability of this approach was illustrated with several examples.

This work also has the potential to be applied to problems such as security of terms with infinite data types and verifying various types of security properties.

If we want to verify security of terms with infinite data types, such as integers, we can use some of the existing methods based on game semantics for verifying safety of such terms, such as counter-example guided abstraction refinement procedure (ARP) [5] or symbolic representation of game semantics [8]. In [7], game semantics based approach is used to verify some other security properties, such as timing and termination leaks. To detect such leaks, slot-game semantics [10] for a quantitative analysis of programs is used.

References

1. Abramsky, S., McCusker, G.: Game Semantics. In: Proceedings of the 1997 Marktoberdorf Summer School: Computational Logic, pp. 1–56. Springer (1998)
2. Barthe, G., D'Argenio, P.R., Rezk, T.: Secure information flow by self-composition. In: IEEE CSFW 2004, pp. 100–114. IEEE Computer Society Press (2004)
3. Clark, D., Hankin, C., Hunt, S.: Information flow for Alogol-like languages. Computer Languages 28(1), 3–28 (2002)
4. Denning, D.E.: Cryptography and Data Security. Addison-Wesley, Reading (1982)
5. Dimovski, A., Ghica, D.R., Lazić, R.S.: Data-Abstraction Refinement: A Game Semantic Approach. In: Hankin, C., Siveroni, I. (eds.) SAS 2005. LNCS, vol. 3672, pp. 102–117. Springer, Heidelberg (2005)
6. Dimovski, A., Lazić, R.: Compositional Software Verification Based on Game Semantics and Process Algebras. Int. Journal on STTT 9(1), 37–51 (2007)
7. Dimovski, A.: Slot Games for Detecting Timing Leaks of Programs. In: Puppis, G., Villa, T. (eds.) GandALF 2013. EPTCS, vol. 119, pp. 166–179. Open Publishing Association (2013)
8. Dimovski, A.: Program Verification Using Symbolic Game Semantics. In: Theoretical Computer Science (TCS) (January 2014)
9. Ghica, D.R., McCusker, G.: The Regular-Language Semantics of Second-order Idealized Algol. Theoretical Computer Science 309(1-3), 469–502 (2003)
10. Ghica, D.R.: Slot Games: a quantitative model of computation. In: Palsberg, J., Abadi, M. (eds.) POPL 2005, pp. 85–97. ACM Press, New York (1998)
11. Heintze, N., Riecke, J.G.: The SLam calculus: programming with secrecy and integrity. In: MacQueen, D.B., Cardelli, L. (eds.) POPL 1998, pp. 365–377. ACM, New York (1998)
12. Joshi, R., Leino, K.R.M.: A semantic approach to secure information flow. Science of Computer Programming 37, 113–138 (2000)
13. Malacaria, M., Hankin, C.: Non-deterministic games and program analysis: An application to security. In: LICS 1999, pp. 443–452. IEEE Computer Society Press, Los Alamitos (1999)
14. McLean, J.: Proving noninterference and functional correctness using traces. J. Computer Security 1(1), 37–58 (1992)
15. Sabelfeld, A., Myers, A.C.: Language-based information-flow security. IEEE Journal on Selected Areas in Communications 21(1), 5–19 (2003)
16. Volpano, D., Smith, G., Irvine, C.: A sound type system for secure flow analysis. Journal of Computer Security 4(2/3), 167–188 (1996)
17. Volpano, D., Smith, G.: Eliminating covert flows with minimum typings. In: IEEE Computer Security Foundations Workshop (CSFW), pp. 156–169. IEEE Computer Society Press (1997)

Stateful Usage Control for Android Mobile Devices*

Aliaksandr Lazouski, Fabio Martinelli, Paolo Mori, and Andrea Saracino

Istituto di Informatica e Telematica,
Consiglio Nazionale delle Ricerche Pisa, Italy
name.surname@iit.cnr.it

Abstract. This paper proposes a framework for regulating data sharing on Android mobile devices. In our approach, the user downloads a copy of the data on his Android device, then the framework controls the data usage by enforcing the usage control policies which have been embedded in the data itself by the data producer. The usage control policy is based on the Usage Control model, whose main feature is to allow the usage of the downloaded data as long as conditions specified in the policy are satisfied. The proposed framework secures the data access procedure relying on both the Android security mechanisms and the introduction of Trusted Platform Module functions. The paper details the proposed framework, presents some preliminary results from the prototype that has been developed, and discusses the security of the prototype.

Keywords: Usage Control, Mobile devices, XACML, Android.

1 Introduction

In the last years, the spreading of mobile devices, such as mobile phones and tablets, has dramatically increased so that nowadays the majority of the population owns at least one of them. New generation mobile devices are managed by operating systems which can be customized by installing applications (apps) offering a plethora of functionalities. Smartphones and tablets are equipped with fast multi-core processors, they have a good storage capacity, and a strong connectivity. Mobile devices can connect to the Internet through several interfaces, e.g., operator network (3G/4G), WiFi, or they can communicate directly with other devices through Bluetooth or NFC interfaces.

Thanks to these features, mobile devices are currently an excellent platform to download and access data, whose usage sometimes should be restricted by security policies.

Currently, Android is the leading operating system for mobile devices and is run by almost 80% of smartphones and tablets [1]. Android is a multi level open source platform, which provides an environment for the execution of mobile applications. Mobile applications are distributed to the final users through repositories (markets), that are managed by trusted parties (e.g., Google Play Store), where developers upload, distribute and sell applications. Android provides a robust security architecture that has been designed to ensure the protection of the platform, i.e., of data, resources and applications, while

---

* This work was supported by the EU FP7 project *Confidential and Compliant Clouds* (CoCo-Cloud), GA #610853.

[1] http://www.gartner.com

S. Mauw and C.D. Jensen (Eds.): STM 2014, LNCS 8743, pp. 97–112, 2014.

reducing the burden on application developers as well as allowing users to control the access rights assigned to applications. In fact, each Android application is executed in a sandbox that prevents it from interacting with other applications, and the access to resources is regulated by a permission system, as detailed in Section 3.1.

However, to regulate the access to downloaded data, the native security features of Android are not sufficient. This paper focuses on controlled data sharing on mobile devices running Android. As a matter of fact, as long as data are stored in the producer domain, they can be protected using traditional access control techniques, but once these data have been downloaded on a mobile device, typically no further controls are performed to regulate their usage. However, many scenarios require that the usage of data is regulated even when they are stored outside the producer's domain.

1.1 Contribution and Motivation

This paper proposes a framework which allows the sharing of data on Android mobile devices while protecting the data by regulating their usage. In particular, the data producer embeds a data usage control policy in the data he shares with another user. The data users exploit our framework to download a copy of the data on their Android devices, and the framework controls their subsequent accesses and the usage of these data by enforcing the usage control policy which is embedded in each data copy. The usage control policy is based on the Usage Control model, defined by Sandhu in [1], and its main feature is that it allows the usage of data as long as a set of conditions are satisfied.

Our approach protects the data from the users of the device and from the applications running on the device. Also, since the device is not always connected to the internet it should be possible to make access decisions locally. Our framework consists of a Data Protection System, that manages the storage and the accesses to the data, and of a policy decision point which is capable to evaluate policies written in UXACML language, an extension of XACML OASIS standard for Usage Control. We implemented the prototype of our stateful data usage control system as a couple of Android applications, called Data Protection System (DPS) app and UXACML Authorization app.

Many real scenarios would benefit of the proposed framework. For example, the data producer could be a team manager who wants to share his business documents with his employees. Since the documents are critical, the manager wants to allow his employees to visualize them on the company's tablets when they are located within the building of the company department, or when they are outside this building and the network interfaces of their devices are switched off. Hence, the manager could use our framework to share documents with his employees, embedding in these documents a policy that allows the visualization of the document according to the previous condition. Other real scenarios like this one can be envisioned in the Bring Your Own Device (BYOD) paradigm, in which employees are allowed to use the same mobile device both for business and private usage. The employers want the employees to separate the two domains, private and business, on their device. Thus, some business functions should be disabled when the employee is using the device for private matters. With the introduction of smartphone and tablets and the increasing popularity of cloud environments,

BYOD topic is of central importance and several security challenges have still to be addressed [2]. The approach described in this paper can be used to prevent the access to data and cloud functionalities, when a business-related security policy is not valid any more.

1.2 Paper Structure

The paper is structured as follows. Section 2 describes some related work. Section 3 describes the standard security support provided by the Android operating system, and the Trusted Platform Module. Section 4 describes the adoption of the usage control model in our scenario along with simple examples of security policies. Section 5 shows the architecture of the proposed framework, describes the prototype implementation along with some performances and security analysis. Finally, Section 6 draws the conclusions.

2 Related Work

The authors of [3] propose a framework to enhance mobile devices security focused on the protection of the resources of the mobile devices from the applications that are executed on these devices. In particular, the framework prevents the misuse of mobile device's resources using a runtime monitor that controls the application behaviour during its execution, and policies are expressed in Conspec [4]. The paper presents a prototype for Symbian OS, running on Nokia E61 and N78 devices, and a prototype for OpenMoko linux running on HTC Universal devices, and evaluates the overhead and the battery consumption introduced by the security support.

The work described in [5] proposes the run-time enforcement of policies to regulate the information flow among applications on Android devices. Policies are expressed through labels, applied to applications or to their components, which specify the secrecy level, integrity level, and declassification and endorsement capabilities of the object it is paired with. The paper describes an implementation on a Nexus S phone running Android 4.0.4, built on the top of Android's activity manager, that intercepts the calls between the components. This framework is different from the one proposed in this paper because it is focused on controlling the information flow among applications.

Another system designed to enhance the security support of Android, CRêPE, is proposed in [6] and [7]. CRêPE is a fine grained context related policy enforcement system, where each policy consists of an access control policy, composed by standard access rules, and an obligation policy, which specifies some actions that must be performed. Each policy is paired with a context, a boolean expression over physical and logical sensor of the mobile device, and when a context expression is evaluated to true the corresponding policy is enforced. The paper describes and evaluates the effectiveness and the performance of a prototype derived from the Android Open Source Project (AOSP).

The work in [8] describes a framework called *Kirin* for security attestation of apps before they are installed on a mobile device. The framework looks for malicious pattern in the application package and avoids the deployment of dangerous apps. Kirin does not perform analysis of the runtime behavior of the application and does not apply any security policy.

Another work focusing on the analysis of access to security critical resources is *TaintDroid* presented in [9]. This framework is based on hooks put in all the methods that handle access to user or device data. The information flow is then tracked, to understand which applications are effectively able to see the tracked data. This framework requires the operative system to be modified.

The work proposed in [10] describes a security framework which enhances the Android permission system allowing the user to choose the permissions to grant to an application and handling correctly the exceptions for revoked permissions, preventing the apps from crashing. With this framework the user can choose effectively which permissions grant to the app. However, the security policies which can be defined through this approach are static and limited to the coarse-grained permission system.

Access control to privacy sensitive information has been addressed in [11], which propose a framework called *TrustDroid* to define access level to specific device resources and operation. TrustDroid also allows to define some context based policies, but this policies only apply to applications installed on the device, thus private data in the wrong context can still be accessed by the user. Moreover a mechanism of remote attestation is missing and it requires modification of the operative system.

A preliminary work concerning sticky policies for mobile devices is presented in [12] where authors claim that context-aware access and usage control can be a significant support for users in mobility. The paper presents a prototype for Android systems, called ProtectMe, which allows to specify sticky policies including access and usage control directives to be enforced on the data they are attached to.

There some significant differences between the work in [12] and the one presented in this paper. Mainly, it is due to the security policy languages that the two frameworks enforce, respectively, PPL [13] and U-XACML [14]. The PPL language is designed to express obligations, i.e., actions that must be enforced by the PPL engine. Instead, the the U-XACML engine handles continuous authorizations and conditions, i.e., constrains on mutable attributes which should be re-evaluated when attributes change and a resource is still in use. A violation of these authorizations and/or conditions implies the access revocation. Then, the U-XACML assumes a distributed authorization infrastructure which requires collaboration of many parties on sharing and updating security attributes. Thus, it is capable to enforce policies which govern usage of all data copies rather than local only. Finally, the work in [12] does not provide performance analysis.

3 Background

We report in this section background notions on the security mechanism on which the proposed framework relies.

3.1 Android Security Overview

The Android framework includes several elements to enforce security on the physical device, applications and user data. The Android native security mechanisms are the Permission System and Application Sandboxing, which enforce, respectively, access control and isolation. Through the permission system, every security critical resource (e.g., camera, GPS,Bluetooth, network, etc.), data or operation is protected by mean of a permission. If an application needs to perform a security critical operation or access a security critical resource, the developer must declare this intention in the app AndroidManifest.xml (manifest for short) file asking the permission for each needed resource or operation. Permissions declared by the application are shown to users when installing the app, to decide if he wants to consider the application secure or not. If the application tries to perform a critical operation without asking the permission for it, the operation is denied by Android. The manifest file is bound to the application by means of digital signature. The integrity check is performed at deploy time, thus the Android system ensures that if an application has not declared a specific permission, the protected resource or operation cannot be accessed. In the last Android versions, users can dynamically revoke and re-grant specific permissions to applications, however this practice requires a level of knowledge and expertise greater than that of average users. In fact, revoking permissions will often result in app misbehaviors including crashes, due to the unhandled exception caused by the missing permission.

On the other hand, isolation is enforced through the synergy of two elements: the Dalvik Virtual Machine and the underlying Linux kernel. In Android every application runs in a virtual machine called Dalvik Virtual Machine (DVM). The DVM is an optimized version of the Java Virtual Machine, where each application has its own memory space, can act like it is the only application running on the system and is isolated from other apps. Moreover each instance of the DVM is registered as a separate user of the Linux kernel. This means that each installed app is considered a user at the kernel level, able to run its own processes and with its own home folder. The home folder of each application stores application files on the device internal memory, thus it is protected from unauthorized access by the Linux kernel itself. In fact, files stored in the home folder can be accessed only by the application itself. However, since the device internal memory is limited, the amount of data that can be stored in the home folder is limited and generally using the internal memory is a deprecated practice.

3.2 Trusted Platform Module

Integrity of the mobile device architecture can be assured through usage of *Trusted Computing*. Verifying device integrity is mandatory to ensure that other applications cannot interfere with the DPS and UXACML Authorization Apps. The *Trusted Computing Platform* (TCP) is an hardware framework that enforces hardware level security on a specific system. Devices protected through trusted computing embed a hardware module called *Trusted Platform Module* (TPM). The TPM includes keys and routines necessaries to verify the integrity of various levels of the device, from the firmware level to the application one.

The Trusted Computing Group is currently proposing a standard for the application of the TPM to mobile devices, such as smartphone and tablet. The system model presented in [15] and depicted in Figure 1 can be matched with the Android architecture. In fact, the Operating System block can be seen as the underlying Linux kernel of Android devices, the Native Applications block is embodied by the native application set provided by Google or the device manufacturer on stock devices e.g. Dialer, Hangout, GMail etc.. Furthermore, the Interpreter block is the DVM

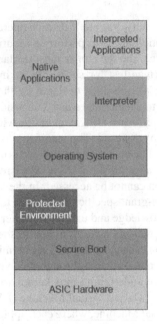

Fig. 1. Secure Mobile Device Architecture Proposed by the TCG

which executes all the applications on the device (Interpreted Applications). The protected environment is the part protected by the TPM where secure information is stored.

The TPM securely stores inside its registers (PCR) the values to perform the integrity checks of the device components. Integrity check is performed by the TPM with a bottom-up approach, in a process which is defined as *Chain of Trust*, where the integrity of each level is considered the *Root of Trust* for the higher level. This process involves a set of measurements on its configuration, which includes a set of hash computations of the code of its kernel and of the running applications. The root-of-trust is rooted to the physical platform TPM. Hence, to measure the initial integrity of the device, starting with the TPM, the following steps are required. Firstly, the TPM applies a set of measurements on the boot-loader, so that from now on, all the steps can be measured from boot to kernel loading and its modules. Then is verified the integrity of the kernel, operative system and finally of the application installed on the device.

When the integrity of a level cannot be verified, the device is considered non-secure from that level to higher ones. If the device cannot be considered secure, the integrity of the DPS and UXACML Authorization apps cannot be ensured. This check is effective against malware or device rooting attempts. In fact, if the user tries to root the device, i.e. tries to obtain root privileges to avoid security policies, the TPM will detect this modification and, consequently, it will block access to data removing the application and all its data (see Section 5). Moreover the external provider of the app will be notified. The same goes for dangerous applications. Any installed application is matched against a database of authorized application signatures. If a new application is installed then the value stored into the TPM is updated only if the app is in the signature database, otherwise the device will be considered non-secure.

Since the mobile TPM has still to be standardized, currently there are no Android devices supporting it. However, the TCP building blocks that have to be included on the Android platform have been described in [16], and are the following: a Root-of-Trust for Measurement (RTM), a Root-of-Trust for Storage and Reporting (RTS/RTR) and a Static Chain of Trust (SCoT). These elements have been developed as extension of the Linux Kernel, realizing a virtual TPM which implements all the interfaces to perform integrity checks and update stored values. However, being a software component this virtual TPM is not able to ensure any security property.

It is worth noticing that the TPM module is a hardware component embedded onto mobile devices, which will be delivered with an Android version able to manage it. The proposed framework will be available only for those devices equipped with TPM. However, the installation of the proposed framework will not require any modification of the existing version of Android, since it will exploit the existing standard interface to exploit the TPM.

4   Usage Control on Android

The framework proposed in this paper is aimed at enabling Data Producers (DPs) to perform a controlled sharing of their data, i.e., it allows other users, data users (DUs), to download a copy of these data (Data Copy, DC) and it imposes some constraints on the usage of these data. The framework has been designed for allowing the sharing through mobile devices running Android operating system. In fact, the data users run our application on their Android devices to download a local copy of the shared data from our sharing server and to access it. The downloaded data copies are paired with their usage control policies, which have been defined by the DP, and our application enforces these policies when data are accessed and stored on Android devices.

4.1   Usage Control Model

The policies enforced on shared data are based on the Usage Control model (UCON) defined in [1]. The core components of the UCON model are: subjects, objects, actions, attributes, authorizations, conditions, obligations. In the following, we briefly describe how they are instantiated in our scenario. However, for a detailed description of the UCON model please refer to [17,18,19].

The *subjects* are the Data Users (DUs) who perform some actions on the local copies of the data (which are the *objects*) that have been downloaded on their mobile devices. In the previous example, the employees are the subjects and the business document is the object. We assume that DUs are registered to Google, as we use the Google account as subject identity. In the reference scenario of this paper the policy covers a small set of security relevant *actions*:

- $visualize(s, o_{dc})$: the DU (s) visualizes the data copy object o_{dc};

- $append(s, o_{dc}, nd)$: the DU (s) append new data nd in the data copy object o_{dc};
- $replicate\&send(s_{from}, s_{to}, o_{dc})$: the DU ($s_{from}$) sends a copy of its data copy object (o_{dc}) to the (device of the) other user s_{to};
- $delete(s, o_{dc})$: the DU (s) deletes the data copy object o_{dc} from the mobile device.

We recall that the set of actions performed by the application could be larger than the previous set because not all the actions performed by the application (and not all their parameters) are security relevant.

Attributes are used to represent subjects' and objects' features. Attributes are mutable when their values are updated as a consequence of actions performed by subjects. Mutable attributes can be updated before the access (*pre-update*), or during (*on-update*), or after (*post-update*) the usage. For example, the subjects' reputation is an attribute that could be updated with a post-update. An object attribute can refer to: i) a specific Data Copy (DC), e.g., "id" or "creation date", ii) a subset of DCs, e.g., "number of data copies belonging to the user U", iii) all DCs derived from the same data object, e.g., "global number of copies".

Immutable attributes of data, e.g., id, creation date, or producer, are embedded in the data object itself, because their values will not change during the object lifetime. Mutable attributes of data, instead, are not embedded in the data object because a large overhead for keeping consistency among all copies of the same attribute would be required. Consequently, mutable attributes of data and users are stored on proper Attribute Managers that are invoked to retrieve the current value of these attributes when required. Since mutable attribute might be read and updated concurrently, Attribute Managers must be able to manage concurrent accesses avoiding inconsistencies. Mutable attribute management is out of the scope of this paper; an example is given in [20].

Authorizations are predicates that involve attributes of the subjects and of the objects. The policy could require that an authorization predicate is satisfied to begin the access (*pre-authorization*), or continuously while the access is in progress (*on-authorization*). In the latter case, as soon as the authorization predicate is no longer satisfied, the access is terminated. *Conditions* are environmental factors which do not depend upon subjects or objects. The evaluation of conditions can be executed before (*pre-condition*) or during (*on-condition*) the action. *Obligations* verify the fulfilment of some mandatory requirements before performing an action (*pre-obligation*), or while performing it (*on-obligation*).

4.2   Policy Example

Let us consider the the previous example, where a team manager wants to share some critical business documents with his employees. The following policy example is expressed using a more readable language then UXACML language:

```
policy-set:
  Target: (o.id = 'document') AND (s.role = 'employee')

  policy-1:
    Target: action = 'visualize(s, o)'
    on-authorization:
          (e.location = 'company-department')
          OR
```

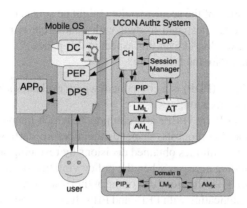

Fig. 2. Usage Control Architecture

```
              (e.inet = 'OFF') AND (e.bluetooth = 'OFF') AND (e.nfc = 'OFF')

policy-2:
  Target: action='replicate&send(s, s', o)'
  pre-authorization:
        (o.nOfCopies < N) AND (e.inet = 'ON') AND (s'.role = 'employee')
  pre-update:
        (o.nOfCopies++)
```

The manager wants to allow his employees to visualize the document on their tablets only when they are located within the building of the company department, or when the network interfaces of their devices are switched off (policy-1). This policy includes an on-authorization predicate which requires that the employee is located within the building of the company department, or that all the network interfaces of his devices are switched off. This predicate must be verified for the whole time the employee visualize the document. In fact, if an employee successfully opens the business document when he is at work, as soon as he leaves the company's building, the framework automatically detects it and closes the business document if at least one of the network interface on his device is switched on.

Another possible usage control policy in this scenario is the one that authorizes one (or more) employees to produce further data copies form their copy, but it allows a maximum of N copies of the same data (policy-2). This policy requires that the device is connected to the internet because the attribute which encodes the number of data copies is global and should be queried/updated from the remote attribute repository.

5   Prototype

This section describes the prototype architecture and implementation, and reports performance and security analysis.

5.1   Architecture Components

Figure 2 shows the components of the architecture. Though main security components reside on the mobile device, the architecture is distributed because the security attributes required for the evaluation of the security policy might be spread over several domains. This architecture has been designed to deal with concurrent retrieval and update of mutable attributes, but we don't cover this aspect in this paper.

The main components are the following:

- Policy Decision Point (PDP) is a component which evaluates security policies and produces the access decision;
- Policy Enforcement Point (PEP) is a component which intercepts invocations of security-relevant access requests, suspends them before starting, queries the PDP for access decisions, enforces obtained decisions by resuming suspended requests, and interrupts ongoing accesses when the policy violation occurs;
- Context Handler (CH) is the front-end of the authorization system, that manages the protocol for communicating with PEPs and PIPs. It converts and forwards messages sent between components in the proper format. During the pre decision phase, the CH also contacts different PIPs and retrieves security attributes;
- Attribute Manager (AM) is a component which manages attributes and knows their current values;
- Policy Information Point (PIP) is a component which provides interface for other security components to query attributes. The PIP communicates then with the specific AM to retrieve attributes;
- Lock manager (LM) is a component which guarantees consistency in concurrent retrieval and updating of mutable attributes It determines whether the attribute query/update should be served or should be delayed by placing it in a queue and executing it later. The LM might be embedded into the AM;
- Session Manager (SM) is a components which is responsible for continuous control and manages ongoing usage sessions;
- Access Table (AT) is a component which keeps meta-data regarding ongoing sessions. It contains a table of the current sessions with their statuses and a table of IDs of the attributes needed to service each session;
- Data Protection System (DPS) is the component which allows the user to access the data. The DPS embeds the PEP in a way such that all the accesses to the data are controlled by the usage control system. The DPS keeps encryption keys to access the data and perform encryption/decryption is the access should be granted to the requester.

5.2   Components Implementation

UCON Authorization System Implementation. The core of our prototype is the UCON authorization system which implements functionality of CH, PDP, PIP, LM, AM, AT, and Session Manager. It was realized as Android application, UXACML Authorization App (see Figure 3), which consists of a set of Android services and each Android service implements specific component or several components of the architecture.

The front-end of the UCON authorization system, the CH, is a bound Android service which implements client-server synchronous interactions. Initially, the PEP binds to the CH and then sends access requests using inter process communication (IPC) of

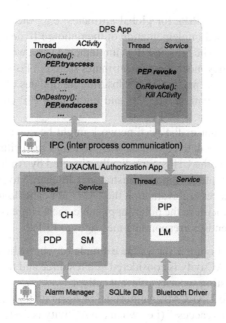

Fig. 3. Usage Control Implementation in Android

Android OS. Communications between the PEP and the CH are blocking, i.e., the code where the PEP is inserted can not continue unless an authorization decision is provided.

The CH may accept several access requests from different applications (PEPs) and each new request is evaluated in a separate thread. The Android OS handles a group of working threads to facilitate efficient evaluation of new requests. Therefore, the UX-ACML Authorization App is powerful to handle multiple calls (access requests) happening at the same time.

After receiving the access request, the CH pulls attributes from PIPs and then sends the access request and the UXACML policy to the PDP for the access evaluation. We modified Balana XACML Engine of OW2 in order to make it running on Android. If the access decision is "permit", the CH calls the Session Manager and the AT to store the metadata regarding new usage session, i.e., the UXACML policy, attributes needed for the continuous access revaluation, address of the PEP where the revocation message should be sent in case of the policy violation, etc. All session-related metadata are stored in the AT, Android SQLite DB, which is private data of the UXACML App and can not be accessed by other Android apps. Access to the AT is done to be thread-safe. Then, the CH subscribes to remote PIPs which holds mutable attributes needed for the continuous access re-evaluation. Finally, the CH responds to the PEP with access decision and this ends the pre-authorization phase.

The CH collects attributes from local and remote PIPs. The local PIP provides interfaces to environmental attributes (e.g, status of a bluetooth connection) and attributes related to local data copies (e.g., number of accesses to the DC stored on the device). Local attributes are stored in PIP's SQLite DB and the LM guarantees the consistent access to these attributes if multiple attribute queries are happening at the same time.

The CH queries remote PIPs for global attributes, e.g., the overall number of the DC in the system. We used implementation of the remote PIP described in [citation removed for blind review]. The remote PIP is implemented as a web-service with locking deadlock-free concurrency mechanism to attributes stored in PostgreSQL DB. Besides, the PostgreSQL triggers allow the CH to subscribe for updates of attributes needed for continuous access re-evaluation. The CH and the remote PIP communicate via wi-fi network.

Indeed, in mobile scenarios the wi-fi network might be down and some remote attribute changes will not be delivered to the CH. To avoid such situations which lead to possible access violation, the CH is periodically triggered by Android Alarm Manager. The UXACML Authorization App administrator is in charge to specify re-evaluation interval. If during the access re-evaluation the CH is not capable to reach remote PIPs and local attributes do not make the policy applicable, the CH fires the access revocation for such sessions and sends corresponding messages to PEPs.

PEP Implementation. Figure 3 shows the example of where the PEP code should be inserted if the Android ACtivity is considered as a resource and time when the ACtivity is visible as the long-lasting security-relevant action.

The PEP binds to the UXACML Authorization App on "tryaccess" and unbinds on the "endaccess" or "revokeaccess" (i.e., when the ACtivity is destroyed). If the resource and actions on it are represented by another abstraction and the lifetime of the resource is longer than that of the activity/service which provides access to it, the binding between the PEP and the UXACML Authorization App is executed upon each security message exchange. The UXACML Authorization App also binds to the PEP if the revocation of usage session is detected. Thus, the PEP receives the revocation message (Android intent) and starts a new thread that handles the real access revocation.

5.3 Performance Analysis

We tested the performance of our prototype in the presence of many concurrently running usage sessions. We installed the UXACML Authorization App and the DPS App with embedded PEP on Motorola Moto G which runs Android 4.4 KitKat and is equipped with 1 GB RAM and Quad-Core 1.2 GHz Cortex-A7 CPU.

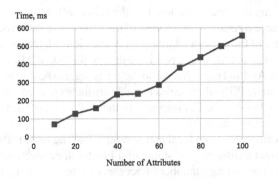

Fig. 4. Overhead of Pre-authorization Phase

First, we measured the overhead which occurs during the pre-authorization phase as a result of the access request construction, attributes retrieval, and evaluation of the policy against the access request (see Figure 4). Without loss of generality, we considered a scenario in which there is a PEP which should authorize the single request. We varied the number of attributes from 10 to 100 which are required by the UCON system to perform the decision process. As a matter of fact, there is a slight growth of t_{pre} with the number of attributes. In our tests, we used local attributes and non-updating UXACML policies (i.e., no attribute updates are needed as a result of access evaluation), while in real systems remote PIPs could be exploited, possibly increasing the time needed for attributes retrieval.

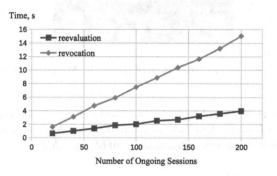

Fig. 5. Overhead of Ongoing Access Phase

Then, we measured the re-evaluation time of many sessions running concurrently varying the number of sessions from 20 to 200. All session used the same 10 attributes which were queried once but all session were re-evaluated independently and sequentially. Figure 5 (blue chart) shows the results obtained. We see that the time needed for re-evaluation of sessions grows linearly in the number of running sessions and for 200 ongoing sessions it is about 4 seconds. In fact, the results shown that the mobile device is powerful to handle a big amount of ongoing sessions.

Further, we measured the revocation time of all sessions whose policies use the same security attribute which changes its value from good to bad and violates the policies. The revocation time of all sessions defines the period of time passed from the point when the CH is triggered for access re-evaluation until PEPs receive revocation messages for all sessions that have to be revoked. Figure 5 (red chart) shows the results obtained. We see that the revocation time of all sessions grows linearly in the number of running session and for revoking 200 sessions we need about 15 seconds. The revocation time of all sessions is several times higher than the time needed just for re-evaluation of the access for these sessions. This is due to heavy resource consumption for the IPC between PEPs and the UXACML Authorization App.

Finally, we measured how many computation resources are consumed by the UXACML Authorization App which runs along with other applications on device and consumes CPU, battery, and memory. Figure 6 shows the resources consumption in the case

Fig. 6. Resources Consumption of UXACML Authorization App

of 100 ongoing usage sessions and when the access re-evaluation is triggered every 30 seconds. With such load the the UXACML Authorization App takes just about 1.4 per cent of the CPU time and needs approximately 30 MB of RAM.

5.4   Security Analysis

This subsection presents a security analysis of the proposed system. The security of our implementation relies on the Android security support, enhanced with the use of a TPM, as discussed in Section 3.2. The proposed system prevents users (including other applications) from directly accessing the DCs downloaded on this device, which are encrypted. As a matter of fact, the DCs stored on the device must be accessed only through our Data Protection System, which enforces the related usage control policies. We consider the following model of attackers:

  i) Users trying to access data stored in the SDCard. Users can browse the SDCard contents through a file manager application.
  ii) Users trying to access encryption keys used to encrypt data stored on the SDCard.
  iii) Users trying to acquire root privileges to access restricted memory space.

The implementation described in this paper assumes to have a mobile device with an embedded TPM, although no Android device currently provides it. The files including the DCs to be protected are stored in the mobile device external memory, i.e. in the SD-Card, and they are encrypted through the AES algorithm. This protects from attackers of type i) who will find encrypted files (and not usable) when accessing the SDCard of the device. The related secret key is stored in the device internal memory, in the home space of the Data Protection System application. Differently from the external memory, this space can only be accessed by the Data Protection System application, so that encrypted files can be decrypted only by the Data Protection System. This security mechanism protects the key from attackers of type ii). Thanks to the inclusion of trusted computing, it is possible to ensure that only the Data Protection System application can access the secret key. In fact, the secret key will be no more accessible as soon as the device has been rooted or unknown dangerous applications have been installed on it. In particular, as soon as the integrity verification fails, the Data Protection System application and all the related files, residing in both the internal and external memory, are removed from the device. Furthermore the Data Protection System application will not be released anymore to the device owner, unless she can prove the device status is secure again, e.g. through a factory reset. This ensures the protection also from an attacker of type iii).

The communications between the Data Protection System and the PDP and between the PDP and the PIP are secured, i.e., the mutual authentication is performed to verify the identity of the communicating applications, and also the integrity of the messages is preserved through the standard Java security library: Java SE Security.

The security policy is paired with each data copy, and it is encrypted and stored with the data itself. In this way, the security policy cannot be modified by the mobile device user or by other applications to obtain unauthorized accesses.

The status of the UXACML Authorization app, e.g., the set of the sessions that are currently opened, is stored in the private space of his app. In this way, neither the device user nor the other applications can modify it.

Finally, if the mobile device user terminates the Data Protection System, and/or the UXACML Authorization app, this only prevents him from accessing the data, since the Data Protection System app is the only way to perform the access to the data.

6 Conclusions

In this paper we have discussed a framework for regulating data sharing on Android mobile devices. In this framework, the data producer embeds a usage control policy in the data, which is downloaded by the user and enforced on the device to prevent unauthorized access to specific pieces of data. The access regulation is performed over time through the usage control paradigm. In particular, the usage control policy is able to interrupt accesses in progress when a previously valid policy is not satisfied any more. We have also presented an implementation of the proposed framework for Android smartphones and tablets, which exploits both the Android native security mechanism and a TPM to ensure system integrity. The TPM inclusion is an assumption, since currently no Android devices with a physical TPM are available, though a standard for TPM on mobile device is currently under the analysis of the TCG. Implementation on an Android-based device with TPM has been scheduled as future work.

References

1. Park, J., Sandhu, R.: The $UCON_{ABC}$ usage control model. ACM Transactions on Information and System Security 7, 128–174 (2004)
2. Morrow, B.: BYOD security challenges: control and protect your most sensitive data. Network Security 2012(12), 5–8 (2012)
3. Costa, G., Martinelli, F., Mori, P., Schaefer, C., Walter, T.: Runtime monitoring for next generation java me platform. Computers & Security 29, 74–87 (2010)

4. Aktug, I., Naliuka, K.: ConSpec: A formal language for policy specification. In: Proceedings of the First International Workshop on Run Time Enforcement for Mobile and Distributed Systems (REM 2007), ESORICS, pp. 107–109 (2007)

5. Jia, L., Aljuraidan, J., Fragkaki, E., Bauer, L., Stroucken, M., Fukushima, K., Kiyomoto, S., Miyake, Y.: Run-time enforcement of information-flow properties on android. In: Crampton, J., Jajodia, S., Mayes, K. (eds.) ESORICS 2013. LNCS, vol. 8134, pp. 775–792. Springer, Heidelberg (2013)

6. Conti, M., Crispo, B., Fernandes, E., Zhauniarovich, Y.: Crêpe: A system for enforcing fine-grained context-related policies on android. IEEE Transactions on Information Forensics and Security 7(5), 1426–1438 (2012)

7. Conti, M., Nguyen, V.T.N., Crispo, B.: CRePE: Context-related policy enforcement for android. In: Burmester, M., Tsudik, G., Magliveras, S., Ilić, I. (eds.) ISC 2010. LNCS, vol. 6531, pp. 331–345. Springer, Heidelberg (2011)

8. Enck, W., Ongtang, M., McDaniel, P.: On Lightweight Mobile Phone Application Certification. In: ACM (ed.) 16th ACM conference on Computer and Communications Security (CCS 2009), pp. 235–254 (2009)

9. Enck, W., Gilbert, P., Chun, B.G., Cox, L.P., Jung, J., McDaniel, P., Sheth, A.N.: Taintdroid: An information flow tracking system for real-time privacy monitoring on smartphones. Commun. ACM 57(3), 99–106 (2014)

10. Zhou, Y., Zhang, X., Jiang, X., Freeh, V.W.: Taming information-stealing smartphone applications (on android). In: McCune, J.M., Balacheff, B., Perrig, A., Sadeghi, A.-R., Sasse, A., Beres, Y. (eds.) Trust 2011. LNCS, vol. 6740, pp. 93–107. Springer, Heidelberg (2011)

11. Bugiel, S., Davi, L., Dmitrienko, A., Heuser, S., Sadeghi, A.R., Shastry, B.: Practical and Lightweight Domain Isolation on Android. In: ACM (ed.) ACM Workshop on Security and Privacy in Smartphones and Mobile Devices (SPSM 2011), pp. 51–61 (2011)

12. Cerbo, F.D., Trabelsi, S., Steingruber, T., Dodero, G., Bezzi, M.: Sticky policies for mobile devices. In: The 18th ACM Symposium on Acces Control Model and Technologies (SAC-MAT 2013), pp. 257–260 (2013)

13. Trabelsi, S., Sendor, J., Reinicke, S.: Ppl: Primelife privacy policy engine. In: 2011 IEEE International Symposium on Policies for Distributed Systems and Networks, pp. 184–185. IEEE Computer Society (2011)

14. Colombo, M., Lazouski, A., Martinelli, F., Mori, P.: A proposal on enhancing XACML with continuous usage control features. In: Proceedings of CoreGRID ERCIM Working Group Workshop on Grids, P2P and Services Computing, pp. 133–146. Springer US (2010)

15. Trusted Computing Group: Tpm 2.0 mobile reference architecture (draft) (April 2014)

16. Bente, I., Dreo, G., Hellmann, B., Heuser, S., Vieweg, J., von Helden, J., Westhuis, J.: Towards permission-based attestation for the android platform. In: McCune, J.M., Balacheff, B., Perrig, A., Sadeghi, A.-R., Sasse, A., Beres, Y. (eds.) Trust 2011. LNCS, vol. 6740, pp. 108–115. Springer, Heidelberg (2011)

17. Zhang, X., Parisi-Presicce, F., Sandhu, R., Park, J.: Formal model and policy specification of usage control. ACM Transactions on Information and System Security 8(4), 351–387 (2005)

18. Zhang, X., Nakae, M., Covington, M.J., Sandhu, R.: Toward a usage-based security framework for collaborative computing systems. ACM Transactions on Information and System Security 11(11), 3:1–3:36 (2008)

19. Lazouski, A., Martinelli, F., Mori, P.: Usage control in computer security: A survey. Computer Science Review 4(2), 81–99 (2010)

20. Lazouski, A., Mancini, G., Martinelli, F., Mori, P.: Architecture, worflows, and prototype for stateful data usage control in cloud. In: 2014 IEEE Security and Privacy Workshop, pp. 23–30. IEEE Computer Society (2014)

A Formal Model for Soft Enforcement: Influencing the Decision-Maker*

Charles Morisset, Iryna Yevseyeva, Thomas Groß, and Aad van Moorsel

Centre for Cybercrime and Computer Security
School of Computing Science, Newcastle University
Newcastle upon Tyne NE1 7RU, UK
`firstname.lastname@newcastle.ac.uk`

Abstract. We propose in this paper a formal model for *soft enforcement*, where a decision-maker is *influenced* towards a decision, rather than forced to select that decision. This novel type of enforcement is particularly useful when the policy enforcer cannot fully control the environment of the decision-maker, as we illustrate in the context of attribute-based access control, by limiting the control over attributes. We also show that soft enforcement can improve the security of the system when the influencer is uncertain about the environment, and when neither forcing the decision-maker nor leaving them make their own selection is optimal. We define the general notion of optimal influencing policy, that takes into account both the control of the influencer and the uncertainty in the system.

1 Introduction

A security policy is a description of what is authorised or not within a system, usually by restricting the actions that are possible in that system. Traditionally speaking, there are two ways to enforce a policy: strong or weak. The former consists in ensuring that non-secure actions cannot be performed, by intercepting and analysing them. The latter consists in analysing, after execution, the different actions, and deciding which ones were correct and which ones were not.

Strong enforcement provides a high level of security, by ensuring that no bad action is performed, but requires for the enforcement mechanism to have a full control over the system, which is not always true. For instance, human users might have a *compliance budget* [1], and will not comply with a policy seen as too restrictive. In addition, uncertainty in the system can lead to enforce the wrong decisions, and a conservative approach could lead to correct actions being denied. On the other hand, weak enforcement provides a high level of productivity, by ensuring that no good action is prevented, which is particularly

---

* This work was partially supported by the EPSRC/GCHQ funded project ChAISe (EP/K006568/1) and the project "Data-Driven Model-Based Decision-Making", part of the NSA funded Centre on Science of Security at University of Illinois at Urbana-Champaign.

S. Mauw and C.D. Jensen (Eds.): STM 2014, LNCS 8743, pp. 113–128, 2014.

crucial when the correctness of an action is uncertain. However, if the decision-maker does not naturally adopt a secure behaviour or makes the wrong decisions due to uncertainty in the system, then non-secure actions could be performed.

We propose here the notion of *soft enforcement*, which offers a middle way, by *influencing* the decision-maker. The strength of the influence ranges from strong enforcement (by being so influential that the decision-maker has no choice but to comply) to weak (by providing no influence so that the decision-maker chooses freely). We show that this approach is particularly useful when no strong enforcement is possible or when there is significant uncertainty in the system.

Contributions. The main contribution of this work is the formal definition of *decision-maker* and *influencer*, together with the characterisation of their interaction through the notion of *context* and *effect*. We introduce the notion of soft enforcement, where the influencer has only a limited influence over the decision-maker, and we illustrate it in Section 3 in the context of access control mechanisms. We also explicitly consider the uncertainty related to the observation of the environment by the different agents, and we illustrate a case where the optimal enforcement strategy is neither strong nor weak in Section 4.3. We believe the model we propose in this paper improves the tradeoff security/flexibility for policy enforcement.

Assumptions. In order to characterise soft enforcement, we assume that influence on decision-makers can be quantified. This assumption is clearly true when the influence comes from a technical aspect, such as controlling access control attributes, as illustrated in Section 3. In addition, we believe we can generalise this assumption when the influence comes from psychological aspects, following psychology work, such as [10,23,5], which provide quantitative evidence that one can influence a human decision-maker. However, these approaches usually consider influence over a population, and assuming that the impact of a particular effect on a single individual can be accurately predicted is clearly a leap from the current state of the art. Hence, when we refer to a decision-maker, we do not necessarily mean a single individual. We also assume that the uncertainty of agent observations can be quantified using bayesian probabilities, and that, at any time, there exists a *true, measurable environment*, although not necessarily by the decision-maker or the influencer.

Scope. A specific problem we do not address in this paper is that of multiple influencers, because it raises the issues of multiple effects resolution and influence loops, as described in Section 5. Although such situations are quite interesting, they require more complex tools (such as composition algebras or game theory), and we believe a model with a single influencer captures many existing systems, and is a significant contribution as such.

Methodology. This is a formal paper in nature, aiming at providing a precise and unambiguous semantics to the quantification of the impact of influence, in a clearly identified setting. The building of the model is inspired from real-world experiments, such as those conducted in [23], but the main validation of this model is theoretical: we are able to formally define the optimal influencing strategy (Equation 1) and to prove its optimality (Proposition 1), which can

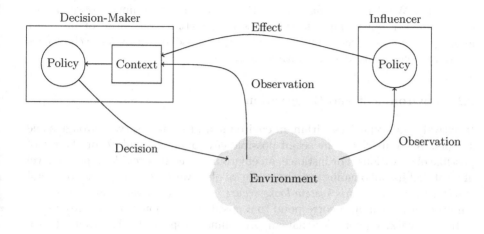

Fig. 1. Relationship between a decision-maker and an influencer

be seen as evidence of the consistency of the model; in addition, we show that strong and weak enforcement can be expressed within our model, and that they are optimal under the intuitive conditions (Section 4.2); Finally, we validate our model by illustrating it with two distinct examples (Section 3 and 4.3).

Structure. In Section 2, we present the basic model for a decision-maker, including the notion of environment, observation, impact and effect. In Section 3, we present an example of decision-making process, based on attribute based access control, and we illustrate the notion of influence, by showing that it might not be possible to always force a decision-maker towards a specific decision. In Section 4, we introduce an explicit notion of influencer, that needs to select an effect based on an observation, and is thus subject to uncertainty. In Section 5, we discuss about the problems arising with the modelling of multiple influencers. Finally, we conclude and discuss future work in Section 6. Note that, to the best of our knowledge, our model is the first formal approach aiming at characterising the influence of a policy enforcer, and as such, there is no explicit related work section. However, we identify several related lines of work in Section 6, especially in the context of extending our model.

2   Decision-Maker

We consider here a multi-agent system, depicted on Figure 1: on the one hand, a decision-maker makes an observation of the environment, analyses it through a context, and makes a decision according to a policy; on the other hand, an influencer also observes the environment, and selects an effect to modify the context of the decision-maker, in order to influence the decision. Note that by policy, we refer to a function governing the behaviour of an agent, which should not be confused with the notion of *security policy*, which describes what decisions are secure. We define in this section the notion of environment, observation, decision-maker, impact and effect; we present in Section 4 the notion of influencer as an agent (i.e., subject to uncertainty); and we raise in Section 5 the challenges to address when considering multiple influencers.

2.1   Environment and Observation

Intuitively, an agent lives within an environment, that it observes through some sensors. We write $\mathcal{E}$ for the set of possible environments, and Θ for the set of possible observations. For instance, an environment could provide a specific level of trust and list all ongoing attacks, while an observation could be a set of literal statements, such as *"this system looks secure"* or *"there are no ongoing attacks"*. An observation can also correspond to a possible valuation of the environment.

In this work, we consider that an environment represents the ground truth, while observations come with some uncertainty. Given an agent α_i, we encode this relationship through the probabilities $p_i(e \mid \theta)$ and $p_i(\theta \mid e)$, representing the conditional probabilities for α_i to be in the environment e when observing θ and of observing θ when being in the environment e, respectively. Note that, for the sake of clarity, we consider that an agent makes a single observation at a time, however each observation could consist of multiple sub-observation, ruled by different probability functions. Hence, an observation should be a seen as a global perception of the current environment.

2.2   Decision-Maker

A decision-maker is an agent responsible for selecting a decision, which can have an impact on the global security policy of the system. We assume here that the decision-maker can be *influenced* through a *context*, which intuitively corresponds to the part of the agent in charge of analysing the observation. Whereas an observation is a probe from the environment, a context is defined within the agent, and organises the observation to the decision-maker. The separation between observation and context is part of the modelling process, and can change from one system to another. For instance, in Section 3, observations and contexts both correspond to attribute valuations, and the context contains those attributes that can be controlled by the influencer. In the nudging approach [23], the context is organised by the "choice architect" (which, to some extent, corresponds to our notion of influencer), and influences the way people make decisions. Some examples given are how voting ballots or pension enrolment forms are designed, or how alternative medical treatments or different educational options are described. The main characteristic of the context is not necessarily the content of the different decisions (for instance, deciding who are the candidates to an election, but rather the way this content is presented (for instance, how candidates are ordered on the ballot). The Mindspace framework [5] identifies multiple factors that are susceptible to influence a decision-maker, such as identifying the source of a message, providing incentives, etc.

In general, a decision-maker is a *probabilistic* agent, typically because a single decision-maker effectively corresponds to a population of users, as said above. More formally, given a decision-maker α_i, we write $\mathcal{C}_i$ for the set of contexts available to α_i, $\mathcal{D}_i$ for the set of decisions available to α_i and[1] $\pi_i : \Theta \times \mathcal{C}_i \to \mathcal{P}(\mathcal{D}_i)$ for the policy associated with α_i. We say that a decision-maker is deterministic given an observation θ and a context c whenever there is a decision d such that $\pi_i(\theta, c, d) = 1$[2]. In this case, we abuse the notation and write $\pi_i(\theta, c) = d$.

2.3   Impact

Each decision selected by a decision-maker α_i can have an *impact* on the environment. For instance, deciding to perform an access or selecting a wireless network has some consequences over the global security of the system. Hence, we consider a *security policy* over the decisions selected by a decision-maker α_i, which we denote by a function $\rho_i : \mathcal{E} \times \mathcal{D}_i \to [0, 1]$, such that given an environment e and a decision d, $\rho_i(e, d)$ equals 1 when d is secure in e, and equals 0 if it is non-secure. Although this modelling allows for gradual levels of security, for instance following [3], in many cases, the impact of a decision is either 0 or 1.

The security policy is defined over the environment, and not over the observation of the decision-maker, meaning that the impact of a decision-maker is calculated from the perspective of the system rather than from that of the decision-maker.

Definition 1 (Impact). *Given an environment e and a context c, the impact of a decision-maker α_i is defined as:*

$$\delta_i(e, c) = \sum_{\theta \in \Theta} p_i(\theta \mid e) \sum_{d \in \mathcal{D}_i} \pi_i(\theta, c, d) \, \rho_i(e, d)$$

The level of security of a decision-maker α_i can then be calculated for a given context c by considering the global impact:

$$\Delta_i(c) = \sum_{e \in \mathcal{E}} p(e) \, \delta_i(e, c).$$

Note that in this case, the probability $p(e)$ for the environment e does not depend on the decision-maker.

If $\Delta_i(c) = 1$, then the agent always behaves securely for the context c. However, in general, it is possible that $\Delta_i(c) < 1$. Indeed, the decision-maker might intentionally select non-secure decisions even with a perfect observation of the environment, or might select non-secure decisions because of inaccurate observations. In either case, the influencer has the responsibility of selecting the context that maximises the level of security of the decision-maker, as described below.

---

[1] Given a set X, we write $\mathcal{P}(X)$ for the probability space associated with X, i.e., for the set of functions $f : X \to [0, 1]$ such that $\sum_{x \in X} f(x) = 1$

[2] Strictly speaking, we should write $\pi_i(\theta, c)(d)$, however, for the sake of clarity, we use here the curried notation when no confusion can arise, and we write $\pi_i(\theta, c, d)$ instead.

2.4 Effect

For a given decision-maker α_i, if the set of contexts is finite, then by definition, there exists at least one effect c^* which maximises the security of the decision-maker, i.e., such that $\Delta_i(c^*) \geqslant \Delta_i(c)$, for any context c.

Since the context corresponds by definition to the input of the decision-maker that can be controlled, ideally, the influencer, who is in charge of enforcing the security policy, only needs to select c^* to ensure the maximum impact. However, in practice, the influencer must take two aspects into account: it might not know the exact environment (and therefore the optimal context c^*), which we consider in Section 4; and it might have a limited control over the context, and therefore might not be able to select the optimal context.

In order to model this latter aspect, we introduce the notion of *effect*, which is a unary function that can modify the context of a decision-maker. Given an agent α_i, we say that an effect applicable to α_i is a function $\eta : \mathcal{C}_i \to \mathcal{C}_i$, and we write $\mathcal{N}_i$ for the set of effects applicable to α_i. Given an environment e and a context c, we can now define the optimal effect η_i^* for the decision-maker α_i:

$$\eta_i^*(e, c) = \arg\max_{\eta \in \mathcal{N}_i} \delta_i(e, \eta(c))$$

In the following, we assume, for the sake of simplicity, that the set of effects $\mathcal{N}_i$ is finite, and we leave for future work the study of infinite sets of effects. Note that $\mathcal{D}_i$ does not change with the application of effects. In other words, influencing an agent does not change the set of decisions possible for that agent. However, an effect can change the probability of a decision from 0 to a value strictly positive, which in practice means that this decision had no chance to be selected before the effect, and is possible after. Hence, although we do not consider here the dynamic creation/suppression of decisions, our approach is flexible enough to consider the dynamic activation/deactivation of decisions.

3 Case Study: Influencing in Access Control

We present in this section a detailed example of decision-maker, observation, context, and effect, based on attribute-based access control. We consider that the policy of the decision-maker follows an access control policy, and therefore the set of decisions corresponds to the possible decisions returned by the policy. Note that we do not aim here to present a full description of attribute-based access control, and we focus only on some elements to illustrate how to define an influencer by controlling a subset of attributes.

3.1 XACML

XACML [19] is a well-known standard for access control, which supports attribute-based requests. A request is a set $q = \{(b_1, v_1), \ldots, (b_n, v_n)\}$, where each b_i is an attribute identifier (e.g., the name of the user, a role, the location of a resource, the time, etc) and each v_i is a value for b_i. Roughly speaking, an access rule consists of a target, which decides if a request is applicable, and of an effect, which is either Permit or Deny. For instance, consider the policy p_1:

$$p_1 : \text{permit-overrides(if } b_1 = v_1 \text{ then Permit, if } b_2 = v_2 \text{ then Deny)}$$

A request q is applicable to first rule if (b_1, v_1) belongs to q, in which case the rule evaluates to Permit; if the attribute b_1 is present in q, but without the value v_1, then r_1 evaluates to Not-Applicable; if b_1 is absent from q, then r_1 evaluates to Indeterminate$\{$P$\}$, thus indicating that the rule could evaluate either to Permit or to Not-Applicable. A policy is then a set of rules, composed together with a policy operator. XACML provides several operators, including permit-overrides, which, intuitively, selects Permit over Deny, and tries to resolve as much uncertainty as possible. We do not provide a full definition of the XACML evaluation mechanism, and we refer to [19,21] for further details.

Hence, we consider the set of decisions $\mathcal{D}_i = \{\text{P}, \text{D}, \text{NA}, \text{IP}, \text{ID}, \text{IPD}\}$, which stand for Permit, Deny, Not-Applicable, Indeterminate$\{$P$\}$, Indeterminate$\{$D$\}$ and Indeterminate$\{$PD$\}$, respectively. An environment corresponds to an access request, and is therefore a set of pairs (b_i, v_i). An observation provides the valuation of the attributes uncontrollable by the influencer, while the context provides the valuation for the other attributes. For instance, as illustrated in Table 1, given two attributes b_1 and b_2 such that only b_1 is controllable by the influencer, an environment can be a set $\{(b_1, v_1), (b_2, v_2)\}$, an observation a set $\{(b_2, v_2')\}$ (where v_2 is not necessarily equal to v_2', in case of uncertainty), and a context a set $\{(b_1, v_1')\}$ (where v_1 is not necessarily equal to v_1', in case the context modifies the environment). Additionally, the observation and the context might remove some attributes.

3.2   Effects

Given a context $c = \{(b_1, v_1), \ldots, (b_n, v_n\}$, we now consider three types of effect:

- id is the identity effect, which leaves the context unchanged, i.e., $id(c) = c$.
- η_{-b} removes b from the context, i.e., $\eta_{-b}(c) = \{(b', v') \in c \mid b \neq b'\}$.
- $\eta_{b,v}$ adds the value v to b in the context, i.e., $\eta_{b,v}(c) = \{(b, v)\} \cup c$.

Clearly, other effects could be considered as well, for instance the effect removing a single value for an attribute, or the effect changing the value of an attribute. Behavioural effects can also be integrated, as considered in [18]. However, this particular set of effects is expressive enough to illustrate our model, and we leave the study of a complete set of effects for access control systems for future work.

We illustrate these effects in Table 1 over the policy p_1 defined above. The second column corresponds to the absence of effect application, and therefore to the decision the decision-maker selects with no influence. The third and fourth columns correspond to the possible effect application when the attribute b_1 is controllable by the influencer, in which case the context c_1 denotes the value of b_1 in the environment, and the observation θ_2 denotes the value of the attribute

Table 1. Application of effects over the policy p_1, where θ_i is an observation of b_i and c_i is the context corresponding to b_i, and where $v_i \neq v_i'$

e	$\pi_i(\theta_2, id(c_1))$	$\pi_i(\theta_2, \eta_{-b_1}(c_1))$	$\pi_i(\theta_1, \eta_{b_1,v_1}(c_1))$	$\pi_i(\theta_1, \eta_{-b_2}(c_2))$	$\pi_i(\theta_1, \eta_{b_2,v_2}(c_2))$
$\{(b_1,v_1),(b_2,v_2)\}$	P	IPD	P	P	P
$\{(b_1,v_1'),(b_2,v_2)\}$	D	IPD	P	IP	D
$\{(b_1,v_1),(b_2,v_2')\}$	P	IP	P	P	P
$\{(b_1,v_1'),(b_2,v_2')\}$	NA	IP	P	ID	D
$\{(b_1,v_1)\}$	P	IPD	P	P	P
$\{(b_1,v_1')\}$	ID	IPD	P	IPD	D
$\{(b_2,v_2)\}$	IPD	IPD	P	IPD	IPD
$\{(b_2,v_2')\}$	IP	IPD	P	IPD	IPD
$\{\}$	IPD	IPD	P	IPD	IPD

b_2 in the environment. The fifth and sixth columns correspond to the case where the attribute b_2 is controllable, and we proceed dually with c_2 and θ_1.

Several observations can be made from Table 1. Firstly, even though this example is relatively simple, all decisions are potentially selectable by the decision-maker, as illustrated in the first column, which means that if both attributes are controllable, the influencer can manipulate the decision-maker into selecting any decision. Secondly, as long as not all attributes are controllable, it is not possible to force the decision-maker to all decisions. For instance, with the first environment, $\{(b_1,v_1),(b_2,v_2)\}$, the decision-maker would normally select Permit, and there is no effect that would force them to select instead Deny or Not-Applicable. Thirdly, some effects can be very strong: for instance, the effect η_{b_1,v_1} systematically forces the decision-maker to select Permit. Altogether, this example illustrates well the idea of soft enforcement: the influencer has a range of influence strength, that depends both on the environment and the effects available.

Of course, the optimal effect depends on the impact function. For instance, if $\rho_i(e, \text{Permit}) = 1$, for any environment e, then clearly the effect η_{b_1,v_1} is optimal. On the other hand, if we want to influence the decision-maker to be as conclusive as possible (i.e., to select either Permit or Deny) while modifying as few decisions as possible, then the effect η_{b_2,v_2} is optimal. The optimal effect can also depend on the environment; for instance, consider the case where, when $b_1 = v_1$, the decision-maker can either observe the true value or $b_1 = v_1'$. If the security policy rewards the decision selected by the uninfluenced decision-maker, then the effect η_{b_1,v_1} is optimal in all environment where $b_1 = v_1$, in order to correct any potential wrong observation from the decision-maker, but not in other environments, in other not to force the decision-maker to select Permit when there is no need to. Hence, the influencer needs to know the current environment in order to select with certainty the optimal effect, which is not necessarily the case if the influencer only has an observation the environment, as described in the next section.

4   Influencing under Uncertainty

As described above, ideally, the influencer can simply select the optimal effect $\eta^*(e, c)$, for an environment e and a context c. In practice, the influencer also observes the environment, and as such might also be uncertain about it. In other words, in general, the influencer cannot select an effect based on the environment, but only based on a given observation. We however consider that the influencer knows the context of the decision-maker, since they control it, and takes into account to select an effect. More formally, an influencer over a decision-maker α_i is an agent α_j associated with a policy $\mu_j : \Theta \times \mathcal{C}_i \to \mathcal{N}_i$.

Note that, for the sake of simplicity, an influencer is a deterministic agent, since we aim at defining the optimal influencer. Hence, whereas a decision-maker is probabilistic in order to denote the limited control we have over such an agent, and the fact that it can correspond to a population of users, an influencer is a completely known agent, acting deterministically.

4.1   Impact

The impact of an influencer is directly computed from the impact of the decision-maker it influences. Although the influencer selects an effect based on a observation, in a similar way than for decision-makers, we calculate the impact in a given environment. In addition, given an influencer α_j, we make explicit its policy μ, in order to consider the optimal policy for α_j, as described below.

Definition 2 (Influencing Impact). *Given an environment e and a context c, the impact of the policy μ for an influencer α_j over a decision-maker α_i is given by:*

$$\delta_j^\mu(e, c) = \sum_{\theta \in \Theta} p_j(\theta \mid e)\, \delta_i(e, \mu(\theta, c, c))$$

where $\mu(\theta, c, c)$ corresponds to the context $\eta(c)$, where $\eta = \mu(\theta, c)$.

The global impact of a policy μ for an influencer α_j is defined in a similar way than that of a decision-maker:

$$\Delta_j^\mu(c) = \sum_{e \in \mathcal{E}} p(e)\, \delta_j^\mu(e, c).$$

Intuitively, the objective of an influencer is to maximise $\Delta_j^\mu(c)$ for a given context c, and we say that the policy μ is *optimal* for a context c if, and only if, for any other policy μ', $\Delta_j^\mu(c) \geqslant \Delta_j^{\mu'}(c)$.

We are now in position to define the optimal policy μ^* for an influencer α_j over a decision-maker α_i.

Proposition 1. *The optimal policy for α_j is defined by, for any θ and any c:*

$$\mu_j^*(\theta, c) = \arg\max_{\eta \in \mathcal{N}_i} \sum_{e \in \mathcal{E}} p_j(e \mid \theta)\, \delta_i(e, \eta(c)) \tag{1}$$

The proof of this proposition can be found in Appendix, and roughly speaking, relies on the application of Bayes' Theorem over $p(e) \cdot p_j(\theta \mid e)$.

4.2   Strong and Weak Enforcement

In practice, the different probabilities between environments and observations might not be known by α_j, making the policy μ_j^* not computable. In this case, the influencer makes a decision based only on the context of the decision-maker and its own observation θ of the environment. Let us consider the two classical methods: weak and strong enforcement.

We write id for the neutral effect (i.e., $id(c) = c$, for any context c, as described in Section 3) and μ_{id} for the policy such that $\mu_{id}(\theta, c) = id$, for any observation θ and any context c. It is easy to see that the impact of this policy is $\Delta_j^{\mu_{id}}(c) = \Delta_i(c)$, since the impact of no influence is equivalent to the impact of the decision-maker alone.

Clearly, as long as the effect id is available to an influencer for all observations, then the optimal strategy μ_j^* has an impact at least as high as that of μ_{id}. In addition, if $\Delta_i(c) = 1$, then μ_{id} is optimal, in other words, if the decision-maker is secure, then there is clearly no need for enforcement.

The other end of the enforcement spectrum consists in forcing the decision-maker towards a specific decision. Let us first assume that, given a context c, there always exists an effect η_d such that $\pi_i(\theta, \eta_d(c), d) = 1$, for any observation θ and any decision d. In other words, η_d forces α_i to select d. Of course, the existence of such an effect is not guaranteed in general, as illustrated in Section 3, especially when the enforcement is decentralised, or when the enforcement mechanism can be overridden or deactivated.

However, even when such an effect exists, selecting it is not necessarily optimal, as we illustrate in Section 4.3. Indeed, the influencer might be wrong and influence towards a non-secure decision. The impact of selecting such an effect depends on the certainty with which the influencer believes how the decision-maker should behave. Let us now assume that α_j only knows the probability function $p_j(e \mid \theta)$, for any environment e and any observation θ, i.e., α_j knows its own uncertainty, but has no knowledge about the uncertainty of the decision-maker. In this case, α_j can first decide what is the "best" decision with the function $best_j : \Theta \rightarrow \mathcal{D}_i$, such that:

$$best_j(\theta) = \arg\max_{d \in \mathcal{D}_i} \sum_{e \in \mathcal{E}} p_j(e \mid \theta)\, \rho_i(e, d)$$

The strong enforcement policy can then be defined as $\mu_j^\uparrow(\theta, c) = \eta_{best_j(\theta)}$, and the impact of this policy is given by, for any environment e and any context c:

$$\delta_j^\uparrow(e, c) = \sum_{\theta \in \Theta} p_j(\theta \mid e)\, \rho_i(e, best_j(\theta))$$

It is worth observing that if, given an observation θ, there is a single environment e such that $p_j(e \mid \theta) = 1$, and given an environment e, there is a single observation θ such that $p_j(\theta \mid e) = 1$, then $\delta_j^\uparrow(e, c) = \max_{d \in \mathcal{D}_i} \rho_i(e, d)$ is clearly maximal. In other words, when the influencer has perfect knowledge of

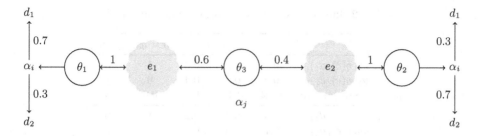

Fig. 2. Example of influence under uncertainty

the environment and has the possibility of forcing the decision-maker to select a given decision, then doing so is optimal. Conversely, when either of the above conditions is not met, the traditional approach of forcing the decision maker to follow a particular decision is not necessarily optimal, as illustrated below.

4.3 Example

We provide here a simple example inspired from a recent experiment presented in [4], on the selection of a wireless network (WiFi). We do not use the full example here, but we extract from it two aspects that are particularly relevant to our model: probabilistic decision-makers and uncertainty of the influencer, and we refer to [17] for further details, in particular for an implementation using Multi-Criteria Decision Analysis. We also took inspiration from Ferreira et al. [7], who empirically study the importance of trusting the name of a WiFi.

Let us consider the following configuration, summarised in Figure 2: two decisions $\mathcal{D} = \{d_1, d_2\}$, two environments $\mathcal{E} = \{e_1, e_2\}$, and a security policy such that $\rho(e_1, d_1) = 1$, $\rho(e_1, d_2) = 0$, $\rho(e_2, d_1) = 0$, and $\rho(e_2, d_2) = 1$. In other words, only d_1 is secure in e_1, and only d_2 is secure in d_2. Let us also consider a decision-maker α_i and a context c such that:

- α_i has full certainty over the environment, i.e., each environment e_k is associated with an observation θ_k, such that $p_i(\theta_k \mid e_k) = p_i(e_k \mid \theta_k) = 1$;
- α_i selects the secure alternative with 70% chance: $\pi_i(\theta_k, c, d_k) = 0.7$ and $\pi_i(\theta_k, c, d_l) = 0.3$, for any $k \in \{1, 2\}$ and any $l \neq k$.

Let α_j be an influencer α_j with some uncertainty over the environment: α_j observes the observation θ_3 such that $p_j(e_1 \mid \theta_3) = 0.6$ and $p_j(e_2 \mid \theta_3) = 0.4$.

Finally, we consider five effects $\mathcal{N}_i = \{id, \eta_{l_1}, \eta_{l_2}, \eta_{d_1}, \eta_{d_2}\}$, where id and η_{d_i} are described in Section 4.2 and correspond to weak and strong enforcement, respectively, and where η_{l_i} is a low influence effect over α_i, which increases by 0.1 the probability of α_i to select d_i, and decreases by 0.1 the probability of α_i to select the other decision. Intuitively, η_{l_i} corresponds to a behavioural effect, that acts on the preferences of the decision-maker, rather than a technological effect. This effect is directly inspired from [17], where the authors considers the

Table 2. Impact of different strategies under uncertainty

	$\eta = id$	$\eta = \eta_{l_1}$	$\eta = \eta_{l_2}$	$\eta = \eta_{d_1}$	$\eta = \eta_{d_2}$
$\pi_i(\theta_1, \eta(c), d_1)$	0.7	0.8	0.6	1	0
$\pi_i(\theta_1, \eta(c), d_2)$	0.3	0.2	0.4	0	1
$p_j(e_1 \mid \theta_3)\, \delta_i(e_1, \eta(c))$	0.42	0.48	0.36	0.6	0
$\pi_i(\theta_2, \eta(c), d_1)$	0.3	0.4	0.2	1	0
$\pi_i(\theta_2, \eta(c), d_2)$	0.7	0.6	0.8	0	1
$p_j(e_2 \mid \theta_3)\, \delta_i(e_2, \eta(c))$	0.28	0.24	0.32	0	0.4
$\delta_j(\theta_3, \eta)$	0.7	**0.72**	0.68	0.6	0.4

impact of changing the colour in which a network is displayed, experimentally proving that people tend to favour networks displayed in green over those displayed in red. As said in the Introduction, we assume in this work that the impact on the decision-maker of such an effect is quantifiable, which is usually demonstrable at the population level, but not necessarily at the individual level. Hence, it should be noted that the simplicity of the impact used for that effect (an increase/decrease of 0.1 for the probability of selecting a decision) is for the purpose of illustrating our model, and in practice, this impact is likely to be more complicated, especially when the effect includes psychological aspects.

Table 2 contains the impact for α_j for each selected effect. The upper part of the table corresponds to the impact if the environment is e_1, while the lower part to the impact if the environment is e_2. We can observe that the optimal effect, given the observation θ_3 and the context c, is η_{l_1}, which corresponds neither to weak nor to strong enforcement. In other words, even though the decision-maker behaves relatively securely and has no uncertainty, it is still worth influencing them, but trying to force them towards one specific decision, without enough certainty about which decision is the correct one, is not optimal.

5   Multiple Influencers

In the model presented so far, each decision-maker is associated with a single influencer. However, in practice, multiple influencers can co-exist: for instance, the employee of a company can be influenced both by the business department, in order to increase productivity, and by the technical department, in order to increase security, or the manager of a resource can be influenced both by the requester of the resource and by its owner. In addition, an influencer could also correspond to a malicious agent, for instance a user selecting a wireless network can be influenced towards a non-secure network by a piece of malware and towards a secure network by a security mechanism. However, the integration of multiple influencers is not straight-forward, and two main issues need to be addressed in order to consider multiple influencers: *multiple effects resolution* and *influencing loops*.

5.1   Multiple Effects Resolution

The policy of a decision-maker takes as input its context onto which the effect of the influencer has been applied. Multiple influencers leads to multiple effects, and the first problem to address when considering multiple influencers is to resolve how these effects are applied on the context.

A first way to address this problem is to consider only commutative effects.In this case, the order with which the effects coming from multiple influencers are applied does not matter. For instance, in the access control scenario described in Section 3, if each influencer controls a distinct set of attributes, then effects coming from different influencers are commutative (although different effects coming from a single influencer are not necessarily commutative). However, if an attribute can be controlled by several influencers, then this is no longer the case. For instance, if one influencer decides to hide the attribute, while another influencer decides to show a specific value for that attribute, then the last effect applied automatically cancels the first one applied. In order to ensure that different parts of the context are controlled by different influencers, the decision-maker can be provided with multiple contexts, one per influencer, which automatically ensures the absence of conflicts between multiple effects.

Another approach to solve the multiple effect resolution problem is to introduce a new agent, responsible for this resolution. Such an agent would act as a single influencer, which would select an effect based on the effects selected by the multiple influencers. Of course, this does not directly solve the problem, since the ordering of the effects still needs to be resolved, but at least, the decision-maker is no longer in charge of it. An analogy can be drawn with the notion of Policy Decision Point (PDP), which is in charge of collecting the access control policies from different sources, and from composing their decisions using policy operators, before forwarding the decision to the Policy Enforcement Point (PEP) [19]. In this analogy, the PDP acts as the single influencer, while the PEP corresponds to the decision-maker (with the notable difference that the PEP is usually forced to follow the decision coming from the PDP).

5.2   Influencing Loops

The second potential problem with multiple influencers is the notion of influencing loop. Indeed, being able to characterise a chain of influence seems appealing to model some real-world scenarios, for instance, when the influence comes through the different levels of management in a company.

At first glance, it would be enough to provide each influencer with a context, and our model would directly allow an influencer to influence another one. For instance, consider the case where α_k influences α_j, which in turn influences α_i: α_k selects an effect over the context of α_j, which then selects an effect over the context of α_i. In this case, α_k is able to influence α_i through α_j. Modelling such an indirect influence is clearly appealing, since it could characterise complex attacks (e.g., influencing the security officer of a company effectively influences all employees of that company), and therefore help defend against them.

However, due to the synchronicity of effect application, two influencers α_j and α_k could influence each other mutually (potentially indirectly), which means that the alternative chosen by α_j depends on that chosen by α_k, which itself depends on that chosen by α_j, thus creating a loop. Hence, this raises the issue of knowing whether this loop has a fix-point, or, in the context of game-theory, whether there is an equilibrium between the strategies of the different influencers.

From the two issues raised above, it follows that in order for a simple model to include multiple influencers, we would need to require effects to be independent or commutative (to address the multiple effects resolution problem), and influencers should not be able to influence each other (to address the influencing loop problem). We however believe that investigating more complex models to release these assumptions is an interesting lead for future work.

6   Conclusion

We have proposed a formal model for the notion soft enforcement, where the agent in charge of enforcing a security policy influences the agent in charge of making the decisions. This notion of influence is characterised by the fact that a decision-maker cannot automatically be forced to comply, as illustrated in Section 3. We have defined the optimal behaviour for an influencer in Proposition 1, and we have illustrated in Section 4.3 that it does not necessarily correspond to weak or strong enforcement, especially when in presence of uncertainty.

Our model requires the impact of an influence effect to be quantifiable, in order to derive the optimal policy. Although this impact is clearly computable when it only concerns a limited control over a technological system (e.g., hiding some attributes in an access control system), it is not necessarily the case in general. Research in psychology tells us that decision-makers can be influenced (e.g., [11,23,10,5]), and there is a growing interest in using behavioural sciences when developing and implementing security products revealed recently (e.g., [15,20,24,18,6]). However, more research is needed to eventually provide a catalog of effects applicable to a decision-maker, together with a measure of their impact. Access control provides an interesting case study, for instance with risk-based access control [3], which takes into account the uncertainty of the decision-making process, or with incentive-based access control (e.g., [16,12]), where decision-makers are given financial incentives to respect the policy.

We believe this model paves the way to an interesting and complex problem: the integration of multiple influencers, as discussed in Section 5. The resolution of multiple effects could for instance be addressed with an algebraic approach (see, e.g., XACML [19,21]), or with a behavioural approach (see, e.g., the notion of additive factor [22]). Similarly, the problem of influencing loop could be addressed by using Game Theory (see, e.g., [14,8]), where an equilibrium would solve a given loop, and the notion of intervening/mediator variable (see, e.g., [13]) could be used to characterise the existence of indirect loops. In particular, the work done in Normative Multi-Agent Systems (e.g., [2]) could help understanding the incentives for the different agents to respect the security norms.

In conclusion, it is worth mentioning that effects can be potentially used by "influencing attackers", which use the same influencing approach, but with the objective of attacking the system. For instance, attribute-hiding attacks is studied in [9], and it is shown that hiding an attribute can lead a decision-maker to permit an access that would have been denied with full knowledge of the environment. Hence, integrating multiple influencers could provide a model characterising the conflicting influences over decision-makers, between security mechanisms and attackers.

References

1. Beautement, A., Sasse, M.A., Wonham, M.: The compliance budget: Managing security behaviour in organisations. In: Proceedings of the 2008 Workshop on New Security Paradigms, NSPW 2008, pp. 47–58. ACM, New York (2008)
2. Boella, G., van der Torre, L.W.N.: A game-theoretic approach to normative multi-agent systems. In: Normative Multi-agent Systems. Dagstuhl Seminar Proceedings, vol. 07122 (2007)
3. Cheng, P.C., Rohatgi, P., Keser, C., Karger, P.A., Wagner, G.M., Reninger, A.S.: Fuzzy multi-level security: An experiment on quantified risk-adaptive access control. In: Security and Privacy 2007, pp. 222–230. IEEE (2007)
4. Coventry, L.M., Briggs, P., Jeske, D., van Moorsel, A.P.A.: Scene: A structured means for creating and evaluating behavioral nudges in a cyber security environment. In: Marcus, A. (ed.) DUXU 2014, Part I. LNCS, vol. 8517, pp. 229–239. Springer, Heidelberg (2014)
5. Dolan, P., Hallsworth, M., Halpern, D., King, D., Metcalfe, I.V.R.: Influencing behaviour: The mindspace way. Journal of Economic Psychology 33(2), 264–277 (2012)
6. Ferreira, A., Huynen, J.-L., Koenig, V., Lenzini, G.: A conceptual framework to study socio-technical security. In: Tryfonas, T., Askoxylakis, I. (eds.) HAS 2014. LNCS, vol. 8533, pp. 318–329. Springer, Heidelberg (2014)
7. Ferreira, A., Huynen, J.-L., Koenig, V., Lenzini, G., Rivas, S.: Socio-technical study on the effect of trust and context when choosing wiFi names. In: Accorsi, R., Ranise, S. (eds.) STM 2013. LNCS, vol. 8203, pp. 131–143. Springer, Heidelberg (2013)
8. Fielder, A., Panaousis, E., Malacaria, P., Hankin, C., Smeraldi, F.: Game theory meets information security management. In: Cuppens-Boulahia, N., Cuppens, F., Jajodia, S., Abou El Kalam, A., Sans, T. (eds.) SEC 2014. IFIP AICT, vol. 428, pp. 15–29. Springer, Heidelberg (2014)
9. Griesmayer, A., Morisset, C.: Automated certification of authorisation policy resistance. In: Crampton, J., Jajodia, S., Mayes, K. (eds.) ESORICS 2013. LNCS, vol. 8134, pp. 574–591. Springer, Heidelberg (2013)
10. Kahneman, D.: Thinking, fast and slow. Farrar, Straus and Giroux (2011)
11. Kahneman, D., Tversky, A.: Prospect theory: An analysis of decision under risk. Econometrica 47(2), 263–291 (1979)
12. Liu, D., Li, N., Wang, X., Camp, L.J.: Beyond risk-based access control: Towards incentive-based access control. In: Danezis, G. (ed.) FC 2011. LNCS, vol. 7035, pp. 102–112. Springer, Heidelberg (2012)
13. MacKinnon, D.P., Lockwood, C.M., Hoffman, J.M., West, S.G., Sheets, V.: A comparison of methods to test mediation and other intervening variable effects. Psychological Methods 7(1), 83 (2002)

14. Manshaei, M.H., Zhu, Q., Alpcan, T., Bacşar, T., Hubaux, J.-P.: Game theory meets network security and privacy. ACM Computing Surveys 45(3), 25 (2013)
15. Martinez-Moyano, I.J., Conrad, S.H., Andersen, D.F.: Modeling behavioral considerations related to information security. Computers & Security 30(6-7), 397–409 (2011)
16. Molloy, I., Cheng, P.-C., Rohatgi, P.: Trading in risk: using markets to improve access control. In: NSPW, pp. 107–125 (2008)
17. Morisset, C., Groß, T., van Moorsel, A., Yevseyeva, I.: Formalization of influencing in information security. Technical Report CS-TR-1423, Newcastle University (May 2014)
18. Morisset, C., Groß, T., van Moorsel, A., Yevseyeva, I.: Nudging for quantitative access control systems. In: Tryfonas, T., Askoxylakis, I. (eds.) HAS 2014. LNCS, vol. 8533, pp. 340–351. Springer, Heidelberg (2014)
19. OASIS. eXtensible Access Control Markup Language (XACML) Version 3.0, Committee Specification 01 (2010)
20. Pfleeger, S.L., Caputo, D.D.: Leveraging behavioral science to mitigate cyber security risk. Computers & Security 31(4), 597–611 (2012)
21. Ramli, C.D.P.K., Nielson, H.R., Nielson, F.: The logic of XACML. Science of Computer Programming 83(0), 80–105 (2014)
22. Sternberg, S.: Discovering mental processing stages: The method of additive factors. In: Methods, Models, and Conceptual Issues: An Invitation to Cognitive Science, pp. 703–863. The MIT Press (1998)
23. Thaler, R.H., Sunstein, C.R.: Nudge: Improving Decisions About Health, Wealth, and Happiness. Yale University Press, New Haven (2008)
24. Vaniea, K., Bauer, L., Cranor, L.F., Reiter, M.K.: Out of sight, out of mind: Effects of displaying access-control information near the item it controls. In: PST, pp. 128–136 (2012)

Proof of Proposition 1. Let us write Δ_j^* for the global impact of μ_j^* for α_j, and given any μ and c, let us show that $\Delta_j^*(c) \geqslant \Delta_j^\mu(c)$. By definition of μ_j^*, we have, for any θ:

$$\sum_{e \in \mathcal{E}} p_j(e \mid \theta)\, \delta_i(e, \mu_j^*(\theta, c, c)) \geqslant \sum_{e \in \mathcal{E}} p_j(e \mid \theta)\, \delta_i(e, \mu(\theta, c, c))$$

where, we recall, $\mu(\theta, c, c)$ stands for $\eta(c)$ with $\eta = \mu(\theta, c)$. Multiplying by $p(\theta)$ on both sides and summing over all θ, we have:

$$\sum_{\theta \in \Theta} p(\theta) \sum_{e \in \mathcal{E}} p_j(e \mid \theta)\, \delta_i(e, \mu_j^*(\theta, c, c)) \geqslant \sum_{\theta \in \Theta} p(\theta) \sum_{e \in \mathcal{E}} p_j(e \mid \theta)\, \delta_i(e, \mu(\theta, c, c))$$

Refactoring, and from Bayes theorem (i.e., $p(e)\, p(\theta \mid e) = p(\theta)\, p(e \mid \theta)$), it follows:

$$\sum_{\theta \in \Theta} \sum_{e \in \mathcal{E}} p(e)\, p(\theta \mid e)\, \delta_i(e, \mu_j^*(\theta, c, c)) \geqslant \sum_{\theta \in \Theta} \sum_{e \in \mathcal{E}} p(e)\, p(\theta \mid e)\, \delta_i(e, \mu(\theta, c, c))$$

from which we can conclude, using the definition of Δ_j^* and Δ_j^μ.

Using Prediction Markets to Hedge Information Security Risks

Pankaj Pandey and Einar Arthur Snekkenes

Norwegian Information Security Lab.
Gjøvik University College, Norway
{pankaj.pandey2,einar.snekkenes}@hig.no

Abstract. Devising a successful risk mitigation plan requires estimation of risk and loss impact. However, the information security industry suffers from the problem of information asymmetry, thus leading to not-so correct estimates for risk and loss impact. Prediction markets have been found to be highly effective in the prediction of future events in several domains such as politics, sports, governance, and so on. Also, many organizations such as Google, General Electric, Hewlett Packard, and others have used prediction markets to forecast various business management issues. Based on the application of prediction markets in other domains and various types of financial markets discussed in the literature, such as macro-markets, weather derivatives and economic derivative markets, we hypothesize that: (i) a well-designed prediction market can be used for risk estimation and estimation of loss impact in information security domain. This will help the decision makers in adopting appropriate risk mitigation strategy; (ii) Prediction markets can further be useful in hedging information security risks by allowing trading of financial instruments linked to the risk of information security events. In this paper, we explore the possibility of information security market where financial and insurance-linked instruments can be traded to facilitate the mitigation of a substantial proportion (if not all) of the information security risk. We present the key design issues relevant to the market for trading of information security related financial instruments. Further, we present a risk assessment of such a market's relevance to its usefulness in hedging information security risks.

1   Introduction

In today's technology driven world, organizations are heavily dependent upon information and communication technology (ICT), and an attack on the ICT infrastructure of an organization may lead to operational disruptions. This disruption in business operations may have a negative impact on several aspects ranging from profitability to the negative impact on brand value and reputation of the organization. Further, a cyber-attack on an organization may be considered a serious management issue and thus leading to a negative impact on the share prices and overall corporate value. Gordon et al. studied the impact of

S. Mauw and C.D. Jensen (Eds.): STM 2014, LNCS 8743, pp. 129–145, 2014.

information security breaches on the share prices of 121 companies for the period of 1995-2007, and they found that news of a cyber-attack had "significant" impact on the share price of the organization [16]. They reported "those who are concerned about the economic impact of information security breaches on the stock market returns of firms apparently have good cause for concern" [16]. The impact of cyber-attacks gets compounded if the attack involves theft of customer data. In another study for Congressional Research Service, researchers found that after a cyber-attack on a company, the company suffers losses in the range of 1-5% in the following trading days [9]. The researchers reported that the share price drop of 1-5% translated into a loss of USD 50-200 Million dollars for shareholders. Jenkins in her report on impact of cyber-attacks on organizations reported that from the beginning of 2011 to the end of April 2013, the cumulative loss of market capitalization stood at USD 53bn on the first day of trading after the news of cyber-attack was broken [36]. Last year, in a massive cyber-attack "Target" lost the data of 70 Million customers. Before the "Target" attack, data of 90 million customers of "TJX Companies" was accessed in 2007. Due to this, by the end of 2007 the company lost more than USD 130 Million in cost of investigation, settlement with banks, card issuers and customers [25]. It is estimated that worldwide due to cyber-attacks and data losses companies lose about USD 1 trillion per year [28].

To protect the interests of investors and shareholders, the Corporate Finance division of Securities and Exchange Commission of U.S.A has issued guidance on concerns on evolving technology and information security threats [3]. Further, the guidance suggests disclosing the relevant *(cyber-) insurance* coverage [3].

With an emphasis on disclosure of insurance policies as a mitigation tool to mitigate information security risks, the focus on cyber-insurance is expected to grow. However, due to several limitations in cyber-insurance products the actual insurance coverage remains limited. According to a study by the Ponemon Institute, only 31% of the companies surveyed are currently covered through cyber-insurance policies [4]. Also, 30% of the respondents in the study said that they do not plan to purchase cyber-insurance coverage. The present-day market of cyber-insurance suffers from problems of low coverage, high premiums and a large number of exclusions, which makes it difficult for a customer to decide on the right policy and adequate coverage. This reduces the incentive for the customers to purchase a cyber-insurance policy to mitigate risks of information security. On the other hand, insurance proceeds are based on the disclosure of loss contingencies and could lead to coverage disputes if the disclosures are prescriptive with respect to coverage conditions. For instance, in 2011 when Sony suffered a range of cyber-attacks and data breaches costing it about USD 177 Million and leading to several putative class action lawsuits against the company [2]; Zurich Insurance, the insurance provider to Sony filed an action against Sony seeking declaration that there is no coverage under various Commercial General Liability policies, among other requests for rulings [30]. Zurich Insurance had itself recognized that "[t] hird-party liability policies such as Commercial General Liability (CGL) policies provide coverage to a company . . .for data security breaches" [10].

In such a scenario, there is a strong need for novel (cyber-financial) instruments to address the financial and other business risks posed by information security events.

Prediction markets have been found to be highly effective in the prediction of future events in several domains such as politics, sports, governance, and so on [39]. Also, many organizations such as Google, General Electric, Hewlett Packard, and others have used prediction markets to forecast various business management issues [39]. Pandey and Snekkenes examined the applicability of prediction markets in information security risk management [31]. Based on the application of prediction markets in other domains and various types of financial markets discussed in the literature, such as macro-markets, weather derivatives, and economic derivatives markets, we hypothesize that: (i) a well-designed prediction market can be used for risk estimation and estimation of loss impact in information security domain. This will help the decision makers in adopting appropriate risk mitigation strategy; (ii) Prediction markets can be useful in hedging information security risks by allowing trading of financial instruments linked to the risk of information security events. In this paper, we explore the possibility of information security market where financial and insurance-linked instruments can be traded to facilitate the mitigation of a substantial proportion (if not all) of the information security risk. We present the key design issues relevant to the market for trading of information security related financial instruments. Further, we present a risk assessment of such a market in its usefulness in hedging information security risks.

The remainder of the paper is structured as follows: Section 2 presents an overview of related work. Section 3 describes the need for novel financial instruments and an open trading market to hedge information security risks. Section 4 presents the design considerations for information security prediction market where different types of cyber-financial instruments can be traded. Section 5 presents an assessment of risks associated with the market for trading of information security instruments. Section 6 concludes the article with conclusion and directions for future research.

2   Related Work

In this section, we present several market models which were proposed or developed to hedge risks associated with various types of contracts trading in those market. As these markets were either proposed or developed with the core idea of risk hedging, they closely match with our idea of the market allowing trading of cyber-financial instruments to hedge information security risks. This section is divided into four subsections. In the first subsection, we briefly describe a prediction market. In the second subsection, we briefly discuss the idea of macro-markets, which was proposed to hedge the macro-economic risks. In the third subsection, we present an overview of weather derivatives market, which allows trading of various types of contracts to hedge weather risks. In the fourth subsection, we discuss the economic-derivatives market, which allowed trading of various types of economic derivatives based on different types of underlying economic data disclosures.

2.1 Prediction Markets

Berg and Rietz defined "Prediction Markets" as markets that are designed and operated with the primary purpose of mining and aggregation of information that is scattered among traders and subsequently this information is used in the form of market values to predict the specific future events [7]. Prediction markets allow trading of contracts whose payoff depends upon the underlying future event. Traders participating in the market, buy and sell the contracts based on their belief that the "future" event will occur. The market price of the contracts is thus an aggregation of trader's expectation on the outcome of the future event and can therefore be used to predict if the event will occur [27].

A significant number of companies have experimented with the use of prediction market to manage the risk. Prediction markets have also been used to predict government policy actions, leading economic indicators, sports events, etc. [20, 27].

There are some examples of applications of prediction markets in other fields of security and terrorism, which have been studied by academic researchers. One such project was the "FutureMAP" project of Defense Advanced Research Project Agency (DARPA), USA [19]. Future Markets Applied to Prediction (FutureMAP) project was started in 2001, and it was meant to be used as an "Electronic Market-Based Decision Support" to improve the existing approaches of collecting intelligence information [20]. However, the project was cancelled in 2003 after being criticized by congress members and media.

2.2 Macro Markets

In 1993, Shiller proposed a new set of markets called macro-markets, which would be a large international trading market allowing trading of futures contracts, long-term claims on major components of income shared by an organization or a large number of people [35]. For instance, in a macro market for USA, an investor could buy a claim on the national income of USA and as long as the claim is held, the investor receives a dividend equal to a specified fraction of national income of USA. Such a claim is comparable to equity in an organization, except that the dividend would equal a share of national income instead of a share in profit of the company. Such a market can be developed for any country or regions such as Asia, European Union and South America. Further, the market for claims on the combined income of several regions of the entire world could be developed. The trading price of the contracts will change with the availability of new information to the traders, same as the rise and fall of share prices of a company when new information about the company is known to the market participants.

The significance of these markets lies in the principle of diversification. People could participate in macro markets to hedge the risk in their own national income, and they can then invest in claims on other countries or regions.

2.3 Weather Derivatives Market

Weather derivatives are financial instruments that are used by organizations and individuals to hedge the risk associated with adverse or unexpected weather conditions. It is important to note that weather derivatives are different from other types of derivatives as the underlying assets (temperature, rain, snow) have no direct value to price the weather derivatives [8, 24]. The weather derivatives are not priced from standard pricing formulas, such as Black-Scholes model, which is used for pricing of standard European style options and other derivatives. Weather derivatives are priced in several ways, such as Historical pricing model (Burn analysis), Index pricing model, Business pricing model, Physical weather models, and a combination of statistical and physical models [8, 24]. A number of energy companies, agriculture companies, (ski) resorts, insurance companies, reinsurance companies, banks and hedge funds participate in the trading of weather derivatives.

Weather derivatives were first publicly traded in 1997 with a pair of over-the-counter (OTC) transactions between Koch Industries and Enron Corp [29]. It was based on a temperature index for Milwaukee, Wisconsin, and it was structured such that Enron would pay USD 10,000 to Koch, for fall in every degree of temperature below the normal temperature during the winter of 1997-1998, while Koch would pay Enron USD 10,000 for the rise in every degree of temperature above the normal temperature.

The standardization to the market of weather derivatives was brought by the Chicago Mercantile Exchange in 1999 when the exchange launched a range of exchange traded futures and options based on the indices of temperatures for various cities in the USA [29]. In 2003 and 2004, CME added contracts on four cities in Europe and two cities in Asia Pacific, respectively [29].

Today, CME allows trading in a range of contracts with underlying assets being temperatures, snowfall, frost and hurricanes. The products offered by CME are based on a range of weather conditions in more than 47 cities in the United States, Canada, Europe, Asia and Australia [1]. Also, CME has products related to hurricane in nine regions of USA [1].PriceWaterhouseCoopers estimated that in the year 2011, the total weather derivatives market was worth $12 billion [14]. Many of the firms specializing in weather derivatives are insurance companies, and the one of the major player in the market is RenRe [14].

2.4 Economic Derivatives Market

Economic derivatives were proposed to allow market participants to take positions on releases of macroeconomic data [13]. These financial contracts were different from the macro market securities proposed by Shiller [35], which were meant to allow hedging against changes in macroeconomic conditions. By contrast, economic derivatives allowed betting on short-term data releases. For example, they may allow trading a combination of digital options to take positions on increase in Non-Farm payrolls between 175,000 and 250,000. Alternatively, if the traders are not willing to bet on a specific range, they can purchase a plain vanilla option.

In Oct 2002, economic derivatives were first introduced by Goldman Sachs and Deutsche Bank [13]. First, it allowed taking positions on US Non-Farm Payrolls (it is a name compiled for goods, manufacturing and construction companies in the USA; farm workers, household employees and employees of non-profit organizations are not included) and later derivatives on other underlying data releases such as ISM manufacturing index (An index based on the surveys of more than 300 manufacturing companies conducted by the Institute of Supply Management), US initial jobless claims, US GDP and international trade balance data were introduced [13]. These derivatives were initially traded over-the-counter in the form of Dutch auctions, where Goldman Sachs acted as counterparty. Subsequently in 2005, auctions were moved to CME where the clearing house offered usual services and central counterparty guarantees which are available in an organized exchange [13].

In 2004, the Commodity Futures Trading Commission of USA granted an exchange license to a new company called HedgeStreet to allow trading of economic derivatives [12]. HedgeStreet offered capped futures and binary options on announcements by Fed, Consumer Price Index, Oil, Gold, Gasoline, Silver, Currencies and many other underlying. The holder of a binary option gets paid a fixed amount. The capped futures are similar to standard futures, but the allowed price movement is capped and floored. This limits the profit as well as the loss.

3 Need for Cyber-financial Instruments and Trading Market

An attack on critical infrastructure and other domains supported by information and communication technology may have a cascading impact. These attacks can easily transcend geographic boundaries of countries and can affect millions of systems in a single event. Currently, the only option available to companies is to buy cyber-insurance products to hedge their information security risks. However, the market of cyber-insurance suffers from several limitations. The cyber-insurance industry suffers from the problem of information asymmetry and lacks historical data that the insurance companies can use to quantify their risk.

Rothschild and Stiglitz examined the market of insurance as one "in which the characteristics of the commodities exchanged are not fully known to at least one of the parties" [34]. They claimed "not only may a competitive equilibrium not exist, but when equilibria exist, they may have strange properties. In the insurance market, sales offers do not specify a price at which customers can buy all the insurance that they want, but instead consist of a price and quantity – a particular amount of insurance that an individual can buy at that price. Furthermore, if individuals were willing or able to reveal their information, everybody could be made better off. By their very being, high-risk individuals cause an externality: the low-risk individuals are worse off than they would be in the absence of the high-risk individuals" [34]. The information asymmetry can exist between insurance buyers and insurance providers, and between the insurance providers and re-insurance companies.

The problem of information asymmetry creates difficulty in quantifying the information security risk leading to underestimation of future losses. Insurers may therefore have to maintain a significant amount of surpluses beyond the premiums. However, considering the cost of capital and regulatory issues, insurers may not be willing to insure high impact information security risks or even if they do, the premiums for such policies will be much higher and with a large number of restrictions on claims. Therefore, there is a need for novel risk-mitigating financial instruments.

Theoretically, capital markets are good alternatives to transfer information security risks. Also, in case of large information security attack (re)insurers would need a large amount of capital to cover the risk, which can be easily absorbed in a capital market. Capital market instruments can bring transparency to the market of risk-transfer, add liquidity to the market and can absorb large risks. The usefulness of an information security (financial) market in mitigating the information security risks will largely depend on properties of the contracts and the underlying events.Some of the generic benefits of capital market instruments over the pure insurance products are as follows:

- Individuals and organizations participating in the market do not need to prove their claim. Traders can freely get-in and out of the positions.
- Capital markets have less or no moral hazard. Moral hazard occurs when the buyer of an insurance policy does not take effective and adequate preventive measures after purchasing the policy and resorts to excessive loss reporting.
- Cyber-insurance policies are currently very restrictive in coverage and are often developed to cater for specific requirements of the client. This creates opaqueness in pricing of policies and coverage. However, since the capital market instruments are traded in an open environment the prices are absolutely transparent.
- Due to the economics of volume, capital markets have lower transaction cost compared to insurance products.
- An open market for trading of cyber-financial instruments will provide relatively easy accessibility to individuals and organizations. Many small companies are usually reluctant to purchase cyber-insurance, and they often have

little incentive in purchasing a policy with broad coverage. However, in the open market, contracts with specific underlying events can be chosen to avoid purchasing coverage on an event that is not required to the buyer.

- Capital markets can provide additional capital required for expansion and strengthening of insurance and reinsurance markets.
- Capital markets have no risk of "adverse selection". Adverse selection is a situation where the actual customers have a distribution that is 'worse' than the whole population as seen from the seller's perspective. For example, if only people that know that they will be/are ill buy medical insurance.

4   Design Considerations for an Information Security Market

According to the work of Spann [37], there are three key design issues: (i) Specification of contracts, (ii) Trading mechanism, and (iii) incentives for participation in the market. Each of these elements is discussed in the following subsections.

4.1   Contract Types

The two most common forms of contracts traded on organized prediction markets, such as CME/Economic Derivatives and HedgeStreet, are binary options and capped futures. The holder of a binary option gets paid a fixed amount. The capped futures are similar to standard futures, but the allowed price movement is capped and floored. This limits the profit as well as the loss. However, different types of market participants prefer different types of financial instruments depending upon their specific needs. Although, the capital market instruments can be defined and categorized in several ways, we classify them into three categories [6]: (i) Derivatives, (ii) Securitization and Insurance-linked Securities, and (iii) Contingent Capital Structures. We restrict ourselves to the first two types of instruments, and contingent capital structures are beyond the scope of this paper.

Derivatives. Derivatives are financial instruments whose value depends upon a market reference (index) or risk factor, such as interest rates, price of a bond, weather data, insurance data, etc. The derivatives can be divided into two groups, namely exchange-traded derivatives and over-the-counter derivatives. The exchange-traded derivatives are traded through an authorized exchange with the clearing house acting as an intermediary on every contract. Over-the-counter derivatives are bespoke contracts traded directly between two parties thus avoiding any intermediary. Both types of derivatives can be used to hedge, speculate or arbitrage. Unlike the insurance contracts which are based on the insurable interest and cannot be traded for profit, derivatives can be used to generate profit on speculations.

Derivatives make it possible to hedge the risks that could not be hedged otherwise [22]. Risks are born by the market participants who are in the best position to bear them, and other market participants can pursue other more profitable activities by hedging the risks that can be hedged with derivatives. Further, derivative markets facilitate gathering of information in incomplete and frictional markets. However, the coverage of non-standard risks through derivatives is very limited, liquidity is a cause of concern, and the derivatives are perceived as risky businesses. Derivatives may pose a systemic risk if a market participant holds an excessively big position relative to the overall market size.

Stultz concluded that the overall benefits of derivatives are much higher than the potential threats [38]. On the other hand, Harrington et al. warned that derivatives for insurance can only be useful if they can lower insurer's cost compared to other methods of risk mitigation for correlated risks, such as purchasing reinsurance [21].

Securitization and Insurance Linked Securities. Securitization is "the process of removing assets, liabilities, or cash flows from the corporate balance sheet and conveying them to third parties through tradable securities" [6]. Securitization was in 1990's taken to the insurance market and insurance-linked securities were developed [17]. Insurance-linked securities are the financial instruments which facilitate the transfer of insurance related risk to the capital market participants. Insurance-linked securities are useful in managing and hedging insurance risks, and to use the capital markets as an alternative source of financing.

In the insurance-linked securitization, bonds are issued by insurance, reinsurance or a corporation and purchased by institutional investors. The underlying risk of the bond is a peak risk, and the pay-off of interest and/or principal amount depends on the occurrence or severity of underlying event. The insurance-linked securities market currently provides various types of instruments such as catastrophe bonds, life securitization bonds, weather bonds, etc. In the information security market, various types of the insurance linked securities such as privacy bonds, bonds on digital rights management, or bonds linked to a catastrophic cyber-attack on critical infrastructures, etc. can be designed to address different types of information security risks. Insurance companies currently providing retail insurance products to individuals and companies to protect them against cyber-attacks, can participate in insurance linked securities market to reduce their underwriting risk and to source more capital from investors.

Insurance linked securities are beneficial for various parties, issuing company, investors and intermediaries. Since the insurer repackages its risk in the form of notes and sells them to investors through special purpose vehicle, the ceding insurer is no longer exposed to the performance of reinsurer, thus reducing the credit exposure of the insurer. Further, insurers earn profit by purchasing the securities that are less likely to be correlated with other assets. Thus, insurance linked securities enhance the risk-reward profile of portfolio [11]. However, there are certain limitations of insurance-linked securities. Creation of insurance linked securities structure can be expensive. This is due to the interest cost, administrative and transaction cost. The administrative and transaction costs include underwriting fees, payments to risk modeling firms, fees charged by rating agencies and various legal fees. Also, the thin markets and lack of good hedging instruments for intermediaries are some of the disadvantages of insurance linked securities. Therefore, insurance linked securities are justifiable for catastrophic events where other risk management instruments are less useful. Information security linked catastrophic bonds can be issued for attacks on critical infrastructure of the country or region.

4.2 Market Mechanisms

The most critical aspect of designing a market is the trading mechanism (platform) through which buyers and sellers are matched. The most prominent trading mechanism is a continuous double auction model. In a continuous double auction model, buyer's bids and seller's asks are queued to be executed. This is the model used in stock markets for equities trading. The bids are sorted in descending order of prices and they by ascending order of posting time. The asks are sorted in ascending order, first by prices and then by posting time. This type of set-up allows matching of asks with pending bids. The continuous double auction model poses no risk to the market institution, incentivizes continuous information revelation, and offers the opportunity to cash out at the current bid price. However, continuous double auction model may suffer from the problem of illiquidity, or wide gaps in bid-ask prices [32].

Continuous Double Auction with Market Maker model is used in sports betting. This model guarantees liquidity by transferring the risk to the market institution. Other traits of Continuous Double Auction model, i.e. continuous revelation of information and an opportunity to exit at the bid price are retained by this model [32].

Pari-mutuel market model is commonly used in horse racing, dog racing, and jai alai games. In a pari-mutuel market, bets are placed on the occurrence of two or more mutually exclusive and exhaustive outcomes in the future. After the event has occurred the money lost by people who bet on the incorrect outcome is redistributed to the people who bet on the correct outcome. The redistribution of the money is directly proportional to the money they bet on the occurrence of the event. Pari-mutuel trading mechanism also guarantees market liquidity with the advantage of no risk to the market institution. However, unlike the continuous double auction with market maker model, it does not incorporate information in a continuous manner indeed it waits until the information is verified with certainty [32].

Hanson proposed a new market mechanism called Market Scoring Rule, which can elicit forecasts over several combinations of outcomes and from individuals as well as from groups [18]. Market scoring rule model combines the advantages of information markets and scoring rules to solve the problems of thin markets and irrational betting as well as the problem of information pooling in simple scoring rules. Though, like the continuous double auction with market maker model, market scoring rules pose a risk to the market institution but the risk is bounded in this case. The market scoring rule mechanism was proposed for use in the "Policy Analysis Market/FutureMAP" project of DARPA [33].

Pennock proposed a novel market mechanism called Dynamic Pari-Mutuel Market, which combines some of the advantages of pari-mutuel market and continuous double auction models [32]. The mechanism combined the properties of infinite liquidity and risk-free nature of a pari-mutuel market with the dynamic nature of continuous double auction model. However, like other market mechanisms this mechanism also has some limitations. One of the major limitation of this market mechanism is that it is one sided in nature, i.e. only buy orders are accepted. Secondly, the pay-off in this model depends on the prices at that time and the final pay-off per contract.

4.3   Participants and Incentives

Designing an efficient and effective market needs to address the incentive structure to motivate traders and investors to participate in such markets, and to truthfully reveal the information (or belief) they have on the underlying event. The structure of incentives and the design of contracts can elicit the collective expectations on a range of parameters, such as probability, mean or median values of an outcome [40].For example, when the outcomes of the underlying event are mutually exclusive, the binary contracts can be used to elicit the anticipated probability of occurrence of the underlying event. When the outcomes are expected in numbers of percentages, index contracts can be used to pay proportionately to the outcome. The price of an index contract represents the mean expectation of market participants on the underlying event. On the other hand, a spread contract with even bets represents the expectation of market participants as a median of outcome. These types of contracts are used to bet on the underlying events where outcomes will exceed a cutoff point.

Every transaction in the information security market will involve two parties. These parties can either be hedgers or speculators (and investors). Hedgers are the market participants trading in the market with the primary objective of reducing or eliminating their information security risks. Speculators (and investors) are expected to participate in the market with the primary objective of making business by trading information security contracts. However, in some situations there may be very thin difference between a hedger and a speculator. Therefore, the main participants in the information security market are expected to be organizations interested in their information security risk, cyber-insurance providers, reinsurance providers, and speculators and investors such as hedge funds, banks, and proprietary traders. The speculators and investors are expected to participate in information security market to diversify their holdings and take advantage of strategies employed by them in other markets, including directional and momentum based strategies. Very rarely contracts are expected to directly exchange between two hedgers as it is rare for two entities to have exactly equal and opposite position.

From the speculator and investors perspective, participation in the information security market provides two benefits. Firstly, the pay-offs from information security contracts are expected to be highly uncorrelated with other forms of financial instruments traded on other markets. Therefore, trading in information security market provides an opportunity for diversification of the portfolio. Secondly, insurance and reinsurance companies can use the information security contracts to issue products with lower transaction cost and minimize their risk.

Insurance and reinsurance companies can offer contracts to hedge their aggregate risk related to information security events. These companies can trade in information security markets to reduce their risk incurred on writing the contracts in retail insurance markets. This provides a hedging opportunity to the large insurance and reinsurance companies.

5 Risk Assessment of Information Security Market

Though the potential of information security (financial) markets are so large, it is important to understand the barriers in the way of the development of information security (financial) market. This section discusses some of the risks associated with the development of a market to allow trading of cyber-financial instruments, consequently allowing hedging of information security risks.

5.1 Issue of Acceptance

The idea of information security (financial) market allowing trading of information security linked events is not so obvious to many people. People may have their reservations with regards to the idea, development of information security linked financial instruments and trading of such instruments in an open market. However, it is important to note that many other financial instruments meant to hedge risks, such as foreign currency swaps were not developed until the early 1980s. A futures market on stock price indices did not exist until 1982. A Weather derivative traded for the first time in 1997 now account for annual transactions worth billions of dollars. Similarly, (carbon) emissions trading market had a slow start. Also, the macro markets proposed by Shiller were never developed to allow actual trading.

5.2 Risk of Failure

Not only do new financial instruments and market designs take a long time to acceptance, they are also prone to high risk of failure. An example of the failure of novel financial instrument and market is the failure of the Consumer Price Index (CPI) futures market.

In 1974, Lovell and Vogel [26] proposed a 'Consumer Price Index Market', when the US inflation was too high. The CPI futures market was proposed to allow investors to hedge the change in real income. This change in real income is the result of rigid nominal income and change in price levels. It took more than a decade to establish a CPI futures market in the US. In 1985, CPI market in the US was established to allow trading of Coffee, Cocoa and Sugar. Despite some activity at the beginning of the market, the market was dead by the end of 1986 [23]. However, a CPI market did succeed in Brazil. The Brazilian market flourished until the Brazilian government shut it down as a measure against inflation. Similar markets were reintroduced in late 1980s; however, they were eventually shut by the government. The point is not that such markets cannot be successful but that they take time to get accepted by others.

An example from the domain of information security is of WabiSabiLabi. WabiSabiLabi was created in 2007; it was an open auction based market where vulnerabilities in software products were traded [5]. However, the company did not succeed and was eventually shut down.

5.3 Lack of Standards on Decision Criteria

Designing a derivative contract for information security events and an index-linked catastrophe bond poses a severe difficulty of decision criteria. We currently lack standards on defining what constitutes an information security attack. Although the development of triggers, such as index linked triggers, can be used to trigger a pay-off but we currently do not have a standard index linked to information security. Though, different types of market participants may prefer different types of cyber-financial instruments, there must be homogeneity in decision criteria on settlement of contracts.

5.4 Market Bubbles

The price of the cyber-financial instruments may be too volatile due to excessive speculation. Thus, bubbles in cyber-financial instruments cannot be ruled out. A price bubble occurs when increasing speculation drives up the price of contracts to unsustainable levels and the eventual burst of the bubble causes a sudden crash in the market. Bubbles are often caused by market participants who are driven by greed of profit. These market participants have had positive returns in the past and with over optimism they drive up the price however in bull markets they flock from the market. The consequences of massive price swing in information security markets, and measures to protect the market participants from such shocks need to be considered and addressed.

For the information security stakeholders, the concern is that the speculative bubbles may drive the market prices away from the "true" market price. This will mislead the decision makers and give incorrect assessment of information. Though, the markets are expected to correct in the long-run, decision makers may not have enough time to wait for a correction in the market. Further, decision makers may not have enough information to differentiate between a speculative (bubble) price and the true price. This will inhibit the whole purpose of using the markets to hedge information security risks.

5.5 Market Manipulation

Like the traditional financial markets, information security markets are also prone to manipulation either for personal gains or to influence the price of financial instruments. The closest example is the case of Roger Duronio, an employee of a brokerage firm PaineWebber [15]. In 2002, Duronio invested USD 22,000 in options and then set off a logic bomb in 1000 computers of the company, betting that the price of stock would fall. This lead to damages worth USD 3 Million. However data loss was prevented with the system redundancy, the price of the stock did not fall, and Duronio was caught.

6 Conclusion and Further Work

We have outlined how financial instruments linked to information security events and an open market allowing trading of these instruments can be beneficial to market participants interested in hedging their financial risk associated with the underlying event. The creation of such a market will allow organizations, insurers and re-insurers to reduce or eliminate the risk they are exposed to the underlying event. We believe that the benefits of creation of an open market allowing trading of financial and insurance-linked instruments are large. With this a substantial proportion (if not, all) of the information security risk can be hedged. In the case of occurrence of the underlying event of the derivative (or any other instrument) the traders are rewarded. On the other hand, positions in cyber-financial instruments with the aim of hedging the information security risks will convey a positive message of willingness of the organization in mitigating the information security risks.

There are several issues that need to be addressed before an open market for trading of cyber-financial instruments can be introduced. Since, the contracts trading in such a market are not asset-backed contracts deriving an appropriate pricing formula will be a key issue. Also, for the settlement of these contracts, decision criteria, contract size, and other requirements have to be developed. Criteria with regards to participation of traders have to be decided early on. For instance, trading of some contracts may be limited to only a specific set of participants. A large number of design, infrastructural and regulatory issues will need to be addressed.

It may also be difficult for organizations to determine the optimal level of exposure to a specific information security event, its impact on the business and benefits of hedging the risk. Also, even if such a market is created the market is highly likely to be illiquid, thus will have limited benefits for the participants. However, this does not mean that we should not pursue scientific study on the creation of an information security (financial) market. We expect the potential benefits of such markets to be much higher than the obstacles seen now.

Our further work will address the various design issues and components of the information security prediction market. In the future, we intend to work on the structure of the market allowing trading of cyber-financial instruments, design of contracts, development of pricing models for information security related financial instruments, contract settlement criteria and other relevant issues.

References

1. Cme group inc., http://www.cmegroup.com/trading/weather/
2. Sony networks hacked post-psn and playstation store restart (last accessed on April 7, 2014), http://www.ibtimes.co.uk/sony-hack-lulzsec-security-psn-playstation-network-hackers-security-breach-3-4-156879
3. Cf disclosure guidance: Topic no. 2 (October 2011), http://www.sec.gov/divisions/corpfin/guidance/cfguidance-topic2.htm (last accessed on April 7, 2014)
4. Managing cyber security as a business risk: Cyber insurance in the digital age. Tech. rep., Ponemon Institute, LLC (August 2013)
5. Anderson, N.: Wabisabilabi wants to be the ebay of 0-day exploits (July 2007), http://arstechnica.com/security/2007/07/wabisabilabi-wants-to-be-the-ebay-of-0-day-exploits/ (last accessed on April 7, 2014)
6. Banks, E. (ed.): Alternative Risk Transfer. Integrated Risk Management through Insurance, Reinsurance and the Capital Markets. John Wiley & Sons Ltd. (2004)
7. Berg, J.E., Rietz, T.A.: Prediction markets as decision support systems. Information Systems Frontiers 5(1), 79–93 (2003)
8. Cao, M., Li, A., Wei, J.: Weather derivatives: A new class of financial instruments. Available at SSRN 1016123 (2003)
9. Cashell, B., Jackson, W.D., Jickling, M., Webel, B.: The economic impact of cyber-attacks. CRS Report for Congress Order Code RL3233, Government and Finance Division, Congressional Research Service (April 2004), http://www.fas.org/sgp/crs/misc/RL32331.pdf
10. Company, Z.A.I.: Data security: A growing liability threat (August 2009), http://www.zurichna.com/NR/rdonlyres/23D619DB-AC59-42FF-9589-C0D6B160BE11/0/DOCold2DataSecurity082609.pdf
11. Cox, S., Pedersen, H.: Catastrophe risk bonds. North American Actuarial Journal 4(4), 56–82 (2000)
12. Dubil, R.: Economic derivatives markets–new opportunities for individual investors: A research agenda. Financial Services Review 16(2) (2007)
13. Gadanecz, B., Moessner, R., Upper, C.: Economic derivatives. BIS Quarterly Review, 69–81 (March 2007), http://www.bis.org/publ/qtrpdf/r_qt0703h.pdf; Published by Bank for International Settlements
14. Gandel, S.: No snow, no problem: How wall street profits from weird weather (January 2012), http://business.time.com/2012/01/24/no-snow-no-problem-how-wall-street-profits-from-weird-weather (last accessed on April 7, 2014)
15. Geller, A.: painedwebber: Geek tried to sink stock with cyber bomb: Feds (December 2002), http://nypost.com/2002/12/18/painedwebber-geek-tried-to-sink-stock-with-cyber-bomb-feds/ (last accessed on April 7, 2014)
16. Gordon, L.A., Loeb, M.P., Zhou, L.: The impact of information security breaches: Has there been a downward shift in costs? J. Comput. Secur. 19(1), 33–56 (2011), http://dl.acm.org/citation.cfm?id=1971852.1971854
17. Goshay, R.C., Sandor, R.L.: An inquiry into the feasibility of a reinsurance futures market. Journal of Business Finance 5(2), 56–66 (1973)

18. Hanson, R.: Combinatorial information market design. Information Systems Frontiers 5(1), 107–119 (2003)

19. Hanson, R.: Designing real terrorism futures. Public Choice 128(1-2), 257–274 (2006), http://dx.doi.org/10.1007/s11127-006-9053-9

20. Hanson, R.: Shall we vote on values, but bet on beliefs? Journal of Political Philosophy 21(2), 151–178 (2013), http://dx.doi.org/10.1111/jopp.12008

21. Harrington, S., Mann, S., Niehaus, G.: Insurer capital structure decisions and the viability of insurance derivatives. The Journal of Risk and Insurance 62(3), 483–508 (1999)

22. Hodgson, A.: Derivatives and their application to insurance: a retrospective and prospective overview. In: Britton, N.R. (ed.) Proceedings of a conference sposnored by ADN Group Australia Limited, Southwood Press Pty. Ltd. (1999)

23. Horrigan, B.R.: The cpi futures: The inflation hedge that won't grow. Business Review, Federal Reserve Bank of Philadelphia (May/June 1987)

24. Jewson, S.: Introduction to weather derivative pricing. The Journal of Alternative Investments 7(2), 57–64 (2004)

25. Kuchler, H., Raval, A.: Target data theft sounds wake-up call for retailers (January 2014), http://www.ft.com/intl/cms/s/0/7d5f28bc-7d81-11e3-81dd-00144feabdc0.html (last accessed on April 7, 2014)

26. Lovell, M.C., Vogel, R.C.: A cpi-futures market. The Journal of Political Economy, 1009–1012 (1973)

27. Luckner, S.: Prediction markets: Fundamentals, key design elements, and applications. In: The 21st Bled eConference, eCollaboration: Overcoming Boundaries Through Multi-Channel Interaction (June 2008)

28. McNicholas, E.R.: Cybersecurity insurance to mitigate cyber-risks and sec disclosure obligations (August 2013), http://www.bna.com/cybersecurity-insurance-to-mitigate-cyber-risks-and-sec-disclosure-obligations/ (last accessed on April 7, 2014)

29. Myers, R.: What every cfo needs to know now about weather risk management, https://www.celsiuspro.com/Portals/0/Downloads/WeatherRisk_What_Every_CFO_Needs_to_Know_Now.pdf

30. NewYork Supreme Court: Zurich American Insurance Company vs Sony Corporation of America, No. 651982/2011 (July 2011)

31. Pandey, P., Snekkenes, E.A.: Applicability of prediction markets in information security risk management. In: Workshop on Security in Highly Connected IT Systems, Munich, Germany (2014)

32. Pennock, D.M.: A dynamic pari-mutuel market for hedging, wagering, and information aggregation. In: Proceedings of the 5th ACM Conference on Electronic Commerce, pp. 170–179. ACM (2004)

33. Polk, C., Hanson, R., Ledyard, J., Ishikida, T.: The policy analysis market: An electronic commerce application of a combinatorial information market. In: Proceedings of the 4th ACM Conference on Electronic Commerce, EC 2003, pp. 272–273. ACM, New York (2003), http://doi.acm.org/10.1145/779928.779994

34. Rothschild, M., Stiglitz, J.: Equilibrium in competitive insurance markets: an essay on the economics of imperfect information. Quarterly Journal of Economics 90, 629 (1976)

35. Shiller, R.J.: Macro markets: Creating institutions for managing society's largest economic risks. Oxford University Press (June 1998) ISBN: 9780198294184

36. Smith, A.: Share prices are rarely hit hard by cyber attacks (October 2013),
    `http://www.ft.com/intl/cms/s/0/`
    `348d7f1a-417e-11e3-9073-00144feabdc0.html` (last accessed on April 7, 2014)
37. Spann, M., Skiera, B.: Internet-based virtual stock markets for business forecasting.
    Management Science 49(10), 1310–1326 (2003)
38. Stulz, R.M.: Should we fear derivatives? Tech. rep., National Bureau of Economic
    Research (2004)
39. Varma, G.K.: Managing risk using prediction markets. The Journal of Prediction
    Markets 7(03), 45–60 (2013)
40. Wolfers, J., Zitzewitz, E.: Prediction markets. Journal of Economic Perspectives
    18(2), 107–126 (2004)

ALPS: An Action Language for Policy Specification and Automated Safety Analysis

Silvio Ranise and Riccardo Traverso

FBK (Fondazione Bruno Kessler), Trento, Italy
{ranise,rtraverso}@fbk.eu

Abstract. Authorization conditions of access control policies are complex and varied as they might depend, e.g., on the current time, the position of the users, selected parts of the system state, and even on the history of the computations. Several models, languages, and enforcement mechanisms have been proposed for different scenarios. Unfortunately, this complicates the verification of safety, i.e. no permission is leaked to unauthorized users. To avoid these problems, we present an intermediate language called Action Language for Policy Specification. Two desiderata drive its definition: (*i*) it should support as many models and policies as possible and (*ii*) it should be easily integrated in existing verification systems so that robust techniques (e.g., model checking or satisfiability solving) can be exploited to safety. We argue (*i*) by using selected examples of access control models and policies taken from the literature. For (*ii*), we prove some theoretical properties of the language that pave the way to the definition of automatic translations to available verification techniques.

1 Introduction

Access control is one of the most important mechanisms to ensure confidentiality (i.e. no unauthorized disclosure of information contained in the resources maintained by a system), integrity (i.e. no unauthorized modification of resources), and availability (i.e. no denials of services) of information in today software systems. It consists of mediating requests performed by users to the resources of a system by granting or denying such requests according to some authorization conditions, usually called policies. Enforcing access control requires that every access to the resources of a system is filtered by the access control system and that all authorized accesses can take place.

Specifying and implementing an access control system is a complex and error-prone task. To alleviate the problems, the development process is usually carried out with a multi-phase approach based on the following three levels of abstractions [6]: the *security policy* level, that defines the conditions under which access is granted or denied; the *security model* level, which is a formal representation of the policies and their effects; and the *security mechanism* level, that defines the procedures implementing the controls imposed by the policy and formally specified in the model. In the literature, several models and policies have been

S. Mauw and C.D. Jensen (Eds.): STM 2014, LNCS 8743, pp. 146–161, 2014.

proposed such as Discretionary, Mandatory, Role-Based, or Attribute-Based, each one with its advantages and weaknesses (see, e.g., [6] for an overview). The availability of several access control models is important for selecting the one which is most suited to express the authorization conditions on the system under consideration.

The main advantage of separating access control development into the three levels identified above is a clear division between access control conditions and the mechanisms used to enforce them. In this way, it is possible to verify the security properties of the policies independently of a particular enforcement mechanism. One of the most important properties to verify is *safety*—i.e. the fact that a policy does not leak rights to unauthorized users [12]. Unfortunately, checking safety is undecidable; for this reason, restrictions of the available models have been proposed in which safety becomes decidable [12]. The drawback is that the restricted models are not expressive enough to be used in realistic scenarios.

The situation is further complicated by the dependence of policies on *contextual information* [6] and the need to update the state of the access control system after granting some permissions [3]. For instance, authorization can be granted or denied depending on the current time of the day; e.g., the teller of a bank may withdraw money only during office hours. As another example, the position of the user requesting access may also be relevant; a patient can be allowed to enter the doctor cabinet only if accompanied by a nurse or the doctor. More complex conditions may depend on the state or the history of the computations of the system. A typical situation is that of Separation of Duty (SoD) constraints for which the same user should not be allowed to execute two (or more) activities: even if the user is entitled to perform any one of them, the system should allow such activities to be performed only under the responsibility of distinct users. Given these kinds of complex authorization conditions, it is not surprising that checking safety becomes a complex task that cannot be done manually even if decidable.

To overcome these difficulties, we propose an intermediate language, called Action Language for Policy Specification (ALPS), in which it is possible to express many security models and policies with contextual constraints, while preserving the decidability of the verification of safety by re-using the cornucopia of available, automated and well-engineered verification techniques.

Outline of the paper. Section 2 introduces ALPS with an example. Section 3 describes our formal model (based on first-order logic) and gives its semantics. Section 4 states and proves some basic properties, that will be used in Section 6 to derive preliminary upper bounds to the complexity of some classes of verification (reachability) problems, expressed in the (core) language ALPS defined in Section 5. Section 7 shows another example application based on workflows with contextual constraints. Finally, Section 8 concludes by a comparison with existing proposals. For lack of space, proofs are omitted and can be found in the accompanying technical report [14].

2   Scenario: Access Control for Smart Spaces

We illustrate the main ideas underlying our approach by using a simple example taken from the field of smart spaces, i.e. physical spaces—such as offices, buildings, museums, and airports—whose access is mediated by software-controlled mechanisms. The main reason for their increasing adoption is the capability to enable flexible policies by permitting administrators to specify authorization conditions that may vary depending on the spatial position of users (e.g., patients are in the waiting room of a medical cabinet), the time of the day (working hours versus evenings), the changes resulting from the execution of actions (e.g., once a patient enters a doctor cabinet, no other patient should be allowed to get in), etc. We consider a simple situation describing a cabinet of a group of doctors that is organized as follows. There are several waiting rooms, each one connected to a group of offices by doors. A person in the cabinet is either a doctor or a patient. Each office in the cabinet is owned by a doctor who arrives between 7 am and 9 am while patients are allowed to get in from 8 am to 7 pm, provided that the doctor is in the office and not busy with another patient. Once a patient leaves the office, the doctor can accept another patient. Doctors can leave their offices anytime and anyone can move from one waiting room to another without constraints. Given this situation, we would like to verify basic properties such as whether it is possible for a patient to be in an office outside of the opening hours, or if a doctor could leave a patient alone in an office.

Below, we explain how the use of our language allows one to separately specify the topology of the space, the persons in the space, and the constraints to access selected parts of the space. Then, we sketch how properties of interest can be automatically checked by re-using available verification tools.

2.1   Formal Specification

Figure 1 shows a formal specification of the ambulatory scenario. The command "**maxtime** 24;" says that time is divided into finitely many and periodically repeating intervals, "separated" by the natural numbers $0, 1, ..., 23$. A time value is any non-negative real number, to be interpreted modulo 24.

The two **type** declarations specify the structure of the space and the kinds of persons in the space. More precisely, the first **type** declarations says that we have two distinct kinds of spaces: offices and waiting-rooms; whereas the second says that we have two distinct kinds of persons: doctors and patients. So, types are interpreted as sets and the sub-typing as the sub-set relation; additionally, sub-sets of a given sets are assumed to be pairwise disjoint. For instance,

type Space , Office (Space) , WaitingRoom (Space) ;

says that Office and WaitingRoom are disjoint sub-sets of Space.

The **immutable** keyword introduces relations that remain constant during the execution of the system: ownership of an office by a doctor and connectedness of two spaces (through a door). The **predicate** keyword introduces relations that may be modified during the execution of the system: the fact that a doctor is busy and the fact that a person is in a given space.

Before describing the actions that can be executed in the ambulatory scenario, we briefly characterize the notion of configuration (state) of the system. A *configuration* of the ambulatory scenario is identified by a value for time (modulo 24), an instance of the topology of the space (Space, Office, and WaitingRoom), a particular set of persons (Person, Doctor, and Patient), the immutable (Owner and Door) and mutable (Busy and In) relations among parts of the space and person that hold—those not listed are implicitly assumed not to hold. (Readers familiar with first-order logic may have noticed the close resemblance with the notion of Herbrand interpretation; see, e.g., [10].) For instance, a configuration θ_0 of the ambulatory with two doctors (d1 and d2), two offices (o1 and o2), and one patient (p), all in the waiting room at 8 am is a pair (t_0, Π_0) where $t_0 = 8$ and Π_0 is a set containing

Space(o1), Space(o2), Space(wr), Office(o1), Office(o2), WaitingRoom(wr), Door(wr, o1), Door(o1, wr), Door(wr, o2), Door(o2, wr), Person(d1), Person(d2), Person(p), Doctor(d1), Doctor(d2), Patient(p), Owner(d1, o1), Owner(d2, o2), In(p, wr), In(d1, wr), In(d2, wr)

We are now in the position to describe the transitions from a configuration to another—introduced by the keyword **action** in Figure 1—that are possible in the ambulatory scenario. Each action is identified by a name and a list of typed parameters and is associated to a pre-condition and a post-condition. The precondition of the action docArrives involving the doctor d, the waiting room w, and the office o is satisfied when the time is any value in the interval between 7 am and 9 am (specified as the inequalities $7 <=$ **time and time** $<= 9$), d is the owner of o (Owner(d, o)), and w is connected to o (Door(w, o)). The postcondition of docArrives requires that the doctor d is in the office o (+In(d,o)) and thus is no more in the waiting room (−In(d, w), which implicitly requires that In(d, w) is part of the pre-condition). For instance, docArrives(d1, wr, o1) can be executed in the configuration $\theta_0 = (t_0, \Pi_o)$ since the value $t_0 = 8$ of **time** is such that $7 \leq t_0 \leq 9$, doctor d1 is the owner of office o1, and the waiting room wr is connected to office o1. Its effect is to remove In(d1,wr) from θ_0 and add In(d1,o1), thereby obtaining the new configuration θ_1 in which the value of time is left unchanged whereas the set of relations that hold after the execution of the action is obtained by replacing In(d1,wr) with In(d1,o1). Notice that this action (as any other action) occurs instantaneously, i.e. the value of time in the configuration is not modified. Similarly to the timed automata of [2], we model the passing of time with a special action that does not change the set of relations holding in a configuration and increases the value of time of an amount which is "compatible" with actions introduced by the keyword **mandatory**. At any configuration, if some mandatory actions are enabled, then one of them must be executed; e.g., the action docArrives takes precedence over the other actions.

The meaning of the remaining actions in Figure 1 is the following: patEnters says that a patient can enter the office of a doctor provided he/she is not busy and the current time is between 7 am and 7 pm; patLeaves says that a patient can leave the office of a doctor at any time (there is no time constraint) making the

maxtime 24;
type Space , Office(Space) , WaitingRoom(Space);
type Person , Doctor(Person) , Patient(Person);
immutable predicate Owner(Doctor , Office) , Door(Space , Space);
predicate Busy(Doctor) , In(Person , Space);

mandatory action docArrives(Doctor d, WaitingRoom w, Office o)
{ 7 <= **time and time** <= 9, Owner(d, o) , Door(w, o) ,
  −In(d, w) , +In(d, o) }
action patEnters(Patient p, Doctor d, Office o, WaitingRoom w)
{ 8 <= **time and time** < 19, In(d, o) , **not** Busy(d) , Door(w, o) ,
  −In(p, w) , +In(p, o) , +Busy(d) }
action patLeaves(Patient p, Doctor d, Office o, WaitingRoom w)
{ In(d, o) , Door(o, w) , −In(p, o) , −Busy(d) , +In(p, w) }
action docLeaves(Doctor d, Office o, WaitingRoom w)
{ **not** Busy(d) , Door(o, w) , −In(d, o) , +In(d, w) }
action waitingRoom(Person p, WaitingRoom w1, WaitingRoom w2)
{ Door(w1, w2) , −In(p, w1) , +In(p, w2) }

Fig. 1. ALPS code listing of a policy for an ambulatory

doctor no more busy; docLeaves says that a doctor can leave the office anytime
provided he/she is not busy with a patient; and waitingRoom says that anyone
can move from one waiting room to another provided these are connected.

2.2   Verification

We would like to use the formal specification in Figure 1 to verify safety in order
to increase our confidence in the security of the specification. For example, we
would like to check if (*P1*) it is possible for a patient to be in an office outside of
the opening hours (i.e. before 7 am or after 7 pm, cf. action patEnters in Figure 1)
or if (*P2*) a doctor could leave a patient alone in an office when the initial
configuration of the system is θ_0 (given above). The problem amounts to explore
all possible sequences of actions that—starting from θ_0—produces a sequence
$\theta_0, \theta_1, ..., \theta_n$ of configurations for some $n \geq 0$ such that θ_n "satisfies" (*P1*) or
(*P2*). The meaning of "satisfies" can be made precise by encoding properties
(*P1*) and (*P2*) as first-order logic assertions and use the standard notions of
satisfaction of arithmetic constraints (for time constraints) and of truth in a
first-order interpretation [10] (for the topology of the space, the set of persons,
the immutable and mutable relations among parts of the space and persons).
Now, property (*P1*) can be encoded as the following two assertions (listed one
per line below):

   Patient(p) , Office(o) , In(p, o) , 0 <= **time and time** < 7
   Patient(p) , Office(o) , In(p, o) , 19 < **time and time** < 24

where the comma is to be read conjunctively, the variables p and o as existentially
quantified. Similarly, property (*P2*) can be encoded as

Doctor (d), Patient (p), Office (o), Owner(d, o),
In(p, o), **not** In(d, o)

where again the variables are implicitly existentially quantified.

In order to solve these verification problems, it is required the exhaustive exploration of all states that are reachable from θ_0 by applying a sequence of actions and then checking if any of these states satisfy the assertions encoding properties $(P1)$ and $(P2)$. While in the scenario considered above this can be done manually, for more complex policies or larger initial configurations, exhaustive exploration needs to be mechanized. Since a property of the policies written in our specification is boundedness (see Theorem 1), we can apply the cornucopia of model checking and planning techniques available in the literature to automatically perform the required exhaustive state-space exploration. In practice, this requires to develop a translator from our specification language to the input language of tools implementing the technique of choice. We have first developed a parser of ALPS specifications by using the Java-based parser generator ANTLR[1]. Then, on top of this, we have implemented a translator to the input language of the Groove model checker.[2] At this point, we were able to automatically check that property $(P1)$ is satisfied whereas $(P2)$ is not, because the patient is not forced to leave the doctor's office after 7 pm, while the doctor is obliged to stay in the office as long as the patient does not leave. There are two main advantages of using Groove. First, the many similarities between ALPS and its input language greatly simplified the definition of the translation and made its correctness (almost) trivial. Second, Groove graphical interface allows for a intuitive visual rendering of the topology of the space.

Mapping our specification language to other languages can also be interesting from a theoretical point of view. In fact, Section 6 below shows how a class of verification problems can be mapped to STRIPS planning problems [9]. In this way, available decidability and complexity results available for the latter [8] can be used to derive interesting results for the former.

3   Model and Semantics

Our specification language (overviewed in Section 2) has been designed to describe access control systems whose state should be updated after granting a permission. For instance, in the ambulatory scenario, after allowing a patient to enter a doctor's office, the doctor becomes busy and no other patient can be allowed to get in. Here, we present the mathematical model underlying our language. Technically, it is based on the action language STRIPS [9] and is extended with the following three features. First, we add the notion of time by equipping each policy specification with a periodic clock (modulo some $T \in \mathbb{N}$). Actions can then be constrained to happen in certain time intervals. This is essential for expressing a wide variety of time-dependent authorization policies. For instance,

---

[1] http://www.antlr.org

[2] http://groove.cs.utwente.nl

in the ambulatory scenario, the action docArrives can only happen between 7 am and 9 am. Second, we use types to specify the structure of users, resources, and contextual information on which authorization conditions are based on. For instance, in the ambulatory scenario, there are two disjoint sub-sets Doctor and Patient of Person. Technically, our notion of type closely resembles that of class in [13] since it characterizes a set of objects with common properties. Our sub-type relation corresponds to the class hierarchy relation in [13]. As shown in Section 4, actions preserve typing. In combination with types, immutable predicates allow us to concisely express the relationships among users, resources, and contextual information underlying a wide range of access control mechanisms. For example, in the ambulatory scenario, Door encodes the (simple) topology of the ambulatory space. In Section 7, we will see how to encode workflows with authorization constraints [5]. The third distinguishing feature of our language consists of mandatory actions, i.e. actions that should be executed with higher priority with respect to "normal" actions. Giving priorities is a crucial mechanism to resolve conflicts in access control policies (see, e.g., [6]).

Before defining policy specifications, we introduce some notation and background notions. We assume the basic syntactic and semantic notions of first-order logic [10].   For a set S and a set $\mathcal{P}$ of predicate symbols we write as$(\mathcal{P}, S)$ to denote the set of atomic statements of the form $P(s_1, \ldots, s_n)$, where $P/n \in \mathcal{P}$ is an n-place predicate and $s_i \in S$ for all $i \in [0 \ldots n]$. In the following, let X be a set of variables such that $\tau \notin X$, and let V be a set of values. We denote $FV(P(x_1, \ldots, x_n))$ the set $\{x_1, \ldots, x_n\} \subseteq X$ containing all free variables occurring in the given atomic statement belonging to as$(\mathcal{P}, X)$. If $f : X \to V$ is an evaluation function, given two atomic statements belonging respectively to as$(\mathcal{P}, X)$ and as$(\mathcal{P}, V)$, then we write $P(x_1, \ldots, x_n) \sqsupseteq_f P(v_1, \ldots, v_n)$ iff $f(x_i) = v_i$ for all $i \in [1 \ldots n]$. We sometimes omit the f and simply write $P(x_1, \ldots, x_n) \sqsupseteq P(v_1, \ldots, v_n)$ to say that there exists such a function f. Furthermore, we extend the concept of evaluation function to sets of atomic statements. Let $A \subseteq$ as$(\mathcal{P}, X)$. We write $f(A)$ to denote the set of all atomic statements $P(v_1, \ldots, v_n) \in$ as$(\mathcal{P}, V)$ such that $P(x_1, \ldots, x_n) \sqsupseteq_f P(v_1, \ldots, v_n)$ for some $P(x_1, \ldots, x_n) \in A$, i.e. the set of all ground atomic statements obtained by replacing each occurrence of each variable $x \in X$ in all atomic statements of A with its evaluation $f(x)$. Finally, for a set $X' \subseteq X$ and a function $g : X \to V$, we denote with $g[X'] \subseteq V$ the image of the subset X' under g.

Let τ be variable symbol. The set Φ^τ of all formulae ϕ of constraints over a variable symbol τ are defined by the following grammar, where $k \in \mathbb{N}$ and $\lhd \in \{<, \leq, =, \geq, >\}$:

$$\phi := \tau \lhd k \mid \phi \wedge \phi \mid \phi \vee \phi \mid \neg \phi$$

The satisfiability of a formula ϕ given an evaluation $t \in \mathbb{R}^{\geq 0}$ for τ, written $t \models_\tau \phi$, is defined in the natural way, by replacing τ with t and evaluating the resulting boolean combination of disequations between constants.

We are now in the position to formalize the notion of Policy Specification.

Definition 1. *A* Policy Specification Σ *is a tuple* $\langle \mathcal{I}, \mathcal{M}, \mathcal{T}, \mathcal{C}, \mathcal{A}_1, \mathcal{A}_2, T \rangle$ *where:*

- $\mathcal{I}$ *and* $\mathcal{M}$ *are sets of predicate symbols with arity 1 or 2 such that* $\mathcal{I} \cap \mathcal{M} = \emptyset$ *and* $\mathcal{T} \subseteq \mathcal{I}$ *is a non-empty subset of predicate symbols with arity 1;*
- $\mathcal{C}$ *is the smallest set of first order formulae over variables* X *and predicates* $\mathcal{P} = \mathcal{I} \cup \mathcal{M}$ *such that:*
    - *for each* $P/1 \in \mathcal{P}$, *there is* $Q/1 \in \mathcal{T}$ *s.t.* $\forall x.P(x) \implies Q(x)$ *is in* $\mathcal{C}$,
    - *the graph having a node* P *per each* $P/1 \in \mathcal{P}$ *and an edge from* P *to* Q *iff* $\forall x.P(x) \implies Q(x)$ *in* $\mathcal{C}$ *and* $P \neq Q$ *is a forest,*
    - *for each* $Q/1 \in \mathcal{T}$, *if* $P_i/1 \in \mathcal{T}$ *with* $0 < i \leq k$ *are the* k *formulae* $\forall x.P_i(x) \implies Q(x)$ *in* $\mathcal{C}$, *then* $\mathcal{C}$ *contains* $\forall x.P_i(x) \implies \neg(P_1(x) \vee \ldots \vee P_{i-1}(x) \vee P_{i+1}(x) \vee \ldots \vee P_k(x))$ *for every such* P_i,
    - *for each* $P'/2 \in \mathcal{P}$, *there are* $Q/1$ *and* $R/1$ *in* $\mathcal{T}$ *such that* $\mathcal{C}$ *contains* $\forall x_1.\forall x_2.P'(x_1, x_2) \implies Q(x_1) \wedge R(x_2)$;
- $\mathcal{A}_1$ *and* $\mathcal{A}_2$ *are set of actions such that* $\mathcal{A}_1 \cup \mathcal{A}_2 = \mathcal{A}$, $\mathcal{A}_1 \cap \mathcal{A}_2 = \emptyset$, $\mathcal{A} \subseteq 2^{\text{as}(\mathcal{P},X)} \times 2^{\text{as}(\mathcal{P},X)} \times 2^{\text{as}(\mathcal{M},X)} \times 2^{\text{as}(\mathcal{M},X)} \times \Phi^\tau$, *and, for each action* ϕ *:* $\langle \alpha, \beta \rangle \Rightarrow \langle \gamma, \delta \rangle \in \mathcal{A}$:
    - *for all* $x \in \text{FV}[\alpha \cup \beta \cup \gamma \cup \delta]$ *there exists a* $P \in \mathcal{T}$ *such that* $P(x) \in \alpha$,
    - *for every* $P(x) \in \gamma \cup \delta$, *there are* $Q'(x) \in \alpha$ *and* $Q \in \mathcal{T}$ *such that* $\mathcal{C} \models \forall x.Q'(x) \implies Q(x)$ *and* $\mathcal{C} \models \forall x.P(x) \implies Q(x)$,
    - *for every* $P'(x_1, x_2) \in \gamma \cup \delta$, *there are* $Q'(x_1), R'(x_2) \in \alpha$ *and* $Q, R \in \mathcal{T}$ *such that* $\mathcal{C} \models \forall x_1.Q'(x_1) \implies Q(x_1)$, $\mathcal{C} \models \forall x_2.R'(x_2) \implies R(x_2)$, *and* $\mathcal{C} \models \forall x_1 \forall x_2.P(x_1, x_2) \implies Q(x_1) \wedge R(x_2)$;
- $T \in \mathbb{N}$.

It is without loss of generality to assume that predicates have arity one or two [4]. The set $\mathcal{I}$ contains predicates that cannot be modified during execution while the set $\mathcal{M}$ contains the predicates that can be modified. The $\mathcal{T}$ contains unary predicates representing types with the sub-typing relation organized in tree-like hierarchies as prescribed by the first-order assertions in $\mathcal{C}$. Actions in $\mathcal{A}_1$ have the highest priority, therefore they will always fire before any other action in $\mathcal{A}_2$ or time delay. Given an action $\phi : \langle \alpha, \beta \rangle \Rightarrow \langle \gamma, \delta \rangle$, ϕ specifies the time intervals during which the rule is enabled for firing, α and β are the positive and negative, respectively, *pre-conditions*, that are required to hold for the action to be enabled, γ is the *add list* and δ is the *delete list* specifying what is to be added and deleted, respectively, to the configuration after executing an action.

The semantics of a Policy Specification $\Sigma = \langle \mathcal{I}, \mathcal{M}, \mathcal{T}, \mathcal{C}, \mathcal{A}_1, \mathcal{A}_2, T \rangle$ is the transition system $\langle \Theta, \Theta_0, \rightarrow \rangle$ where Θ is the set of all possible configurations, $\Theta_0 \subseteq \Theta$ is the set of initial configurations, and $\rightarrow$ is the transition relation induced by the actions in Σ.

Definition 2. *A configuration (or state)* $\theta \in \Theta$ *for* Σ *is a pair* $\langle \Pi, t \rangle$, *where:*

- $\Pi \subseteq \text{as}(\mathcal{P}, V)$ *is the set of all (ground) atomic statements which hold in the current state;*
- *for each* $v \in V$, *there is a* $P \in \mathcal{T}$ *such that* $P(v) \in \Pi$;

– $t \in \mathbb{R}^{\geq 0}$ *such that* $0 \leq t < T$ *is the current time.*

An initial configuration $\theta_0 \in \Theta_0 \subseteq \Theta$ *is a configuration* $\langle \Pi, t \rangle$ *such that each and every formula in* $\mathcal{C}$ *is satisfiable by* Π.

When checking the satisfiability of the preconditions for an action $a = \phi : \langle \alpha, \beta \rangle \Rightarrow \langle \gamma, \delta \rangle \in \mathcal{A}$, we do not only make sure that the atomic statements in α and β are respectively true and false in the current configuration, but also that those in δ hold. This is because, intuitively, if we want to remove some atomic statements from Π as an effect, we first have to make sure that they actually belong to the set.

Definition 3. *For an action* $a = \phi : \langle \alpha, \beta \rangle \Rightarrow \langle \gamma, \delta \rangle \in \mathcal{A}$, *a configuration* $\theta = \langle \Pi, t \rangle$, *and a function* $f : X \to V$, *we say that* θ *satisfies the guard (or preconditions) of* a, *written* $\theta \models_f^{\mathrm{Grd}} a$, *iff* $t \models_\tau \phi$ *and:*

- *for every* $\mathrm{P}(x_1, \ldots, x_n) \in \alpha \cup \delta$, *there exists a* $\mathrm{P}(v_1, \ldots, v_n) \in \Pi$ *such that* $\mathrm{P}(x_1, \ldots, x_n) \sqsupseteq_f \mathrm{P}(v_1, \ldots, v_n)$;
- *for every* $\mathrm{P}'(x_1', \ldots, x_n') \in \beta$, *there is no* $\mathrm{P}'(v_1', \ldots, v_n') \in \Pi$ *such that* $\mathrm{P}'(x_1', \ldots, x_n') \sqsupseteq_f \mathrm{P}'(v_1', \ldots, v_n')$.

We omit f and write $\theta \models^{\mathrm{Grd}} a$ to indicate that there exists an f such that $\theta \models_f^{\mathrm{Grd}} a$.

Definition 4. *Given two configurations* $\theta = \langle \Pi, t \rangle$ *and* $\theta' = \langle \Pi', t' \rangle$ *in* Θ, *there is a transition* $\theta \to \theta'$ *iff either one of the following is satisfied:*

(Action Transition). *For an action* $a = \phi : \langle \alpha, \beta \rangle \Rightarrow \langle \gamma, \delta \rangle \in \mathcal{A}$, *we have a transition* $\theta \to^a \theta'$ *iff the following conditions hold:*
- *if* $a \in \mathcal{A}_2$, *then there is no* $a_1 \in \mathcal{A}_1$ *such that* $\theta \models^{\mathrm{Grd}} a_1$, *i.e., actions in* $\mathcal{A}_1$ *have an higher priority;*
- *there is an* $f : X \to V$ *such that* $\theta \models_f^{\mathrm{Grd}} a$ *and* $\Pi' = (\Pi \setminus f(\delta)) \cup f(\gamma)$.

(Time Transition). *Given* $\Delta \in \mathbb{R}^{\geq 0}$, *we have a transition* $\theta \to^\Delta \theta'$ *iff* $T > 0$, $\Pi = \Pi'$, $t' = (t + \Delta) \mod T$, *and there are no* $\Delta' < \Delta \in \mathbb{R}^{\geq 0}$ *and* $a_1 \in \mathcal{A}_1$ *such that* $\langle \Pi, (t + \Delta') \mod T \rangle \models^{\mathrm{Grd}} a_1$.

We use $\to^*$ to denote the reflexive and transitive closure of $\to$. We say that a configuration $\theta \in \Theta$ is reachable iff there exists $\theta_0 \in \Theta_0$ such that $\theta_0 \to^* \theta$.

4   Basic Properties of the Model

We now state some important properties of our model. Transitions transform a configuration into a new one.

Proposition 1. *The tuple* $\theta' = \langle \Pi', t' \rangle$ *resulting from the firing of an action* $a = \phi : \langle \alpha, \beta \rangle \Rightarrow \langle \gamma, \delta \rangle$ *from a configuration* $\theta = \langle \Pi, t \rangle \in \Theta$ *is necessarily a configuration.*

Additionally, the transition preserves the *well-typing* of configurations, i.e. applying an action to a configuration satisfying the assertions in $\mathcal{C}$ yields a new configuration also satisfying $\mathcal{C}$. Checking if a configuration $\langle \Pi, t \rangle$ is well-typed is decidable in polynomial time by a simple reduction to the satisfiability problem for Boolean Horn formulae, which is known to be solvable in linear time [7].

Proposition 2. *Given a system $\Sigma = \langle \mathcal{I}, \mathcal{M}, \mathcal{T}, \mathcal{C}, \mathcal{A}_1, \mathcal{A}_2, T \rangle$, $\mathcal{C}$ is satisfiable by Π for any reachable configuration $\theta = \langle \Pi, t \rangle \in \Theta$.*

Once the set V of values has been fixed by the policy specification Σ, the firing of actions in Σ cannot add/remove values to/from V.

Proposition 3. *Let Σ be a policy specification defined over a set V of values. For any $\theta = \langle \Pi, t \rangle \in \Theta$, the set of all values appearing in atomic statements of Π is equal to V.*

Finally, we identify under which conditions a policy specification Σ is *essentially finite-state* [1], i.e. it is possible to define an equivalence relation $\equiv$ over the set of configurations Θ generated by Σ such that $(a) \equiv$ has a finite number of equivalence classes and (b) if θ_1 and θ_2 are in Θ such that $\theta_1 \equiv \theta_2$ and $\theta_1 \to \theta_3$, then $\theta_2 \to \theta_4$ for some $\theta_4 \equiv \theta_2$. In our case we can abstract away the real-valued clock of configurations via a time region construction, along the lines of that in the seminal paper by Alur and Dill on Timed Automata [2].

Proposition 4. *Let Σ be a policy specification. If $\mathcal{P}$ and V are finite sets, then Σ is essentially finite state.*

5   Action Language for Policy Specification

To simplify the writing of policy specification, we introduce the language Action Language for Policy Specification (ALPS), whose grammar is in Figure 2.

We now define the Policy Specification $\Sigma = \langle \mathcal{I}, \mathcal{M}, \mathcal{T}, \mathcal{C}, \mathcal{A}_1, \mathcal{A}_2, T \rangle$ induced by a list of declarations in ALPS.

A declaration **maxtime** n states that T equals n in the system being defined (the nonterminal $\langle nat \rangle$ represents natural numbers).

The set $\mathcal{T}$ is defined by a list of **type** declarations, each defining a number of comma separated unary predicates. The nonterminal $\langle pred\text{-}symbol \rangle$ represents predicate symbols, i.e., capitalized words with letters and numbers. For a type declaration **type** P1(Q1), ..., Pn(Qn) we make sure each predicate Pi for i between 1 and n belongs to both sets $\mathcal{I}$ and $\mathcal{T}$. Furthermore, for each Pi(Qi), we require Qi to be declared as a **type** and include a constraint $\forall x.\text{Pi}(x) \implies \text{Qi}(x)$ in $\mathcal{C}$. When Qi is omitted it is assumed to be equal to Pi, making the predicate Pi only a subtype of itself.

A predicate P is included in $\mathcal{I}$ if the **immutable** modifier is specified, otherwise it is included in $\mathcal{M}$. The **predicate** declarations are treated as those for **type**. Applying Definition 1 allows one to easily compute all the assertions in $\mathcal{C}$. Notice that it is forbidden to declare predicate symbols twice (either in **type**

$\langle system \rangle$	::=	$\langle time\text{-}decl \rangle$ $\langle type\text{-}decls \rangle$ $\langle pred\text{-}decls \rangle$ $\langle actions \rangle$
$\langle time\text{-}decl \rangle$	::=	'maxtime' $\langle nat \rangle$ ';'
$\langle type\text{-}decls \rangle$	::=	$\langle type\text{-}decl \rangle$ $[\langle type\text{-}decls \rangle]$
$\langle type\text{-}decl \rangle$	::=	'type' $\langle unary\text{-}pred\text{-}types \rangle$ ';'
$\langle unary\text{-}pred\text{-}types \rangle$	::=	$\langle unary\text{-}pred\text{-}type \rangle$ [',' $\langle unary\text{-}pred\text{-}types \rangle]$
$\langle unary\text{-}pred\text{-}type \rangle$	::=	$\langle pred\text{-}symbol \rangle$ ['(' $\langle pred\text{-}symbol \rangle$ ')']
$\langle pred\text{-}decls \rangle$	::=	$\langle pred\text{-}decl \rangle$ $[\langle pred\text{-}decls \rangle]$
$\langle pred\text{-}decl \rangle$	::=	['immutable'] 'predicate' $\langle pred\text{-}types \rangle$ ';'
$\langle pred\text{-}types \rangle$	::=	$\langle pred\text{-}type \rangle$ [',' $\langle pred\text{-}types \rangle]$
$\langle pred\text{-}type \rangle$	::=	$\langle unary\text{-}pred\text{-}type \rangle$
	|	$\langle pred\text{-}symbol \rangle$ '(' $\langle pred\text{-}symbol \rangle$ ',' $\langle pred\text{-}symbol \rangle$ ')'
$\langle actions \rangle$	::=	$\langle action \rangle$ $[\langle actions \rangle]$
$\langle action \rangle$	::=	['mandatory'] 'action' $\langle id \rangle$ '(' $\langle parms \rangle$ ')' '{' $\langle conds \rangle$ '}'
$\langle parms \rangle$	::=	$\langle parm \rangle$ [',' $\langle parms \rangle]$
$\langle parm \rangle$	::=	$\langle pred\text{-}symbol \rangle$ $\langle id \rangle$
$\langle conds \rangle$	::=	$\langle cond \rangle$ [',' $\langle conds \rangle]$
$\langle cond \rangle$	::=	$\langle time\text{-}cond \rangle$ | $\langle atom \rangle$ | 'not' $\langle atom \rangle$ | '+' $\langle atom \rangle$ | '-' $\langle atom \rangle$
$\langle atom \rangle$	::=	$\langle pred\text{-}symbol \rangle$ '(' $\langle id \rangle$ ')' | $\langle pred\text{-}symbol \rangle$ '(' $\langle id \rangle$ ',' $\langle id \rangle$ ')'
$\langle time\text{-}cond \rangle$	::=	'time' ('<' | '<=' | '=' | '>=' | '>') $\langle nat \rangle$
	|	'(' $\langle time\text{-}cond \rangle$ ('and' | 'or') $\langle time\text{-}cond \rangle$ ')'
	|	'(' 'not' $\langle time\text{-}cond \rangle$ ')'
$\langle confs \rangle$	::=	$\langle atom \rangle$ [',' $\langle confs \rangle]$

Fig. 2. ALPS grammar

or **predicate** declarations) and, for each subtype declaration P(Q), the type Q must be declared before P. Thanks to the latter condition we can enforce that the associated type graph is a forest, as required by Definition 1.

Each **action** definition generates an action $\phi : \langle \alpha, \beta \rangle \Rightarrow \langle \gamma, \delta \rangle$ as follows. The optional modifier **mandatory** states that the action should belong to $\mathcal{A}_1$ instead of $\mathcal{A}_2$. The nonterminal $\langle id \rangle$ represents identifiers, that is words with letters, numbers, and a lowercase initial letter. They are used to give names to rules, to represent variables, and also values. Before writing the actual firing pre- and post-conditions for the rule, the free variables being used have to be listed and typed as specified by the nonterminal $\langle parms \rangle$. Each parameter P x is then mapped to $P(x) \in \alpha$ in Σ, where P has to belong to the set $\mathcal{T}$.

All time conditions listed in the body of a rule are considered to be in conjunction. The formula ϕ is derived in the natural way by translating **and, or,** and **not** respectively in $\wedge$, $\vee$, and $\neg$, and by replacing **time** with τ. When time conditions are absent, ϕ is always true. Even though the production $\langle time\text{-}cond \rangle$ requires to always specify parentheses and to use **time** at left-hand side of comparisons, as a simplification we often omit parentheses by assuming the usual precedence rules when the meaning is clear and we use **time** at right-hand side. Conditions of the form P(x) and Q(y,z) are mapped respectively to atomic statements $P(x) \in \alpha$ and $Q(y, z) \in \alpha$. Similarly, negated conditions **not** P(x) and **not** Q(y,z) are mapped to atomic statements in β. Finally, post-conditions (i.e. those preceded by + and −), are respectively mapped to atomic statements in γ and δ. The resulting tuple $\phi : \langle \alpha, \beta \rangle \Rightarrow \langle \gamma, \delta \rangle$ must of course still satisfy all requirements from Definition 1.

A configuration can be represented through a comma-separated list of ground statements according to production $\langle confs \rangle$. Both variables X and values V are represented via identifiers $\langle id \rangle$. We map the set of all identifiers appearing in actions to the former, and the set of all the ones appearing in a given configuration to the latter. It follows that X and V are both finite sets. Thus, by Proposition 4, we can state the following result.

Theorem 1. *Given a valid specification* $\langle system \rangle$, *the resulting policy specification* Σ *is essentially finite-state.*

6   Safety as Reachability

Since safety can be reduced to reachability [12], Theorem 1 suggests to use available verification techniques (e.g., model checking or planning) for the automated safety analysis of ALPS policies. For this reason, we focus here on reachability problems, i.e. checking if there exists a finite sequence of actions that lead a policy from an initial configuration to one satisfying a given *goal*. As a first step towards the development of automated techniques, we derive upper bounds to the complexity of the safety problem of ALPS policies.

Definition 5. *A goal* $\mathcal{G}$ *for a policy specification* $\langle \mathcal{I}, \mathcal{M}, \mathcal{T}, \mathcal{C}, \mathcal{A}_1, \mathcal{A}_2, T \rangle$ *is a tuple* $\langle \phi, \alpha, \beta \rangle$ *such that* $\phi \in \Phi^\tau$ *and* $\alpha, \beta \subseteq as(\mathcal{M}, X)$.

We extend the notion of guard satisfiability $\models^{\text{Grd}}$ from Definition 3 to goals, which can be seen as actions without post-conditions. For a configuration θ and a guard $\mathcal{G} = \langle \phi, \alpha, \beta \rangle$, we write $\theta \models^{\text{Grd}} \mathcal{G}$ if θ satisfies (via some evaluation function) the time constraint ϕ, the positive guard α, and the negative guard β.

Definition 6 (Reachability Problem). *A reachability problem instance is a three-tuple* $\langle \Sigma, \theta_0, \mathcal{G} \rangle$ *where* Σ *is a policy specification,* $\theta_0 \in \Theta_0$ *is an initial configuration for* Σ, *and* $\mathcal{G}$ *is a goal.*
Given the reachability problem instance $\langle \Sigma, \theta_0, \mathcal{G} \rangle$, *the reachability problem is to determine whether there is a configuration* $\theta \in \Theta$ *s.t.* $\theta_0 \rightarrow^* \theta$ *and* $\theta \models^{\text{Grd}} \mathcal{G}$ *(recall the definition of* $\rightarrow$ *in Section 3).*

It is possible to reduce the reachability problem to the planning problem defined in [8]. The reduction encodes an ALPS specification together with an initial configuration into what [8] calls a (first-order) planning domain. The latter (see [8] for details) generalizes the basic notions of operators (i.e. actions with pre-condition, add list, and delete list), states (i.e. configurations), plans (i.e. executions), goals, and planning (i.e. reachability) problem introduced in

STRIPS [9]. Time, types, and priorities are not provided by planning domains however, and the difficulty in the translation lies in encoding them. We take into account the first two, but—for the sake of brevity—we disregard mandatory actions, leaving them to future work.

Theorem 2. *The reachability problem for policy specification derived from ALPS specifications without mandatory actions is in* 2-EXPSPACE. *In absence of time, i.e. when* **maxtime** *is set to 0, the problem is in* EXPSPACE. *When delete lists are also missing, the problem is in* NEXPTIME. *Further, if also we forbid negated pre-conditions, the problem is in* EXPTIME.

The complexity for the general case is higher than the expected EXPSPACE from [8]—in particular we refer to the case without function symbols, with finitely many constants, where operators are given in the input, and delete lists are allowed—because the reduction results in an exponential increase of the size of the system, since each action is encoded via $2 \cdot T$ operators at most and T is exponential in the input. When **maxtime** is set to 0, there is no need to encode time and related guards, so that complexity goes down to EXPSPACE— the same of the most general case in [8]. By forbidding both time and delete lists—we cannot forbid only delete lists since they are needed to encode time in the reduction—complexity drops to NEXPTIME. By forbidding also negated preconditions, complexity goes down to EXPTIME.

7   Access Control for Workflows

In Section 2, we showed a first application of ALPS to specifying access control policies for smart spaces. Here, we illustrate how ALPS can express workflows in which the execution of tasks is constrained by authorization requirements as in [5]. (The accompanying technical report [14] shows a third application of ALPS to the specification of Administrative Role-Based Access Control policies.)

For concreteness, we consider an example of constrained workflow for the processing of purchase orders from [5]. There are six tasks: CrtPO to create a purchase order requesting goods from a supplier, ApprPO to approve an order before dispatching to the supplier, SignGRN and CtrsignGRN to acknowledge delivery by signing and countersigning (respectively) a note, CtrPay to create a payment file on receipt of the supplier's invoice, ApprPay to approve the payment. Tasks are executed by user for a given purchase order and their execution is constrained as follows: CrtPO precedes all other tasks, ApprPO precedes all other tasks but CrtPO, SignGRN precedes both CtrsignGRN and ApprPay, and CtrPay precedes ApprPay (notice, for example, that the order of execution of SignGRN and CrtPay is not pre-determined). Additionally, the following authorization requirements must be enforced. The user that approves a purchase order (ApprPO) must be more senior than the user that creates it (CrtPO). The user that creates a purchase order (CrtPO) must sign for the goods (SignGRN)—this is an example of Binding of Duty. The user that countersigns the note (CrtsignGRN) must be different from the user that signed it (SignGRN)—this is an example of Separation of Duty. The user that creates the purchase order (CrtPO) cannot create the payment for those goods (CrtPay). Finally, the user that approves the payment (ApprPay) must be more senior than the user creating the payment (CrtPay).

```
maxtime 0;
type Val, U(Val), O(Val);
immutable predicate Eq(Val, Val), Prec(U, U);
predicate
    CrtPO(O),       CrtPO(U, O),       ApprPO(O),       ApprPO(U, O),
    SignGRN(O),  SignGRN(U, O),  CtrsignGRN(O),  CtrsignGRN(U, O),
    CrtPay(O),    CrtPay(U, O),      ApprPay(O),      ApprPay(U, O);

action placeOrder(U u, O o)
{ not CrtPO(o), +CrtPO(o), +CrtPO(u, o) }
action approveOrder(U ou, U au, O o)
{ not ApprPO(o), CrtPO(ou, o), Prec(ou, au),
  +ApprPO(o), +ApprPO(au, o) }
action signGoods(U ou, O o)
{ not SignGRN(o), ApprPO(o), +SignGRN(o), +SignGRN(ou, o) }
action ctrsignGoods(U su, U csu, O o)
{ not CtrsignGRN(o), SignGRN(su, o), not Eq(su, csu),
  +CtrsignGRN(o), +CtrsignGRN(csu, o) }
action createPayment(U ou, U pu, O o)
{ not CrtPay(o), ApprPO(o), CrtPO(ou, o), not Eq(ou, pu),
  +CrtPay(o), +CrtPay(pu, o) }
action approvePayment(U pu, U au, O o)
{ not ApprPay(o), CrtPay(pu, o), Prec(pu, au), CtrsignGRN(o),
  +ApprPay(o), +ApprPay(au, o) }
```

Fig. 3. ALPS code listing of an example workflow

To specify this situation in ALPS (see Figure 3), we observe that we do not need to express timing constraints and we disable time transitions by setting **maxtime** to 0. We introduce two types of values Val: U for users and O for orders. To model authorization requirements, we use two predicates: a binary predicate Eq to test for equality (Eq(x, y)) and inequality (**not** Eq(x, y)) to express Binding and Separation of Duty constraints, respectively, and a binary predicate Prec to model the seniority relation of the users. The only atomic statements regarding Eq in initial configurations are of the form Eq(v, v), one for each value v; similarly, we have a finite set of atomic statements of the form Prec(u1, u2) for each pair (u1,u2) of users such that u2 is more senior than u1. We model each task by a binary predicate and a unary predicate with the same name (notice that we consider as distinct predicates sharing the same identifier but with different arities). For instance, ApprPO(u,o) means that user u has approved the purchase order o whereas ApprPO(o) means that the task

ApprPO has been executed on the purchase order o. Unary predicates associated to task have been introduced to be able to express conditions on actions involving universal quantification on users, that otherwise would be impossible to specify in ALPS. To illustrate why this is so, consider the following condition: there is no user u who has executed CrtPO for a given purchase order o, which is equivalent to all user u has not executed CrtPO for o. It is not difficult to realize that there is no expression belonging to the production ⟨cond⟩ in the grammar involving the binary predicate CrtPO of ALPS in Figure 2 encoding such a condition; it becomes possible when using the unary predicate.

The creation of a purchase order is modeled with the placeOrder action. Whenever there are a user u and an order o such that o has not yet been placed, we mark it as placed with +CrtPO(o) and associate to it the user who made it. The approval of an order (cf. action approveOrder) is similar to placeOrder with the following two differences. First, we require the purchase order to be already placed by some user ou, as required by the constraints on the execution of the tasks. Second, the user au who approves the order must be more senior than ou as required by the authorization constraints. The remaining actions in Figure 3 have been derived similarly by taking into account both the causal relation on the execution of tasks and the authorization constraints.

Initial configurations only need to declare some values, such as (at least) a purchase order with some users, together with the truth assignments for Eq and Prec. The workflow is satisfiable when there exists an assignment of users to tasks such that each task execution constraint is satisfied and it is possible to reach a configuration where ApprPay(au,o) holds for some user au and some order u. Indeed, since every action/task checks that the previous ones in the workflow have been performed, the fact that the last one was means that all other tasks have been performed too and that all constraints were satisfied. This is an instance of the *workflow satisfiability problem* [5] and can be reduced to the reachability problem defined in Section 6 whose upper bound complexity is NExpTime by Theorem 2. Notice that a more precise complexity result for the workflow satisfiability problem is known, i.e. NP-complete by a reduction to a graph colorability problem [15].

8   Discussion

We presented a formal model and a core language ALPS to describe access control models and policies that are available in the literature. To illustrate its flexibility, we showed ALPS encodings of authorization scenarios taken from smart spaces (Section 2) and authorization-aware workflows (Section 7). We also showed how safety for these scenarios can be encoded as reachability in our framework. We derived decidability and (upper bounds) complexity results for the reachability by a reduction to known results in (first-order) planning [8]. Although our complexity characterization (Theorem 2) is not strict as those available in the literature, they provide a first characterization that can later be refined by defining more precise reductions in the same framework.

The work described in this paper is a first step towards the development of automated analysis techniques for access control policies by leveraging state-of-the-art verification techniques such as model checking or planning. We believe that our approach should facilitate the adaptation and cross-fertilization of ideas developed in these fields and the re-use of well-engineered verification tools. In particular, we plan to investigate how to develop a scalable safety analysis technique for the access control policies in smart spaces specified in [11] by using the translator to the model checker Groove as described towards the end of Section 2.2.

Another interesting line of research is to explore how ALPS can be extended with operators to combine authorization constraints similar to those available in the eXtensible Access Control Markup Language (XACML).[3] A limited form of modular specification for access control policies can be obtained by using Boolean operators (see, e.g., [6]) and it is thus already available in the current version of ALPS.

References

1. Abdulla, P.A.: Well (and better) quasi-ordered transition systems. Bulletin of Symbolic Logic 16(4), 457–515 (2010)
2. Alur, R., Dill, D.L.: A theory of timed automata. Theoretical Computer Science 126(2), 183–235 (1994)
3. Becker, M.Y., Nanz, S.: A Logic for State-Modifying Authorization Policies. ACM Trans. on Info. and Sys. Sec. 13(3), 1–28 (2010)
4. Boolos, G.S., Burgess, J.P., Jeffrey, R.C.: Computability and Logic. Cambridge University Press (2002)
5. Crampton, J.: A reference monitor for workflow systems with constrained task execution. In: 10th ACM SACMAT, pp. 38–47. ACM (2005)
6. De Capitani di Vimercati, S., Foresti, S., Jajodia, S., Samarati, P.: Access Control Policies and Languages. Int. J. of Comp. Science and Eng. 3(2), 94–102 (2007)
7. Dowling, W.F., Gallier, J.H.: Linear-time algorithms for testing the satisfiability of propositional horn formulae. J. of Logic Progr. 1(3), 267–284 (1984)
8. Erol, K., Nau, D.S., Subrahmanian, V.S.: Complexity, Decidability and Undecidability Results for Domain-Independent Planning: A Detailed Analysis. Artificial Intelligence 76, 75–88 (1991)
9. Fikes, R.E., Nilsson, N.J.: Strips: A new approach to the application of theorem proving to problem solving. Artificial Intelligence 2(3), 189–208 (1972)
10. Fitting, M.: First-Order Logic and Automated Theorem Proving. In: Graduate Texts in Computer Science, 2nd edn., Springer, Heidelberg (1996)
11. Frohardt, R., Chang, B.-Y.E., Sankaranarayanan, S.: Access Nets: Modeling Access to Physical Spaces. In: Jhala, R., Schmidt, D. (eds.) VMCAI 2011. LNCS, vol. 6538, pp. 184–198. Springer, Heidelberg (2011)
12. Harrison, M.A., Ruzzo, W.L., Ullman, J.D.: Protection in Operating Systems. Communications of ACM 19(8), 461–471 (1976)
13. Lenzerini, M.: Class Hierarchies and Their Complexity. In: Advances in Database Programming Languages, pp. 43–65. ACM (1990)
14. Ranise, S., Traverso, R.: ALPS: An Action Language for Policy Specification and Automated Safety Analysis, Technical Report (2014), http://goo.gl/vVPFKS
15. Wang, Q., Li, N.: Satisfiability and Resiliency in Workflow Authorization Systems. ACM TISSEC 13(4) (2010)

---

[3] https://www.oasis-open.org/committees/tc_home.php?wg_abbrev=xacml

A Formal Definition of Protocol Indistinguishability and Its Verification Using Maude-NPA[*]

Sonia Santiago[1], Santiago Escobar[1], Catherine Meadows[2], and José Meseguer[3]

[1] DSIC-ELP, Universitat Politècnica de València, Spain
{ssantiago,sescobar}@dsic.upv.es
[2] Naval Research Laboratory, Washington DC, USA
meadows@itd.nrl.navy.mil
[3] University of Illinois at Urbana-Champaign, USA
meseguer@illinois.edu

Abstract. Intuitively, two protocols $\mathcal{P}_1$ and $\mathcal{P}_2$ are *indistinguishable* if an attacker cannot tell the difference between interactions with $\mathcal{P}_1$ and with $\mathcal{P}_2$. In this paper we: (i) propose an intuitive notion of indistinguishability in Maude-NPA; (ii) formalize such a notion in terms of state unreachability conditions on their *synchronous product*; (iii) prove theorems showing how —assuming the protocol's algebraic theory has a *finite variant (FV) decomposition*– these conditions can be checked by the Maude-NPA tool; and (iv) illustrate our approach with concrete examples. This provides for the first time a framework for automatic analysis of indistinguishability *modulo* as wide a class of algebraic properties as FV, which includes many associative-commutative theories of interest to cryptographic protocol analysis.

1 Introduction

The security of cryptographic systems has traditionally been reasoned about using two different types of models. The first is the *computational model*, in which the cryptographic system is attacked by a probabilistic polynomial-time adversary. In this model one normally proves some sort of *indistinguishability property* which guarantees, e.g., that an attacker who interacts with two different instances of a protocol involving different data should not be able to tell the difference. The second is commonly known as the *Dolev-Yao model* in which cryptographic operations are modeled as abstract function symbols. This lends itself well to model checking, so it is normally used to verify conditions that can be formulated as state reachability properties, e.g., that the attacker should not be able to obtain a secret in the clear (known as *simple secrecy* in the literature).

---

[*] Santiago Escobar and Sonia Santiago have been partially supported by the EU (FEDER) and the Spanish MINECO under grants TIN 2010-21062-C02-02 and TIN 2013-45732-C4-1-P, and by Generalitat Valenciana PROMETEO2011/052. José Meseguer has been partially supported by NSF Grant CNS 13-10109.

S. Mauw and C.D. Jensen (Eds.): STM 2014, LNCS 8743, pp. 162–177, 2014.

Recently the interest in formulating and applying indistinguishability properties for Dolev-Yao models has been growing. There are a number of reasons for this. The first is that cryptography has advanced to the point at which it is not only possible to provide computational proofs of security for algorithms, but also for the protocols that use those algorithms as well. If Dolev-Yao tools can be extended to prove indistinguishability, this increases the likelihood that both approaches can be used together in an effective way to ensure protocol security. The second is that there is a growing class of privacy-protection protocols for which simple secrecy is clearly inadequate. Such protocols protect low-entropy data such as votes, medical records, or network routes; even partial leakage of this information could be harmful. The third is the result of recent work on automatic generation of cryptographic algorithms. In this work, multiple possible algorithms are generated out of a library of components and then checked for security. This may involve the use of Dolev-Yao like tools to weed out insecure algorithms or even verify the security of correct ones, as in [3].

When a Dolev-Yao tool is used to check for subtle properties such as indistinguishability, it is important that it offers as detailed a picture of the properties of the cryptographic operations as possible. This is done by including information about their algebraic properties, that is, the equations obeyed by the function symbols. For example, if a cryptographic system uses exclusive-or, one should be able to take into account the associative-commutative, identity, and self-cancellation properties of exclusive-or. Such algebraic properties have been studied extensively in the literature, although there are still some classes of properties that are not that well understood.

At this point, there are four main problems being explored in relation to Dolev-Yao indistinguishability. The first is how best to formulate in the Dolev-Yao model a property such as indistinguishability that in its broadest sense is *not* a reachability property. The second is how to incorporate equational theories in this reasoning. The third is how to increase the range and complexity of the types of protocols we can reason about. The fourth is when and how to ensure that Dolev-Yao indistinguishability implies computational indistinguishability. In this paper we address the first two of these problems, although we note that the second is closely related to the fourth, and can be used to facilitate its solution. We summarize our contributions below:

Formulating Indistinguishability in Dolev-Yao. We propose an intuitive notion of indistinguishability related to the notion of *uniformity* used in Proverif [6] in that it is defined, not in terms of equivalence between two protocols, but of equivalence between *roles* of two protocols. In this case roles from the two protocol versions $\mathcal{P}_1$ and $\mathcal{P}_2$ are paired together and executed in a synchronous fashion (called a *synchronous product* in our case). We then define our notion as the conjunction of two more basic properties, namely *Indistinguishable Messages* (IM) and *Indistinguishable Attacker Event Sequences* (IAES). Intuitively, the IM property says that the attacker, when performing the same actions for $\mathcal{P}_1$ and for $\mathcal{P}_2$, can never reach two corresponding stages in such action sequences such that it can learn the *same* message from $\mathcal{P}_1$ at both stages, but *different* messages from P_2 at those same stages, or viceversa. The IAES property says that the attacker *can perform the same interaction steps* with P_1 and P_2, which requires a bisimulation between the two protocols. We prove a result with respect to the semantics of the Maude-NPA protocol analysis tool [13], showing that the conjunction of IM and IAES can be formulated in terms of reachability properties in Maude-NPA.

Incorporating Equational Theories. Our approach extends naturally to any algebraic theory E that can be decomposed as $E = E_0 \cup B$, with the equations E_0 oriented as rewrite rules modulo B, and the decomposition (B, E_0) satisfying the *finite variant* (FV) property. In this case we prove theorems showing that the IM and IAES properties can be checked by the Maude-NPA tool. The class of theories with finite variant decompositions contains a large number of theories of interest to cryptographic protocol analysis, including exclusive-or, Abelian groups, and a number of theories describing the properties of modular exponentiation. Thus previous work on analysis of protocols modulo finite variant decompositions is *naturally* extended to the verification of indistinguishability under many possible equational theories.

Finally, we illustrate the IM and IAES properties with two examples.

Example 1. Consider two protocols P_1 and P_2 using the exclusive-or (XOR) operator "$\oplus$". Below we give the exchange of messages for each protocol:

$$(P_1) \; A \to B : m_1 \oplus m_1 \qquad\qquad (P_2) \; A \to B : m_1 \oplus m_2$$

where m_1 and m_2 are two constants denoting different messages. Since the attacker can perform the XOR cancellation (i.e. $M \oplus M = 0$), and can generate the XOR unit element 0, then it can distinguish P_1 and P_2 by performing the following actions:

$$(P_1) \; 1. \; A \to I(B) : m_1 \oplus m_1 \; (=_{XOR} 0) \quad (P_2) \; 1. \; A \to I(B) : m_1 \oplus m_2$$

Thus these protocols do not satisfy the IM property, since in P_1 the attacker generates 0 from two different action sequences, whereas in P_2 it does not.

Example 2. Consider a protocol similar to the first step of the Encryption Key Exchange (EKE) protocol [5] in which, unlike the original EKE, the attacker can distinguish whether a decryption succeeds or not. The algebraic properties of this protocol consist of the cancellation of encryption and decryption. In this protocol, Alice sends to Bob her name (A) concatenated with the encryption of her public key *pkey(A)* with a password *pw(A,B)* they have agreed on before.

$$A \to B : A \, ; \, \{pkey(A)\}_{pw(A,B)}$$

Consider two cases in which the honest principals perform the same step shown above, but in P_1 the attacker knows the right password *pw(A,B)*, whereas in P_2 it knows a random password *pg(i)*. The intruder can distinguish between P_1 and P_2 by performing the following actions, where steps 2, 3, and 4 denote deductions performed by the intruder:

(P_1) 1. $A \to I(B) : A \, ; \, \{pkey(A)\}_{pw(A,B)}$ (P_2) 1. $A \to I(B) : A \, ; \, \{pkey(A)\}_{pw(A,B)}$
(P_1) 2. $I : \{pkey(A)\}_{pw(A,B)}$ (P_2) 2. $I : \{pkey(A)\}_{pw(A,B)}$
(P_1) 3. $I : pw(A,B)$ (P_2) 3. $I : pg(i)$
(P_1) 4. $I : decryption\ succeeds$ (P_2) 4. $I : decryption\ fails$

That is, in step 4 in $\mathcal{P}_1$ the attacker can obtain the message *pkey(A)* in the clear, by decrypting the message sent in step 2 *pw(A,B)*, whereas in $\mathcal{P}_2$ such decryption fails. Hence the protocols are not bisimilar and so fail to satisfy IAES.

Paper Organization. We first discuss related work in Section 2 and recall some technical preliminaries in Section 3. In Section 4 we recall the forwards semantics of Maude-NPA defined in [14]. In Section 5 we present our formal definition of indistinguishability using the fowards semantics given in Section 4 as a reference model and prove that it can be analyzed in Maude-NPA assuming that the equational theory used for $\mathcal{P}_1$ and $\mathcal{P}_2$ has a finite variant decomposition. Section 6 explains how to analyze indistinguishability properties in Maude-NPA. We summarize our conclusions in Section 7.

2   Related Work

Work in extending the Dolev-Yao model to support the definition and verification of indistinguishability properties goes as far back as the early eighties, when Michael Merritt developed a theory of *hidden automorphisms* [19]. The first to apply a tool to analyze protocols for indistinguishability was Gavin Lowe [18], who used the FDR model checker to analyze security of password-base protocols against off-line guessing attacks.

Abadi and Fournet gave in [1] the definition of two kinds of indistinguishability: static equivalence and observational equivalence, in terms of the applied π-calculus presented in that paper. Roughly speaking, static equivalence describes a passive observer's inability to distinguish between two protocols, while observational equivalence describes an active attacker's inability to distinguish between two protocols.

More recently Cortier and Delaune [12] have shown that *trace equivalence* implies observational equivalence for *determinate* applied π-calculus processes. Roughly speaking, a process is determinate if it exhibits no non-deterministic choice points, and two processes are trace equivalent if for any trace produced by one process there is a trace produced by the other process indistinguishable from the first trace by the attacker. In our approach, the IM property assumes the existence of traces in both sides of a protocol pairing and simply compares the messages. Thus, IM is closer to static equivalence than trace equivalence, where you need to prove the existence of such traces. On the other hand, the IAES property ensures the existence of traces with the same behavior. Indeed, IM does not imply IAES, since the latter is tested after the former is proved.

Trace equivalence is decidable in the bounded session model, and a number of algorithms and tools have been developed, covering a wide class of equational theories [4,8,9,7,10]. However to our knowledge there has been very little work (if any) on trace equivalence involving AC theories.

Although trace equivalence is decidable for the bounded session model, it is not straightforward to implement in search-based tools that are typically used to evaluate cryptographic protocols. This is because trace equivalence is an example of a *hyperproperty* [11] : it is not defined in terms of sets of traces, but sets of pairs of traces, and thus cannot be defined in terms of reachability or unreachability of particular classes of states. However, integration of indistinguishability into state exploration tools has a number of potential benefits, since one automatically obtains support for whatever feature the tool offers, e. g., support for the unbounded session model and equational theories involving AC.

Checking for hyperproperties such as trace or observational equivalence can be implemented in a search-based tool by specifying a stronger property that can be formulated in terms of state reachability. Such an approach was taken by Lowe in [18]; a protocol was secure against guessing attacks if the attacker could not generate certain types of terms. This was later shown in [22] to imply a property similar to the observational equivalence of [1].

The most prominent application of this approach to cryptographic protocol verification has been in the Proverif tool via the notion of *uniformity*, shown to imply observational equivalence in [6]. It is used to define the indistinguishability of two processes that differ only in certain terms. Uniformity requires that the two processes be executed in lock-step as a *bi-process* and projection of the bi-process to each of its components is a bisimulation. The authors prove that uniformity is equivalent to a state unreachability property, and thus can be evaluated using ProVerif. ProVerif can be used to verify uniformity for *subterm convergent* rewrite theories; Arapinis *et al.* [2] have developed methods for extending this to some theories that include a restricted encoding of AC axioms (in particular, some terms must be ground).

The approach we use in our paper is closest to that of ProVerif; we define a pairing between two protocols and define security in terms of reachability conditions on the protocol pairing. One major difference is in the support of AC theories without any encoding restrictions, as long as they have decompositions with the finite variant property. This is inherited from Maude-NPA. There are also differences in the approach we take to specification and implementation of security properties. In ProVerif, the intruder is given the ability to evaluate a predicate that outputs "bad" if there is a violation of uniformity. One then checks for uniformity by proving that no state containing "bad" is reachable. This gives Proverif the ability to reduce everything to just one property.

In our approach we use an unmodified Dolev-Yao intruder with no ability to evaluate predicates. This is motivated by our preference to avoid increasing the complexity of Maude-NPA's Dolev-Yao model unless absolutely necessary, and thus to express our security requirements in the original Maude-NPA framework. In particular, the IM property implicitly includes a test on equality, but it is expressed as a property of the attack state, not as an intruder predicate. We are however, considering developing more general intruder predicate testing functionality as future work, and if we decide to do this we will revisit this issue.

3   Preliminaries

We follow the classical notation and terminology from [23] for term rewriting and from [20,21] for rewriting logic and order-sorted notions. We assume an *order-sorted signature* $\Sigma = (\mathsf{S}, \leq, \Sigma)$ with partially ordered set of sorts $(\mathsf{S}, \leq)$. We also assume an S-sorted family $\mathcal{X} = \{\mathcal{X}_\mathsf{s}\}_{\mathsf{s} \in \mathsf{S}}$ of disjoint variable sets with each $\mathcal{X}_\mathsf{s}$ countably infinite. $\mathcal{T}_\Sigma(\mathcal{X})_\mathsf{s}$ is the set of terms of sort s, and $\mathcal{T}_{\Sigma,\mathsf{s}}$ is the set of ground terms of sort s. We write $\mathcal{T}_\Sigma(\mathcal{X})$ and $\mathcal{T}_\Sigma$ for the corresponding order-sorted term algebras. The subterm of t at position p is $t|_p$, and $t[u]_p$ is the result of replacing $t|_p$ by u in t. Application of substitution σ to a term t is denoted $t\sigma$.

A *Σ-equation* is an unoriented pair $t = t'$, where $t, t' \in \mathcal{T}_\Sigma(\mathcal{X})$ have a common typing $\mathsf{t} : \mathsf{s}$, $\mathsf{t}' : \mathsf{s}$, $\mathsf{s} \in \mathsf{S}$. Given a set E of Σ-equations, order-sorted equational logic induces a congruence relation $=_E$ on terms $t, t' \in \mathcal{T}_\Sigma(\mathcal{X})$; see [21]. We write $CSU_E(t = t')$ for a complete set of unifiers of t and t' modulo E.

A *rewrite rule* is an oriented pair $l \to r$, where $l \notin \mathcal{X}$, $Var(r) \subseteq Var(l)$, and $l, r \in \mathcal{T}_\Sigma(\mathcal{X})$ have a common typing $\mathsf{l} : \mathsf{s}$, $\mathsf{r} : \mathsf{s}$, $\mathsf{s} \in \mathsf{S}$. An *(unconditional) order-sorted rewrite theory* is a triple (Σ, E, R) with Σ an order-sorted signature, E a set of Σ-equations, and R a set of rewrite rules. The relation $\to_{R,E}$ on $\mathcal{T}_\Sigma(\mathcal{X})$ is defined as: $t \xrightarrow{p}_{R,E} t'$ (or $\to_{R,E}$) if p is a position of t, $l \to r \in R$, $t|_p =_E l\sigma$, and $t' = t[r\sigma]_p$ for some σ. A term u is in $\to_{R,E}$-normal form if there is no v such that $u \to_{R,E} v$.

Given an (unconditional) order-sorted rewrite theory (Σ, E, R) such that E has a finitary and complete unification algorithm, the narrowing relation $\rightsquigarrow_{R,E}$ on $\mathcal{T}_\Sigma(\mathcal{X})$ is defined as $t \xrightarrow{p}_{\sigma, R, E} t'$ if p is a non-variable position of t, $l \to r \in R$, $\sigma \in CSU_E(t|_p = l)$, and $t' = (t[r]_p)\sigma$.

A *decomposition* (Σ, B, E_0) of an equational theory E is a rewrite theory that satisfies the following properties: (i) B is regular, sort-preserving and uses top-sort variables, (ii) B has a finitary unification algorithm, and (iii) the rules E_0 are *convergent* modulo B, i.e., sort-decreasing, confluent, terminating, and coherent modulo B. Given a decomposition $E = (\Sigma, B, E_0)$, the normal form of a term t is denoted by $t\downarrow_{E_0,B}$. Given a decomposition $E = (\Sigma, B, E_0)$, a variant of a term t is a pair (t', θ) such that $t' =_B (t\theta)\downarrow_{E_0,B}$. A decomposition (Σ, B, E_0) has the *finite variant (FV) property* if there is a complete and finite set of variants for each term (see [15] for details). If a decomposition (Σ, B, E_0) of an equational theory E has the *finite variant property*, there is an algorithm to compute a finite complete set $CSU_E(t = t')$ of E-unifiers [15].

A transition system is written $\mathcal{A} = (A, \to)$, where A is a set of states, and $\to$ is a transition relation between states, i.e., $\to \subseteq A \times A$. A rewrite theory $\mathcal{R} = (\Sigma, B, R)$ specifies a transition system $\mathcal{T}_\mathcal{R}$ whose states are elements of the initial algebra $\mathcal{T}_{\Sigma/B}$, and whose transitions are specified by the set of rewrite rules R. Given two transition systems $\mathcal{A} = (A, \to_\mathcal{A})$ and $\mathcal{B} = (B, \to_\mathcal{B})$, a *simulation* from $\mathcal{A}$ to $\mathcal{B}$, written $\mathcal{A} H \mathcal{B}$, is a relation $H \subseteq A \times B$ such that $a H b$ and $a \to_\mathcal{A} a'$ implies that there exists $b' \in B$ such that $a' H b'$ and $b \to_\mathcal{B} b'$. A simulation H from $(A, \to_\mathcal{A})$ to $(B, \to_\mathcal{B})$ is a *bisimulation* if H^{-1} is a simulation from $(B, \to_\mathcal{B})$ to $(A, \to_\mathcal{A})$.

4   Forwards Semantics for Maude-NPA

Maude-NPA [13] performs a *backwards narrowing-based reachability analysis*. However, our notion of indistinguishability is more naturally defined in Maude-NPA in terms of a *rewriting-based forwards analysis*. In this section, we briefly recall the forwards semantics and refer the reader to [14] for further information.

4.1   Maude-NPA's Strand Space Model

In this section we give an overview of Maude-NPA's use of the strand space model to specify protocols and states. This model, with some minor differences, is the same as that used in the backwards semantics.

Given a protocol $\mathcal{P}$, states are modeled as elements of an initial algebra $\mathcal{T}_{\Sigma_{\mathcal{P}}/E_{\mathcal{P}}}$, where $\Sigma_{\mathcal{P}}$ is the signature defining the sorts and function symbols (for the cryptographic functions and for all the state constructor symbols) and $E_{\mathcal{P}}$ is a set of equations specifying the *algebraic properties* of the cryptographic functions and the state constructors. Therefore, a state is an $E_{\mathcal{P}}$-equivalence class $[t] \in \mathcal{T}_{\Sigma_{\mathcal{P}}/E_{\mathcal{P}}}$ with t a ground $\Sigma_{\mathcal{P}}$-term.

In Maude-NPA, a state consists of a multiset of partially executed *strands* S_i and a set of terms in the intruder's knowledge, i.e. a state is a term of the form $\{S_1 \& \cdots \& S_n \& \{IK\}\}$ where $\&$ is an associative-commutative union operator.

The *intruder knowledge* $\{IK\}$ is represented as a set of facts using the comma as an associative-commutative union operator with identity operator *empty*. In the forwards semantics knowledge facts are all of the from $m \in \mathcal{I}$ (the intruder knows m) where m is a message expression.

A *strand* [16] specifies the sequence of messages sent and received by a principal executing the protocol and is represented as a sequence of $\{+,-\}$–labeled messages $[msg_1^{\pm}, \ldots, msg_{k-1}^{\pm}, msg_k^{\pm}]$ such that msg_i^- (also written $-msg_i$) represents an *input* message, msg_i^+ (also written $+msg_i$) represents an *output* message, and each msg_i is a term of a special sort Msg. Strands are used to represent both the actions of honest principals (with a strand specified for each protocol role) and the actions of an intruder (with a strand for each operation an intruder is able to perform on terms).

In the following, a protocol specification is defined as a collection of honest and intruder strand *patterns* together with the algebraic theory of the protocol.

Definition 1 (Protocol Specification). *Given a protocol $\mathcal{P}$, its protocol specification is a triple $((\Sigma_{\mathcal{P}}, E_{\mathcal{P}}), HPS_{\mathcal{P}}, IS_{\mathcal{P}})$ where $(\Sigma_{\mathcal{P}}, E_{\mathcal{P}})$ is the algebraic theory of $\mathcal{P}$, and $HPS_{\mathcal{P}}$ and $IS_{\mathcal{P}}$ denote the set of honest and intruder strands of $\mathcal{P}$, respectively.*

4.2   Forwards Semantics

In a forward reachability analysis, state changes are defined by means of a set $R_{F\mathcal{P}}$ of *rewrite rules*, so that the rewrite theory $(\Sigma_{\mathcal{P}}, E_{\mathcal{P}}, R_{F\mathcal{P}})$ characterizes the behavior of protocol $\mathcal{P}$ modulo the equations $E_{\mathcal{P}}$ [1] . These rewrite rules are generated from principal and intruder strands as explained below.

The forwards execution of a protocol begins with an "empty" initial state, that is a state with the empty set of strands and intruder knowledge. The protocol is executed to determine whether or not an *attack state* can be reached, where an attack state is a ground instance of a state pattern defined by the user. One progresses by applying *rewrite rules* to states.

For each different kind of principal and intruder strand a set of rewrite rules is associated as follows. Given a strand $[m_1^\pm, \ldots, m_n^\pm]$, n different rewrite rules are applied to incrementallly "build" the strand step by step. See [14] for more details and a formal definition of the forwards semantics.

For example, the intruder encryption capability denoted by the strand $[-(K), -(M), +(e(K, M)]$ has the following associated rewrite rules:

$$\{SS \,\&\, \{K{\in}\mathcal{I}, IK\}\} \to \{SS \,\&\, [-(K)] \,\&\, \{K{\in}\mathcal{I}, IK\}\}$$
$$\{SS \,\&\, [-(K)] \,\&\, \{M{\in}\mathcal{I}, IK\}\} \to \{SS \,\&\, [-(K), -(M)] \,\&\, \{M{\in}\mathcal{I}, IK\}\}$$
$$\{SS \,\&\, [-(K), -(M)] \,\&\, \{IK\}\} \to \{SS \,\&\, [-(K), -(M), +(e(K, M)] \{e(K, M){\in}\mathcal{I}, IK\}\}$$

where SS denotes a set of strands and IK a set of intruder knowledge facts.

The forwards execution of a protocol induces a transition system as follows.

Definition 2 (Transition System Induced by a Protocol). *Given a protocol* $\mathcal{P}$ *characterized by the forward rewrite theory* $(\Sigma_{\mathcal{P}}, E_{\mathcal{P}}, R_{F\mathcal{P}})$ *such that* $(\Sigma_{\mathcal{P}}, B, E_0)$ *is a decomposition of* $(\Sigma, E_{\mathcal{P}})$, *we can associate to it a transition system* $\mathcal{L}_{\mathcal{P}}$ *whose states are B-equivalence classes of terms in* E_0, B-*canonical form and whose transitions are of the form:*

$$[t]_B \to [t']_B$$

where $t \to_{R_{F\mathcal{P}}, B} u$ *and* $t' =_B u\!\downarrow_{E_0, B}$.

Unlike the case with process calculi, no information is removed from a state and the history of previous actions can be recovered from a state. Therefore there is no need to record this information through labels in order to obtain a labeled transition system. However, labels can be added if desired (e.g. as a compact way of encoding essential information).

5   Formalization of Indistinguishability in Maude-NPA

Intuitively, two protocols are indistinguishable if an intruder cannot tell the difference between them. In this section we provide the framework that will allow the definition and verification of indistinguishability in Maude-NPA. To define such a framework, in Section 5.1 we first formalize, by the concept of a *protocol pairing*, the notion of pairs of protocols that are similar enough to

---

[1] The rules $R_{F\mathcal{P}}$ model *protocol transitions*. In addition, *equations* $E_{\mathcal{P}}$ are assumed to have a *decomposition* $(\Sigma_{\mathcal{P}}, B, E_0)$ with $E_{\mathcal{P}} = B \cup E_0$ which has the FV property, where E_0 are *not* transitions, but *oriented equations*.

each other so that the issue of their indistinguishability can arise. Then, in Section 5.2 we formalize the idea of *similar interactions* of the attacker with a protocol pairing $\mathcal{P}_1, \mathcal{P}_2$ by the concept of the *synchronous product* $\mathcal{P}_1 \otimes \mathcal{P}_2$. Finally, in Section 5.3 we define the indistinguishability of a protocol pairing in Maude-NPA as the conjunction of two simpler properties called IAES and IM.

5.1   Protocol Pairing

The notion of indistinguishability implies comparing two protocols $\mathcal{P}_1$ and $\mathcal{P}_2$ to ensure that an intruder *cannot distinguish* the behaviors of $\mathcal{P}_1$ and $\mathcal{P}_2$. In practical applications $\mathcal{P}_1$ and $\mathcal{P}_2$ are somewhat different *versions* of a given protocol with some significant *differences*. In this section, we formalize, by the concept of a *protocol pairing*, the notion of such pair of protocols in Maude-NPA.

Definition 3 (Protocol Pairing). *A protocol pairing $\mathcal{P}_1, \mathcal{P}_2$ is a pair of protocol specifications of the form $((\Sigma_{\mathcal{P}_1}, E_{0_{\mathcal{P}_1}} \cup B_{\mathcal{P}_1}), HPS_{\mathcal{P}_1}, IS_{\mathcal{P}_1}), ((\Sigma_{\mathcal{P}_2}, E_{0_{\mathcal{P}_2}} \cup B_{\mathcal{P}_2}), HPS_{\mathcal{P}_2}, IS_{\mathcal{P}_2})$ such that:*

1. *$\mathcal{P}_1$ and $\mathcal{P}_2$ share the same algebraic signature and equations, i.e. $(\Sigma_{\mathcal{P}_1}, E_{0_{\mathcal{P}_1}} \cup B_{\mathcal{P}_1}) = (\Sigma_{\mathcal{P}_2}, E_{0_{\mathcal{P}_2}} \cup B_{\mathcal{P}_2}) = (\Sigma, E_0 \cup B)$ having a decomposition (Σ, B, E_0).*
2. *$HPS_{\mathcal{P}_1}$ and $HPS_{\mathcal{P}_2}$ have strands for the same roles, with the same length and the same polarities (+ or −) at each position in the strand.*
3. *$IS_{\mathcal{P}_1}$ and $IS_{\mathcal{P}_2}$ have strands for the same operations, with the same length and the same polarities (+ or −) at each position in the strand.*

We assume both $HPS_{\mathcal{P}_1}$ and $HPS_{\mathcal{P}_2}$, and $IS_{\mathcal{P}_1}$ and $IS_{\mathcal{P}_2}$ have disjoint variables.

We will also require that strands in certain pairs both be identical up to change of variables, depending on the indistinguishability model used. For example, in the standard model based on cryptographic definitions of indistinguishability the same attacker interacts with two different versions of the protocol, so any two paired intruder strands must be identical up to change of variables. In Lowe's password guessing model the same attacker with different password guesses interacts with the same version of the protocol, so we require that any two paired strands be identical up to change of variables, except that describing the attacker's guess of the password.

The differences between $\mathcal{P}_1$ and $\mathcal{P}_2$ can be specified by having different messages in the same j-th strands of $\mathcal{P}_1$ and $\mathcal{P}_2$, at the same positions in the strands. Below we illustrate the notion of protocol pairing using the following example.

Example 3. Let us consider the two protocols $\mathcal{P}_1$ and $\mathcal{P}_2$ of Example 1 shown above. Note that both $\mathcal{P}_1$ and $\mathcal{P}_2$ share the same algebraic signature and equations (XOR), and have the same set of intruder strands, and differ only in the set of honest principal strands, as explained below. More specifically, the sets $HPS_{\mathcal{P}_1}$ and $HPS_{\mathcal{P}_2}$ of honest strands of $\mathcal{P}_1$ and $\mathcal{P}_2$, respectively, are as follows:

$$HPS_{\mathcal{P}_1} = \{ [(m_1 \oplus m_1)^+] \} \qquad HPS_{\mathcal{P}_2} = \{ [(m_1 \oplus m_2)^+] \}$$

where m_1 and m_2 are two constants denoting different messages, and $\oplus$ is the exclusive-or operator. Therefore, $\mathcal{P}_1, \mathcal{P}_2$ is a protocol pairing.

5.2 Synchronous Product of Protocols

Given a protocol pairing $\mathcal{P}_1, \mathcal{P}_2$ as explained above, the analysis of its indistinguishability assumes that the attacker interacts in an analogous way with both protocols at each step. That is, if it performs an action a in $\mathcal{P}_1$, then it does so in $\mathcal{P}_2$ too. In this section we formalize the idea of *similar interactions* of the attacker with a protocol pairing $\mathcal{P}_1, \mathcal{P}_2$ by the concept of the *synchronous product* $\mathcal{P}_1 \otimes \mathcal{P}_2$. Intuitively, a synchronous product is a new protocol obtained from a protocol pairing in which both protocols from the pairing are executed in a synchronous manner.

In order to provide a formal definition of a synchronous product of protocols, we first define the synchronous product of strands.

Definition 4 (Synchronous Product of Strands). *Given two strands* $Str_1 = [m_1^{\pm}, \ldots, m_n^{\pm}]$, *and* $Str_2 = [m_1'^{\pm}, \ldots, m_n'^{\pm}]$ *corresponding to the same protocol role or intruder action, and with the same polarities at each position in the strand, the synchronous product of* Str_1 *and* Str_2, *written* $Str_1 \otimes Str_2$, *is a strand of the form* $[(m_1 \otimes m_1')^{\pm}, \ldots, (m_n \otimes m_n')^{\pm}]$, *with* $\otimes$ *a new operator.*

Let SS_1 *and* SS_2 *be two sets of strands that have n strands corresponding to the same protocol roles or intruder actions. The synchronous product of* SS_1 *and* SS_2, *written* $SS_1 \otimes SS_2$, *is a set of strands of the form* $\{Str_{1_i} \otimes Str_{2_j}\}_{0 \leq i,j \leq n}$, *such that* $Str_{1_i} \in SS_1$, $Str_{2_j} \in SS_2$, *and* Str_{1_i} *and* Str_{2_j} *correspond to the same protocol role or intruder action.*

Let us now define the synchronous product of protocols as follows.

Definition 5 (Synchronous Product of Protocols). *Given a protocol pairing* $\mathcal{P}_1, \mathcal{P}_2$, *its synchronous product, denoted by* $\mathcal{P}_1 \otimes \mathcal{P}_2$, *is a new protocol as explained below. Basically, the signature is extended with new sorts and symbols to support the specification of a pair of protocols.*

- *First, the theory decomposition* (Σ, B, E_0) *shared by* $\mathcal{P}_1$ *and* $\mathcal{P}_2$ *is renamed to* $(\widehat{\Sigma}, \widehat{B}, \widehat{E_0})$, *just by a renaming* $s \mapsto \widehat{s}$ *(where* $s \in S$ *and* $\widehat{s} \in \widehat{S}$, *of the partially ordered set of sorts so that:* $\widehat{\mathsf{Msg}} = \mathsf{SingleMsg}$, *and* $\widehat{s} = s$ *otherwise, and with* $s < s'$ *iff* $\widehat{s} < \widehat{s'}$. *The operators* $\widehat{\Sigma}$ *are renamed accordingly, so that* $f : s_1 \cdots s_n \to s$ *is renamed to* $f : \widehat{s_1} \cdots \widehat{s_n} \to \widehat{s}$, *and the equations* B *and* E_0 *are renamed to* $\widehat{B}$ *and* $\widehat{E_0}$ *just by renaming the sorts of their variables by the mapping* $s \mapsto \widehat{s}$.
- *A new sort* Msg *is added as the new top sort of the connected component for messages, so that* $\mathsf{SingleMsg} < \mathsf{Msg}$.
- *A new operator* $\_ \otimes \_ : \mathsf{SingleMsg}\ \mathsf{SingleMsg} \to \mathsf{Msg}$ *is added to* $\Sigma_{\otimes}$.
- *Its protocol specification is the triple* $\mathcal{P}_1 \otimes \mathcal{P}_2 = ((\Sigma_{\otimes}, \widehat{E_0} \cup \widehat{B}), HPS_{\mathcal{P}_1} \otimes HPS_{\mathcal{P}_2}, IS_{\mathcal{P}_1} \otimes IS_{\mathcal{P}_2})$, *where* $HPS_{\mathcal{P}_1}$, $HPS_{\mathcal{P}_2}$, $IS_{\mathcal{P}_1}$, *and* $IS_{\mathcal{P}_2}$ *are renamed to have disjoint variables.*

Therefore, if (Σ, B, E_0) *is the original theory decomposition, then the theory of the synchronous product is* $(\Sigma_{\otimes}, \widehat{B}, \widehat{E_0})$.

Example 4. For example, given the protocol pairing $\mathcal{P}_1, \mathcal{P}_2$ of Example 3 the set $HPS_{\mathcal{P}_1 \otimes \mathcal{P}_2}$ of protocol strands of the synchronous product $\mathcal{P}_1 \otimes \mathcal{P}_2$ is as follows:

$$HPS_{\mathcal{P}_1 \otimes \mathcal{P}_2} = \{ [((m_1 \oplus m_1) \otimes (m_1 \oplus m_2))^+] \}$$

The indistinguishability of a protocol pairing $\mathcal{P}_1, \mathcal{P}_2$ in Maude-NPA is characterized in terms of the synchronous product $\mathcal{P}_1 \otimes \mathcal{P}_2$, as we explain in Section 5.3. To be analyzed in Maude-NPA the equational theory of the synchronous product $\mathcal{P}_1 \otimes \mathcal{P}_2$ should have a finite variant decomposition. The following result states that, if the rewrite theory used by two protocols $\mathcal{P}_1$ and $\mathcal{P}_2$ has a finite variant decomposition, then so does the rewrite theory of $\mathcal{P}_1 \otimes \mathcal{P}_2$.

Theorem 1. *For a synchronous product $\mathcal{P}_1 \otimes \mathcal{P}_2$, the rewrite theory $(\Sigma_\otimes, \widehat{B}, \widehat{E_0})$ has the finite variant property iff the rewrite theory (Σ, B, E_0) does also.*

Proof. Since $(\widehat{\Sigma}, \widehat{B}, \widehat{E_0})$ is just a sort-renamed copy of (Σ, B, E_0) it has the FV property. Note that $(\widehat{\Sigma}, \widehat{B}, \widehat{E_0}) \subseteq (\Sigma_\otimes, \widehat{B}, \widehat{E_0})$ is a theory inclusion, and $\Sigma_\otimes$ terms are either $\widehat{\Sigma}$-terms, which have all a finite set of variants, or terms in $\mathcal{T}_{\Sigma_\otimes}(\mathcal{X}) - \mathcal{T}_{\widehat{\Sigma}}(\mathcal{X})$, which are either variables, whose only variant is itself, or terms of the form $t \otimes t'$, with $t, t' \in \mathcal{T}_{\widehat{\Sigma}}(\mathcal{X})$. Let $bd(t)$ and $bd(t')$ be the bounds (see [15]) on reduction sequences to their normal forms for t and t', respectively. Then $bd(t \otimes t') \leq bd(t) + bd(t')$, and thus $(\Sigma_\otimes, \widehat{B}, \widehat{E})$ has the FV property. □

Using Definition 2, the forward analysis of a synchronous product $\mathcal{P}_1 \otimes \mathcal{P}_2$ induces a transition system $\mathcal{L}_{\mathcal{P}_1 \otimes \mathcal{P}_2}$.

In the following, we define two projection functions that will be used below to connect the behavior of a synchronous product of protocols with the behavior of each protocol.

Definition 6 (Projection Functions). *Let Σ and $\Sigma_\otimes$ be as in Definition 5, and let $\widehat{\mathcal{X}} = \{\mathcal{X}_{\widehat{s}}\}_{\widehat{s} \in \widehat{S}}$, and $\mathcal{X} = \{\mathcal{X}_s\}_{s \in S}$. We then define functions $\pi_1, \pi_2 : \mathcal{T}_{\Sigma_\otimes}(\widehat{\mathcal{X}}) \to \mathcal{T}_\Sigma(\mathcal{X})$ recursively as follows:*

$$\pi_1(x{:}\widehat{s}) = \pi_2(x{:}\widehat{s}) = x{:}s$$
$$\pi_1(t_1 \otimes t_2) = t_1 \qquad \pi_2(t_1 \otimes t_2) = t_2$$
$$\pi_1(f(t_1, \ldots, t_n)) = f(\pi_1(t_1), \ldots, \pi_1(t_n)) \text{ for } f \neq \otimes$$
$$\pi_2(f(t_1, \ldots, t_n)) = f(\pi_2(t_1), \ldots, \pi_2(t_n)) \text{ for } f \neq \otimes$$

These projection functions are homomorphically extended to states, transitions and transition systems.

Proposition 1. *Given two protocols $\mathcal{P}_1$ and $\mathcal{P}_2$, its synchronous product $\mathcal{P}_1 \otimes \mathcal{P}_2$ and their associated transition systems $\mathcal{L}_{\mathcal{P}_1}, \mathcal{L}_{\mathcal{P}_2}$, and $\mathcal{L}_{\mathcal{P}_1 \otimes \mathcal{P}_2}$ as defined above, the projection functions in Definition 6, $\pi_1 : \mathcal{L}_{\mathcal{P}_1 \otimes \mathcal{P}_2} \to \mathcal{L}_{\mathcal{P}_1}$, and $\pi_2 : \mathcal{L}_{\mathcal{P}_1 \otimes \mathcal{P}_2} \to \mathcal{L}_{\mathcal{P}_2}$ are both simulations.*

Proof. Easy from analysis of the rules $R_{F\mathcal{P}_1}$, $R_{F\mathcal{P}_2}$, and $R_{F(\mathcal{P}_1 \otimes \mathcal{P}_2)}$. □

5.3 Indistinguishability in Maude-NPA

We now define IM and IAES as follows.

Definition 7 (Indistinguishable Messages (IM)). *A protocol pairing* $\mathcal{P}_1, \mathcal{P}_2$ *with underlying equational theory* $(\Sigma, E_0 \cup B)$ *satisfies the* indistinguishable messages (IM) *property iff for any initial state* St_0 *of* $\mathcal{L}_{\mathcal{P}_1 \otimes \mathcal{P}_2}$, *there exists no sequence of transitions* $St_0 \to St_1 \cdots St_{n-1} \to St_n$ *such that the intruder knowledge in* St_n *contains two facts* $(m_1 \otimes m_2) \in \mathcal{I}$ *and* $(m_1' \otimes m_2') \in \mathcal{I}$ *such that either (i)* $m_1 =_E m_1'$ *but* $m_2 \neq_E m_2'$, *or (ii)* $m_2 =_E m_2'$ *but* $m_1 \neq_E m_1'$, *where* $E = E_0 \cup B$.

Definition 8 (Indistinguishable Attack Event Sequences (IAES)). *Given a protocol pairing* $\mathcal{P}_1, \mathcal{P}_2$ *and the two projections* $\pi_1 : \mathcal{L}_{\mathcal{P}_1 \otimes \mathcal{P}_2} \to \mathcal{L}_{\mathcal{P}_1}$ *and* $\pi_2 : \mathcal{L}_{\mathcal{P}_1 \otimes \mathcal{P}_2} \to \mathcal{L}_{\mathcal{P}_2}$, *we say that* $\mathcal{P}_1, \mathcal{P}_2$ *have* indistinguishable attack event sequences (IAES) *iff* π_1 *and* π_2 *are bisimulations.*

Corollary 1. *Given a protocol pairing* $\mathcal{P}_1, \mathcal{P}_2$ *and the two projections* $\pi_1 : \mathcal{L}_{\mathcal{P}_1 \otimes \mathcal{P}_2} \to \mathcal{L}_{\mathcal{P}_1}$ *and* $\pi_2 : \mathcal{L}_{\mathcal{P}_1 \otimes \mathcal{P}_2} \to \mathcal{L}_{\mathcal{P}_2}$, *if* π_1 *and* π_2 *are bisimulations then protocols* $\mathcal{P}_1$ *and* $\mathcal{P}_2$ *are bisimilar.*

In Section 6 we explain in detail how the IAES and IM properties explained above are analyzed in practice in Maude-NPA.

6 Indistinguishability Verification in Maude-NPA

In this section we explain how the theoretical framework for indistinguishability verification presented in Section 5 can be implemented in Maude-NPA. In Section 4 we presented the rewriting-based forwards operational semantics of Maude-NPA, which is used as a reference model to define our notion of indistinguishability in Maude-NPA, as explained in Section 5. However, Maude-NPA performs a *backward narrowing-based reachability analysis* that we briefly recall in Section 6.1 (see [13] for further details). Thus the IM and IAES properties are analyzed in Maude-NPA by performing backward narrowing-based reachability analysis from certain attack patterns, as explained in Section 6.2 below.

6.1 Backwards Reachability Analysis in Maude-NPA

Maude-NPA explores *symbolic state patterns* $[t(x_1, \ldots, x_n)] \in T_{\Sigma_{\mathcal{P}}/E_{\mathcal{P}}}(X)$ on the free $(\Sigma_{\mathcal{P}}, E_{\mathcal{P}})$-algebra over a set of variables X. In this way, a state pattern $[t(x_1, \ldots, x_n)]$ represents not a single concrete state but a possibly infinite set of such states, namely, all the instances of the pattern $[t(x_1, \ldots, x_n)]$ where the variables $x_1, \ldots, x_n$ have been instantiated by concrete ground terms.

As in Section 4, a state is represented as a set of strands and the intruder knowledge. However, in the backwards semantics there are two kinds of intruder facts: *positive* knowledge facts (the intruder knows m, i.e., $m \in \mathcal{I}$), and *negative* knowledge facts (the intruder *does not yet know* m but *will know it in a future state*, i.e., $m \notin \mathcal{I}$), where m is a message expression.

In the symbolic backwards semantics *strands* evolve over time; the symbol $|$ is used to divide past and future. That is, in a strand $[\ m_1^{\pm}, \ldots, m_i^{\pm}\ |\ m_{i+1}^{\pm}, \ldots,\ m_k^{\pm}\ ]$, messages $m_1^{\pm}, \ldots, m_i^{\pm}$ are the *past messages*, and messages $m_{i+1}^{\pm}, \ldots, m_k^{\pm}$ are the *future messages* ($m_{i+1}^{\pm}$ is the immediate future message).

State changes are described by means of a set $R_{B\mathcal{P}}$ of *rewrite rules*, so that the rewrite theory $(\Sigma_{\mathcal{P}}, E_{\mathcal{P}}, R_{B\mathcal{P}})$ characterizes the behavior of protocol $\mathcal{P}$ modulo the equations $E_{\mathcal{P}}$ for backwards execution. The rules $R_{B\mathcal{P}}$ are generic rules plus rules generated for each principal and intruder strand in the given protocol. See [14] or [13] for more detail and a formal definition of the backwards semantics.

The *backwards* reachability analysis performed by Maude-NPA consists in symbolically running the protocol "in reverse" by narrowing modulo the equations $E_{\mathcal{P}}$. This can be achieved by using the set of rules $R_{B\mathcal{P}}^{-1}$ (where $v \longrightarrow u$ is in $R_{B\mathcal{P}}^{-1}$ iff $u \longrightarrow v$ is in $R_{B\mathcal{P}}$), and performing backwards *narrowing* steps of the form $S \rightsquigarrow_{R_{B\mathcal{P}}^{-1}, E_{\mathcal{P}}} S'$ to search for an *initial state pattern* from an *attack pattern* symbolically describing an attack situation, If Maude-NPA finds an initial state, then the protocol is insecure, and if it terminates without finding an initial state, then it proves the protocol is secure w.r.t. the attack pattern.

The following result, proved in [14], allows us to use reachability in the backwards semantics to prove reachability in the forwards semantics.

Theorem 2 (Soundness and Completeness). ([14], Theorems 1 and 2) *The backwards narrowing-based reachability analysis performed by Maude-NPA is sound and complete with respect to the forwards rewriting-based reachability analysis presented in Section 4.2.*

6.2   Analysis of Indistinguishability properties in Maude-NPA

In Section 5.3 we defined our notion of indistinguishability as the conjunction of two more basic properties, namely, *Indistinguishable Messages* (IM) and *Indistinguishable Attacker Event Sequences* (IAES), using the forwards operational semantics of Maude-NPA explained in Section 4. In this section we prove a result with respect to the symbolic backwards semantics of the Maude-NPA protocol analysis tool presented in 6.1, showing that the conjunction of IM and IAES of a protocol pairing $\mathcal{P}_1, \mathcal{P}_2$ can be expressed as the unreachability of several different attack patterns for the synchronous product $\mathcal{P}_1 \otimes \mathcal{P}_2$.

In the following, for each property we describe a set of attack patterns in Maude-NPA's syntax denoting states violating that property. If Maude-NPA proves that at least one of the patterns is reachable from an initial state, then it proves that the protocol pairing violates the property and, therefore, the intruder can distinguish between both protocol variants. If the tool proves that no attack pattern is reachable (by terminating without finding an initial state), then it proves that the protocol pairing satisfies the property. Necessary and sufficient conditions for IM and IAES respectively are given in the two theorems below.

Theorem 3. *Let $\mathcal{P}_1, \mathcal{P}_2$ be a protocol pairing. Then $\mathcal{P}_1$ and $\mathcal{P}_2$ satisfy the IM property iff no initial state can be symbolically backwards reached from an attack state of $\mathcal{P}_1 \otimes \mathcal{P}_2$ of either one of the following forms:*

(1) $\{SS \mathbin{\&} \{(m_1 \otimes m_2) \in \mathcal{I},\ (m_1 \otimes m_2') \in \mathcal{I}, (m_2 \neq_E m_2'), IK\}\}$, *or*
(2) $\{SS \mathbin{\&} \{(m_1 \otimes m_2) \in \mathcal{I},\ (m_1' \otimes m_2) \in \mathcal{I}, (m_1 \neq_E m_1'), IK\}\}$

Proof. Trivial by the soundness and completeness of the backwards operational semantics w.r.t. the forwards operational semantics (see Theorem 2). □

Theorem 4. *Let* $\mathcal{P}_1, \mathcal{P}_2$ *be a protocol pairing satisfying the IM property. Then* $\mathcal{P}_1, \mathcal{P}_2$ *satisfy the IAES property iff no initial state can be symbolically backwards reached from any attack state of either of the forms:*

(1) $\{\ SS \mathbin{\&} [\ L\ |\ -(m_1 \otimes m_2),\ L'\ ] \mathbin{\&} \{(m_1 \otimes m_2') \in \mathcal{I},\ (m_2 \neq_E m_2'),\ IK\}\}$, *or*
(2) $\{\ SS \mathbin{\&} [\ L\ |\ -(m_1 \otimes m_2),\ L'\ ] \mathbin{\&} \{(m_1' \otimes m_2) \in \mathcal{I},\ (m_1 \neq_E m_1'),\ IK\}\}$

Proof. ($\Rightarrow$) We reason by contradiction. Suppose $\mathcal{P}_1, \mathcal{P}_2$ satisfy IAES and an attack of type (1) exists. By the soundness and completeness of the backwards narrowing performed by Maude-NPA there is a ground substitution θ such that from an initial state of $\mathcal{P}_1 \otimes \mathcal{P}_2$ we can reach a ground state, via the forwards semantics, of the form $t = \{\widetilde{SS}\ \theta \mathbin{\&} [L\theta] \mathbin{\&} \{(m_1\theta \otimes m_2'\theta) \in \mathcal{I}, \widetilde{IK}\ \theta\}\}$, where $\widetilde{SS}$ are instances of *already executed* strand fragments in SS, and $\widetilde{IK}\ \theta$ are the instances of *positive* knowledge facts in IK, and with $m_2'\theta \neq_E m_2\theta$.

Because $(m_1\theta \otimes m_2\theta) \in \mathcal{I}$, $\mathcal{P}_1$ can make a transition

$$\pi_1(t) \rightarrow \{\pi_1(\widetilde{SS}\ \theta) \mathbin{\&} [\pi_1(L\theta), -m_1\theta] \mathbin{\&} \{m_1\theta \in \mathcal{I}, \pi_1(\widetilde{IK}\ \theta)\}\} \qquad (\dagger)$$

But, since π_1 is a bisimulation, this means that $\mathcal{P}_1 \otimes \mathcal{P}_2$ can make a transition

$$t \rightarrow \{SS\theta \mathbin{\&} [L, -(m_1\theta \otimes m_2\theta)] \mathbin{\&} \{(m_1\theta \otimes m_2\theta) \in \mathcal{I}, IK\}\} \qquad (\ddagger)$$

which is only possible if there is a fact $(m_1\theta \otimes m_2\theta) \in \mathcal{I}$ in IK, violating the IM assumption. The proof for an attack of type (2) is entirely similar.

($\Leftarrow$) Suppose no attacks of type (1) or (2) exist but, say $\pi_1 : \mathcal{P}_1 \otimes \mathcal{P}_2 \rightarrow \mathcal{P}_1$ (the case for π_2 is similar) is *not* a bisimulation. Thus there is a ground state t reachable from the initial state via the forwards semantics such that $\mathcal{P}_1$ can make a transition $\pi_1(t) \rightarrow u$ but there is no transition $t \rightarrow v$ in $\mathcal{P}_1 \otimes \mathcal{P}_2$ with $\pi_1(v) = u$. This can only happen for a *message receive* transition in a *user strand*. Therefore, the transition must be of the form ($\dagger$) above, but there is *no* transition of the form ($\ddagger$) above. Thus the received message $m_1\theta \in \mathcal{I}$ in $\pi_1(t)$ comes from a pair $(m_1\theta \otimes m_2'\theta) \in \mathcal{I}$ in t such that $m_2'\theta \neq_E m_2\theta$, contradicting the assumption that no attack of type (1) exists. □

6.3   Experimental Evaluation

We have begun exploring the implementation of indistinguishability verification in Maude-NPA following the method presented in this paper, and performed a preliminary   evaluation   (source   files   and   output   available   at http://www.dsic.upv.es/~ssantiago/indist.html). Although we were unable to achieve termination of some analyses, we have proved in Maude-NPA the non-indistinguishability of some pairs of protocols such as the protocol involving an

XOR operator of Example 1 and a complete version of the EKE protocol following the style of Example 2. We also investigated reasons for non-termination due to state space explosion. One is that the attack states used are quite general. As future work, we plan to study sound and complete ways to replace them by more specific atttack states. Another is that these analyses make a heavy use of inequalities modulo equational theories. ProVerif includes methods for solving inequality constraints early in the search, but they do not apply to theories with AC operators. Thus we hold off on evaluating inequalities until the end of the search. However, work on evaluating inequality constraints for theories with AC is beginning to appear (see e.g. [17]). We expect to explore this issue further in our future work.

7 Conclusions

We have formalized an intuitive notion of indistinguishability as the conjunction of the IM and IAES properties defined in terms of the synchronous products of two protocols and shown it to be *checkable* automatically by Maude-NPA. This is a significant step forward in indistinguishability research, because, for the first time, there is a tool that can perform such automatic checks *modulo* a very wide class of theories, namely, all theories with the finite variant property that can have axioms B such as AC or C, which include theories like Abelian Groups, several theories of homomorphic encryption, exclusive-or, and modular exponentiations essential for many privacy-preserving protocols. We have also illustrated with concrete examples how this kind of indistinguishability analysis can be performed by Maude-NPA.

As usual, much work remains ahead. First of all, our indistinguishability notion can be further strengthened in various ways that should also be formalized and mechanized in Maude-NPA. For example, it can be extended to cover other issues that may allow the intruder to distinguish two protocols, such as the sorts of the messages. Second, an interesting line of future work in this sense is the handling of protocols with branching, which would allow us to check indistinguishability properties for a wider class of protocols. Third, a more detailed comparison with other indistinguishability notions should be carried out. This is nontrivial, since they depend on different protocol models. Fourth, much more experimentation is needed to test and improve our capacity to prove indistinguishability for protocol pairings.

References

1. Abadi, M., Fournet, C.: Mobile values, new names, and secure communication. In: POPL, pp. 104–115 (2001)
2. Arapinis, M., Bursuc, S., Ryan, M.D.: Reduction of equational theories for verification of trace equivalence: Re-encryption, associativity and commutativity. In: Degano, P., Guttman, J.D. (eds.) POST 2012. LNCS, vol. 7215, pp. 169–188. Springer, Heidelberg (2012)

3. Barthe, G.B., Crespo, J.M., Grégoire, B., Kunz, C., Lakhnech, Y., Schmidt, B., Béguelin, S.Z.: Fully automated analysis of padding-based encryption in the computational model. In: ACM Conference on Computer and Communications Security, pp. 1247–1260 (2013)
4. Baudet, M.: Deciding security of protocols against off-line guessing attacks. In: Proc. ACM CCS 2005, pp. 16–25. ACM (2005)
5. Bellovin, S., Merritt, M.: Encrypted key exchange: Password-based protocols secure against dictionary attacks. In: Proceedings of the 1992 Symposium on Research in Security and Privacy, pp. 72–84. IEEE (1992)
6. Blanchet, B., Abadi, M., Fournet, C.: Automated verification of selected equivalences for security protocols. J. Log. Algebr. Program. 75(1), 3–51 (2008)
7. Chadha, R., Ciobâcă, Ş., Kremer, S.: Automated verification of equivalence properties of cryptographic protocols. In: Seidl, H. (ed.) ESOP 2012. LNCS, vol. 7211, pp. 108–127. Springer, Heidelberg (2012)
8. Cheval, V., Comon-Lundh, H., Delaune, S.: Automating security analysis: symbolic equivalence of constraint systems. In: Giesl, J., Hähnle, R. (eds.) IJCAR 2010. LNCS, vol. 6173, pp. 412–426. Springer, Heidelberg (2010)
9. Cheval, V., Comon-Lundh, H., Delaune, S.: Trace equivalence decision: negative tests and non-determinism. In: Proc. ACM CCS 2011, pp. 321–330 (2011)
10. Cheval, V., Cortier, V., Plet, A.: Lengths may break privacy – or how to check for equivalences with length. In: Sharygina, N., Veith, H. (eds.) CAV 2013. LNCS, vol. 8044, pp. 708–723. Springer, Heidelberg (2013)
11. Clarkson, M., Schneider, F.: Hyperproperties. J. Computer Security 18(6), 1157–1210 (2010)
12. Cortier, V., Delaune, S.: A method for proving observational equivalence. In: CSF, pp. 266–276. IEEE Computer Society (2009)
13. Escobar, S., Meadows, C., Meseguer, J.: Maude-NPA: Cryptographic protocol analysis modulo equational properties. In: Aldini, A., Barthe, G., Gorrieri, R. (eds.) FOSAD 2007/2008/2009. LNCS, vol. 5705, pp. 1–50. Springer, Heidelberg (2009)
14. Escobar, S., Meadows, C., Meseguer, J., Santiago, S.: A rewriting-based forwards semantics for Maude-NPA. In: Proc. HotSoS (to appear, 2014), Preliminary version available at: http://www.dsic.upv.es/~sescobar/papers/HotSoS2014.pdf
15. Escobar, S., Sasse, R., Meseguer, J.: Folding variant narrowing and optimal variant termination. J. Log. Algebr. Program. 81(7-8), 898–928 (2012)
16. Thayer Fabrega, F.J., Herzog, J., Guttman, J.: Strand Spaces: What Makes a Security Protocol Correct? Journal of Computer Security 7, 191–230 (1999)
17. Gutiérrez, R., Meseguer, J., Rocha, C.: Order-sorted equality enrichments modulo axioms. In: Durán, F. (ed.) WRLA 2012. LNCS, vol. 7571, pp. 162–181. Springer, Heidelberg (2012)
18. Lowe, G.: Analysings protocol subject to guessing attacks. Journal of Computer Security 12(1), 83–98 (2004)
19. Merritt, M.: Cryptographic Protocols. PhD thesis, Georgia Inst. of Technology (1984)
20. Meseguer, J.: Conditional rewriting logic as a united model of concurrency. Theor. Comput. Sci. 96(1), 73–155 (1992)
21. Meseguer, J.: Membership algebra as a logical framework for equational specification. In: Parisi-Presicce, F. (ed.) WADT 1997. LNCS, vol. 1376, pp. 18–61. Springer, Heidelberg (1998)
22. Newcomb, T., Lowe, G.: A computational justification for guessing attack formalisms. Technical report No. RR-05-05. Oxford University Computing Laboratory (October 2005)
23. TeReSe (ed.): Term Rewriting Systems. Cambridge Univ. Press, Cambridge (2003)

Hybrid Enforcement of Category-Based Access Control

Asad Ali and Maribel Fernández

Department of Informatics, King's College London, Strand WC2R 2LS, UK
asad.2.ali@kcl.ac.uk

Abstract. Access control policies are often partly static, i.e. no dependence on any run-time information, and partly dynamic. However, they are usually enforced dynamically - even the static parts. We propose a new hybrid approach to policy enforcement using the Category-Based Access Control (CBAC) meta-model. We build on previous work, which established a static system for the enforcement of (static) hierarchical Role-Based Access Control (RBAC) policies. We modify the previous policy language, JPol, to specify static and dynamic categories. We establish an equivalence between static categories and static roles (in RBAC), therefore we are able to use the previous design patterns and static verification algorithm, with some changes, to enforce static categories. For dynamic categories, we propose a new design methodology and generate code in the target program to do the necessary run-time checks.

1 Introduction

Access control policy enforcement is the task of ensuring that the implementation of a system is such that each request to access a resource is either granted or denied according to the policy which specifies the rights users have to access resources. Barker's access control meta-model [2], which we refer to as Category-Based Access Control (CBAC), contains a small amount of primitives, which can be specialised to produce equivalent forms of other models for policy specifications. One example is the popular Role-Based Access Control (RBAC) model [7], where each user has one or more roles, and each role has an associated list of permissions on resources.

Our focus is on the recently emerged hybrid approach to policy enforcement, which seeks to leverage the benefits of both the static and dynamic approaches (refer to [9] for a comparison of the latter two approaches and [5] for an example of the hybrid approach). In practice, we find that parts of a policy do not depend on run-time information, thus are static. However, to the best or our knowledge, these parts are still enforced dynamically in today's available access control systems, such as RBAC (in e.g., Java Web Security [3,8]). One significant reason for this is that, in the context of Object-Oriented programs where a policy restricts calls to some methods in some classes, it is very difficult to know by statically analysing code which user, with which of their associated static access

S. Mauw and C.D. Jensen (Eds.): STM 2014, LNCS 8743, pp. 178–182, 2014.
© Springer International Publishing Switzerland 2014

rights, can execute any method call found in the code. Without knowing this, it is impossible to check, statically, if the call is allowed.

For static policies (using RBAC), this has been solved through the use of a new program design methodology; this is discussed in previous work [1]. In CBAC, a category can also be static exactly like a static role, hence we can reuse the previous solution. However, we need to consider, in addition, enforcement of dynamic permissions.

We propose a hybrid solution to CBAC policy enforcement for Java programs by extending our previous work. This is done firstly through an extension of our previous design patterns resulting in the new CBAC MVC patterns, which integrate static and dynamic categories into the program as a set of Model-View-Controller (MVC) [10] classes. Each set acts as an interface specific to an associated category. The flow of the program directs users either to the interface of one of their assigned static categories, from which they can access interfaces of the dynamic categories which are related to the chosen static category, otherwise to other areas of the program which do not access resources. Secondly, we extend the static enforcement checks presented in our previous work. Finally, we generate code into classes associated to dynamic categories to check at runtime if access requests should be granted or denied depending on the user-to-category assignments in the policy (i.e. if the user is computed to be a member of a category permitted to invoke the action).

To the best of our knowledge, this is the first hybrid verifier available for general policies specified using CBAC.

2   Concept Overview

We now describe the concepts that add to those in our previous work [1], which arise in the context of dynamic policies and hybrid enforcement.

Firstly, the policy contains categories, to which permissions to invoke an action in a resource class are assigned and also users are assigned. Dynamic information is added through the use of *dynamic categories*, as well as static information through static categories. User membership to dynamic categories depends on conditions utilising dynamic information (see situational/event identifiers in [2]), but not in the case of static categories. Therefore, the latter are equivalent to static roles, hence we can re-use several concepts from our previous work. Furthermore, categories can be related in two ways. The first is hierarchically, where either a static category *subsumes* the permissions of a subordinate static category, or a dynamic category *subsumes* the permissions of a subordinate static or dynamic category. The second is by a *can-be* relation, whereby a user in a *static or dynamic category* can switch to a *can-be* related *dynamic category* as a result of a condition on dynamic information being fulfilled e.g. the system entering an 'emergency' state. Note that as in our previous work, user definitions and consequently user-to-category assignments are not part of the policy specification in our system. This is so that new users can be added to the system and user membership to categories can change, thus introducing a degree of flexibility.

Secondly, the two kinds of category are implemented into the program as interfaces exactly like role interfaces, using our previous patterns which we now rename *CBAC MVC* and add the dynamic category MVC classes. The patterns also specify *links* between category interfaces, which are implementations of the two relations between categories described above. Simply put, for a category c_1 and the set composed of all of its senior and *can-be* related categories, there is an invocation in c_1's interface of the interface of each category in the set. We call every invocation of this kind a *link*. The last addition to the patterns is that of a reference monitor, which we call a *categoriser*. The programmer must implement this to compute at run-time if a user invoking a specific action is in a dynamic category permitted to invoke that action. This is left open to the programmer as a result of the generality required by CBAC.

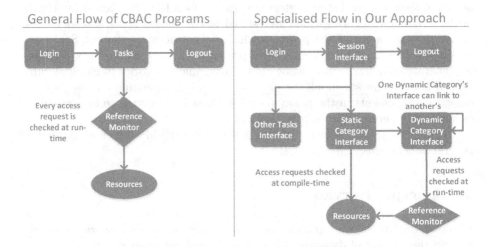

Fig. 1. General and specialised flow in our approach of CBAC programs

The flow of the target program reflects the changes made in the patterns, as shown in Figure 1 which is described as follows. An authenticated user enters the session interface which means that their static categories have been retrieved. They can then choose any of these to display and interact with its interface, or choose an other task interface. From a static category interface associated to c_1, the user can choose to display the interface of dynamic category c_2, where either c_1 *can-be* c_2 or c_2 *subsumes* c_1. This is due to the implementation, as *links*, of the relations specified between categories above. The same applies from the interface of c_2 to the interface of another dynamic category c_3, and so on. Action invocations in static category interface classes will be checked at compile-time. For dynamic categories, this will be checked at run-time by the categoriser.

Thirdly, we extend our static analysis. At compile-time, we check that each action call in every class in a static category interface abides by the permission-to-category assignments in the policy. This can be done because of our design patterns. This flow enables us to know for each action call in a class in a category interface, which category is calling that action - that category interface's owner (i.e. single associated category). For static category interfaces, this means that no run-time check is necessary, because its action calls will have been checked with the permission-to-category assignments in the policy and the user-to-category assignment do not depend on any dynamic information - the user is always a member of an assigned static category.

For dynamic category interfaces, we also need to check that at run-time, each action call abides by the user-to-category assignments in the policy i.e. the user is computed to be in a category which contains the permission to invoke that action. In our approach, this is achieved by the programmer-provided categoriser. We then generate code before each action call, for an *if* condition containing a call to the categoriser. The call will provide to the categoriser the name of the called action, the name of the class in which the called action is defined, the class in which the action was called and the security context information which will contain the dynamic information required by CBAC (e.g. the identity of the user). The categoriser will compute all the categories that the user is in at that time using the security context information. Then it will check if at least one of the computed categories is permitted to invoke the called method. It will return true if this is the case and thus the action will be invoked, else it will return false and the action will not be invoked. We leave the implementation of the categoriser open to the programmer; reference monitors are well-studied in the literature (see, for example, [6]).

3   Results

The main strength of our work is that it can leverage the benefits of both static and dynamic enforcement approaches. The programmer has assurances at compile-time that the policy is enforced correctly in the program, significantly reducing testing time and making programs easier to debug, but the policy is still able to express dynamic information which is enforced also. The impact of policy enforcement on run-time resources is reduced since static parts of the policy are enforced at compile-time only. For classes associated to dynamic categories, as well as being checked at run-time, their action invocations are checked at compile-time (along with classes associated to static categories) to ensure no actions can be invoked that are not assigned to that category. This helps the programmer to correctly implement the tasks, which contain the action invocations, associated to categories. For dynamic category classes, this can also reduce the number of policy violations that can occur at run-time. Another strength is that because the policy in our approach follows the CBAC meta-model, it can be used in any environment where a specialisation of CBAC is used to specify the policy, of which there are a multitude [4].

References

1. Ali, A., Fernández, M.: Static enforcement of role-based access control. In: Ravara, A., Ter Beek, M. (eds.) Proceedings of the 10th International Workshop on Automated Specification and Verification of Web Systems. EPTCS (2014)
2. Barker, S.: The next 700 access control models or a unifying meta-model? In: Proceedings of the 14th ACM Symposium on Access Control Models and Technologies, SACMAT 2009, pp. 187–196. ACM, New York (2009)
3. Basin, D., Doser, J., Lodderstedt, T.: Model driven security: From UML models to access control infrastructures. ACM Trans. Softw. Eng. Methodol. 15(1), 39–91 (2006)
4. Bertolissi, C., Fernández, M.: Category-based authorisation models: Operational semantics and expressive power. In: Massacci, F., Wallach, D., Zannone, N. (eds.) ESSoS 2010. LNCS, vol. 5965, pp. 140–156. Springer, Heidelberg (2010)
5. Bodden, E., Lam, P., Hendren, L.: Partially evaluating finite-state runtime monitors ahead of time. ACM Trans. Program. Lang. Syst. 34(2), 7:1–7:52 (2012)
6. Fernandez, E.B., Sorgente, T., Larrondo-Petrie, M.M.: Even more patterns for secure operating systems. In: Proceedings of the 2006 Conference on Pattern Languages of Programs, PLoP 2006, pp. 10:1–10:9. ACM, New York (2006)
7. Ferraiolo, D., Kuhn, R.: Role-based access control. In:15th NIST-NCSC National Computer Security Conference, pp. 554–563 (1992)
8. Gosling, J., Joy, B., Steele, G., Bracha, G.: Java(TM) Language Specification, The (3rd Edition) (Java (Addison-Wesley)). Addison-Wesley Professional (2005)
9. Hamlen, K.W., Morrisett, G., Schneider, F.B.: Computability classes for enforcement mechanisms. ACM Trans. Program. Lang. Syst. 28(1), 175–205 (2006)
10. Krasner, G.E., Pope, S.T.: A cookbook for using the model-view controller user interface paradigm in Smalltalk-80. J. Object Oriented Program. 1(3), 26–49 (1988)

Lime: Data Lineage in the Malicious Environment*

Michael Backes, Niklas Grimm, and Aniket Kate

Saarland University, Germany
backes@cs.uni-saarland.de, s9nigrim@stud.uni-saarland.de,
aniket@mmci.uni-saarland.de

Abstract. Intentional or unintentional leakage of confidential data is undoubtedly one of the most severe security threats that organizations face in the digital era. The threat now extends to our personal lives: a plethora of personal information is available to social networks and smartphone providers and is indirectly transferred to untrustworthy third party and fourth party applications. In this work, we present a generic data lineage framework LIME for data flow across multiple entities that take two characteristic, principal roles (i.e., owner and consumer). We define the exact security guarantees required by such a data lineage mechanism toward identification of a guilty entity, and identify the simplifying non-repudiation and honesty assumptions. We then develop a novel accountable data transfer protocol between two entities within a malicious environment by building upon oblivious transfer, robust watermarking, and signature primitives.

1 Introduction

In the digital era, information leakage through unintentional exposures, or intentional sabotage by disgruntled employees and malicious external entities, present one of the most serious threats to organizations. According to an interesting chronology of data breaches maintained by the Privacy Rights Clearinghouse (PRC), in the United States alone, $868, 045, 823$ records have been breached from $4, 355$ data breaches made public since 2005 [1]. It is not hard to believe that this is just the tip of the iceberg, as most cases of information leakage go unreported due to fear of loss of customer confidence or regulatory penalties: it costs companies on average \$214 per compromised record [2].

We find that most data leakage scenarios can be associated to an absence of accountability mechanisms during data transfers: leakers either do not focus on protection, or they intentionally expose confidential data without any concern, as they are convinced that the leaked data cannot be linked to them. In other words, when entities know that they can be held accountable for leakage of some information, they will demonstrate a better commitment towards its required protection.

This accountability can be directly associated with *provably* detecting a transmission history of data across multiple entities starting from its origin. This is known as data provenance, data lineage or source tracing. The data provenance methodology, in the form of robust watermarking techniques [5] or adding fake data [7], has already been suggested in the literature and employed by some industries. However, most efforts have been ad-hoc in nature and there is no formal model available. Additionally, most

---

* The full version of the paper is available online [4].

S. Mauw and C.D. Jensen (Eds.): STM 2014, LNCS 8743, pp. 183–187, 2014.

of these approaches only allow identification of the leaker in a non-provable manner, which is not sufficient in many cases.

Our Contributions. In this paper, we formalize this problem of provably associating the guilty party to the leakages, and work on the data lineage methodologies to solve the problem of information leakage in various leakage scenarios.

As our first contribution, we define LIME, a generic data lineage framework for data flow across multiple entities in the malicious environment. We observe that entities in data flows assume one of two roles: owner or consumer. We introduce an additional role in the form of auditor, whose task is to determine a guilty party for any data leak, and define the exact properties for communication between these roles. In the process, we identify an optional non-repudiation assumption made between two owners, and an optional trust (honesty) assumption made by the auditor about the owners.

The key advantage of our model is that it enforces *accountability by design*; i.e., it drives the system designer to consider possible data leakages and the corresponding accountability constraints at the design stage. This helps to overcome the existing situation where most lineage mechanisms are applied only after a leakage has happened.

As our second contribution, we present an accountable data transfer protocol to verifiably transfer data between two entities. To deal with an untrusted sender and an untrusted receiver scenario associated with data transfer between two consumers, our protocols employ an interesting combination of the robust watermarking, oblivious transfer, and signature primitives. We also implement our protocol and demonstrate the practicality for real-life data transfer scenarios such as outsourcing. Due to space reasons we treat some of the contributions only in the full version of this paper [4].

2   The Lime Framework

As we address a general case of data leakage in data transfer settings, we propose the simplifying model LIME (**L**ineage **i**n the **m**alicious **e**nvironment). With LIME we assign a clearly defined role to each involved party and define their inter-relationships. This allows us to define the exact properties that our transfer protocol has to fulfill in order to allow a provable identification of the guilty party in case of data leakage.

Model. As LIME is a general model and should be applicable to all cases, we abstract the data type and call every data item *document*. There are three different roles that can be assigned to the involved parties in LIME: data *owner*, data *consumer* and *auditor*. The data owner is responsible for the management of documents and the consumer receives documents and can carry out some task using them or transfer them to other consumers. The auditor is not involved in the transfer of documents, he is only invoked when a leakage occurs and then performs all steps that are necessary to identify the leaker. All of the mentioned roles can have multiple instantiations when our model is applied to a concrete setting. We refer to a concrete instantiation of our model as *scenario*.

In the following we show relations between the different entities and introduce optional trust assumptions. We only use these trust assumptions because we find that they are realistic in a real world scenario and because it allows us to have a more efficient data transfer in our framework. In the full version of the paper [4] we explain how our framework can be applied without any trust assumptions.

When documents are transferred from one owner to another one, we can assume that the transfer is governed by a *non-repudiation assumption*. This means that the sending owner trusts the receiving owner to take responsibility if he should leak the document.

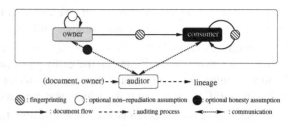

Fig. 1. The LIME framework

As we consider consumers as untrusted participants in our model, a transfer involving a consumer cannot be based on a non-repudiation assumption. Therefore, whenever a document is transferred to a consumer, the sender embeds information that uniquely identifies the recipient. We call this *fingerprinting*. If the consumer leaks this document, it is possible to identify him with the help of the embedded information.

As presented, LIME relies on a technique for embedding identifiers into documents, as this provides an instrument to identify consumers that are responsible for data leakage. We require that the embedding does not affect the utility of the document. Furthermore, it should not be possible for a malicious consumer to remove the embedded information without rendering the document useless. A technique that can offer these properties is *robust watermarking*. We use the definition by Adelsbach et al. [3].

A key position in LIME is taken by the auditor. He is not involved in the transfer, but he takes action once a leakage occurs. He is invoked by an owner and provided with the leaked data. If the leaked data was transferred using our model, there is identifying information embedded for each consumer who received it. Using this information the auditor can create an ordered chain of consumers who received the document which we call *lineage* of the leaked document. The last consumer in the lineage is the leaker. In the process of creating the lineage each consumer can reveal new embedded information to the auditor to point to the next consumer – and to prove his own innocence.

We can assume that the auditor trusts the owner to be honest. Honesty in this case means, that the owner does not leak a document and blame another party. We can make this assumption as the owner is concerned with the document's privacy in the first place. However, the auditor does not trust the consumers. In a real world setting the auditor can be any authority, for example a governmental institution, police, a legal person or even some software. We show the flow of documents, the optional non-repudiation and honesty assumptions and the cases in which fingerprinting is used in Fig. 1.

Threat Model and Design Goals. Although we try to address the problem of data leakage, LIME cannot guarantee that data leakage does not occur in the first place; once a consumer has received a document, nothing can prevent him from publishing it. We offer a method to provably identify the guilty party once a leakage has been detected. By introducing this *reactive* accountability, we expect that leakage is going to occur less often, since the identification of the guilty party will in most cases lead to negative consequences. As our only goal is to identify guilty parties, the attacks we are concerned about are those that disable the auditor from provably identifying the guilty party.

The crucial phase in our model is the transfer of a document involving untrusted entities, so we clearly define which properties we require our protocol to fulfill. We call the two parties *sender* and *recipient*. We expect a transfer protocol to fulfill the following properties and only tolerate failures with negligible probabilities.

1. **Correctness:** When both parties follow the protocol steps correctly and only publish their version of the document, the guilty party can be found.
2. **no Framing:** The sender cannot frame recipients for the sender's leakages.
3. **No Denial:** If the recipient leaks a document, he can be provably associated with it.

We also require our model to be collusion resistant, i.e. it should be able to tolerate a small number of colluding attackers [8].

3   Accountable Data Transfer

In this section we specify how one party transfers a document to another one, what information is embedded and which steps the auditor performs to find the guilty party in case of data leakage. We assume a public key infrastructure to be present, i.e. both parties know each others signature verification key. The employed oblivious transfer subprotocol can be instantiated with any implementation from the literature, e.g. [6].

Trusted Sender. In the case of a trusted sender it is sufficient for the sender to embed identifying information, so that the guilty party can be found. As the sender is trusted, there is no need for further security mechanisms. In the following, we describe a transfer protocol that fulfills the properties of correctness and no denial as defined in Section 2. As the sender is trusted to be honest, we do not need the no framing property.

The sender, who is in possession of some document D, creates a watermarking key k, embeds a triple $\sigma = (C_S, C_R, \tau)$ consisting of the two parties' identifiers and a timestamp τ into D to create $D_w = \mathcal{W}(D, \sigma, k)$. He then sends D_w to the recipient, who will be held accountable for this version of the document. As the sender also knows D_w, this very simple protocol is only applicable if the sender is completely trusted; otherwise the sender could publish D_w and frame the recipient.

Untrusted Sender. In the case of an untrusted sender we have to prevent the sender from cheating, i.e. we have to fulfill the no framing property. To achieve this property, the sender divides the original document into n parts and for each part he creates two differently watermarked versions. He transfers one of each of these two versions to the recipient via OT_1^2. The recipient is held accountable only for the document with the parts that he received, but the sender does not know which versions that are. The probability for the sender to cheat is hence $\frac{1}{2^n}$. We present the exact protocol in Fig. 2.

Data Lineage Generation. The auditor is used to find the guilty party in case of a leakage. He is invoked by the owner of the document and is provided with the leaked document. In order to find the guilty party, the auditor proceeds in the following way:

1) The auditor initially takes the owner as the current suspect. 2) The auditor appends the current suspect to the lineage. 3) The auditor sends the leaked document to the current suspect and asks him to provide the detection keys k_1 and k_2 for the watermarks in this document as well as the watermark σ. If a non-blind watermarking scheme is used, the auditor additionally requests the unmarked version of the document. 4) If, with key k_1, σ cannot be detected, the auditor continues with 9. 5) If the current suspect is trusted, the auditor checks that σ is of the form (C_S, C_R, τ) where C_S is the identifier of the current suspect, takes C_R as current suspect and continues with 2. 6) The auditor

sender holding D		recipient requesting D_w
generate watermarking keys	$\Longleftarrow$	compute $\sigma = [C_S, C_R, \tau]_{sk_{C_R}}$ and
$k_1, k_2 \leftarrow GenKey^{WM}(1^\kappa)$		send σ
compute $D' = \mathcal{W}(D, \sigma, k_1)$		
split D into n parts $D_1 \ldots D_n$		for $i \in \{1 \ldots n\}$
for $i \in \{1 \ldots n\}$		pick random $b_i \leftarrow_R \{0, 1\}$
for $j \in \{0, 1\}$		as input for ith instance of OT_2^1
$D_{i,j} = \mathcal{W}(D_i, j, k_2)$		set $\bar{b} = b_1 \cdots b_n$
$m_{i,j} = [\tau, i, j]_{sk_{C_S}}$		
generate AES key $ek_{i,j}$		
$c_{i,j} = enc(\langle D_{i,j}, m_{i,j} \rangle, ek_{i,j})$		
send $c_{i,j}$	$\Longrightarrow$	
Use $ek_{i,0}$ and $ek_{i,1}$ as input for	$ek_{i,b_i} \Longrightarrow$	for $i \in \{1 \ldots n\}$
the ith instance of OT_2^1	for $i \in \{1 \ldots n\}$	$\langle D_{i,b_i}, m_{i,b_i} \rangle = dec(c_{i,b_i}, ek_{i,b_i})$
	(n parallel OT_2^1)	join $D_{1,b_1}, \ldots, D_{n,b_n}$ to obtain D_w ⇓

Fig. 2. Protocol for untrusted senders

verifies that σ is of the form $[C_S, C_R, \tau]_{sk_{C_R}}$ where C_S is the identifier of the current suspect. He also verifies the validity of the signature. 7) The auditor splits the document into n parts and for each part he tries to detect 0 and 1 with key k_2. If none of these or both of these are detectable, he continues with 9. Otherwise he sets b'_i as the detected bit for the ith part. He sets $\bar{b}' = b'_1 \ldots b'_n$. 8) The auditor asks C_R to prove his choice of $\bar{b} = b_1 \cdots b_n$ for the given timestamp τ by presenting the $m_{i,b_i} = [\tau, i, b_i]_{sk_{C_S}}$. If C_R is not able to give a correct proof (i.e., m_{i,b_i} is of the wrong form or the signature is invalid) or if $\bar{b} = \bar{b}'$, then the auditor takes C_R as current suspect and continues with 2. 9) The auditor outputs the lineage. The last entry is responsible for the leakage.

In the full version of the paper [4] we provide a proof of correctness and evaluation results of an implementation of the presented protocol. We also discuss additional features of our approach and elaborate on related work.

References

1. Chronology of data breaches, http://www.privacyrights.org/data-breach
2. Data breach cost, http://www.symantec.com/about/news/release/article.jsp?prid=20110308_01
3. Adelsbach, A., Katzenbeisser, S., Sadeghi, A.-R.: A computational model for watermark robustness. In: Camenisch, J.L., Collberg, C.S., Johnson, N.F., Sallee, P. (eds.) IH 2006. LNCS, vol. 4437, pp. 145–160. Springer, Heidelberg (2007)
4. Backes, M., Grimm, N., Kate, A.: Lime: Data lineage in the malicious environment (2014), http://arxiv.org/abs/1408.1076
5. Mascher-Kampfer, A., Stögner, H., Uhl, A.: Multiple re-watermarking scenarios. In: IWSSIP, pp. 53–56 (2006)
6. Naor, M., Pinkas, B.: Efficient oblivious transfer protocols. In: SODA, pp. 448–457 (2001)
7. Papadimitriou, P., Garcia-Molina, H.: Data leakage detection. IEEE Transactions on Knowledge and Data Engineering, 51–63 (2011)
8. Pfitzmann, B., Waidner, M.: Asymmetric fingerprinting for larger collusions. In: CCS, pp. 151–160 (1997)

NoPhish: An Anti-Phishing Education App*

Gamze Canova, Melanie Volkamer, Clemens Bergmann, and Roland Borza

Technische Universität Darmstadt
name.surname@cased.de

Abstract. Phishing is still a prevalent issue in today's Internet. It can have financial or personal consequences. Attacks continue to become more and more sophisticated and the advanced ones (including spear phishing) can only be detected if people carefully check URLs. We developed a game based smartphone app – *NoPhish* – to educate people in accessing, parsing and checking URLs; i.e. enabling them to distinguish trustworthy and non-trustworthy websites. Throughout several levels information is provided and phishing detection is exercised.

1 Introduction

The financial benefit of phishing [1] is an incentive for phishers to keep luring victims into disclosing their sensitive information. The anti-phishing working group registered more than 100.000 unique phishing attacks in the second half of 2013, i.e. impersonated websites [2]. Furthermore, they report that the average up-time of such websites is about 28 hours. During this time potential victims are still likely to fall for an attack. People could be supported by tools such as the Netcraft Extension. However, such tools can never provide 100% accuracy [3]. Therefore, the tools' checks need to be complemented by humans checking the URLs. Many people lack the required knowledge to properly check URLs [4,5] and assess the trustworthiness of a given website. Some people are not even aware of faked messages and websites at all [6,4]. Several solutions have been proposed to address the problem of lacking knowledge e.g. tutorials or guides[1], quizzes[2] and games[3][4]. Tutorials are read-intensive if they cover all the different channels (such as email or SMS) and URL spoofing tricks phishers exploit. The quizzes – if at all – do not explain why answers are correct/incorrect. The game Anti-Phishing Phyllis only focuses on the email channel. Anti-Phishing Phil 1 and 2 [3] are already rather advanced in terms of different URL spoofing tricks; but can still be improved by including awareness aspects, addressing different channels, explaining the structure of a URL more precisely, addressing more categories of URL spoofing tricks, and providing knowledge about HTTPS.

---

* Long version available on request.

[1] https://www.bsi-fuer-buerger.de/BSIFB/DE/GefahrenImNetz/Phishing/phishing_node.html

[2] https://www.staysecureonline.com/staying-safe-online/

[3] http://www.wombatsecurity.com/antiphishingphyllis

[4] http://jackieweber.net/Projects/phil.html

S. Mauw and C.D. Jensen (Eds.): STM 2014, LNCS 8743, pp. 188–192, 2014.

Our goal was to develop a new game – *NoPhish* – an anti-phishing education app that addresses these issues to provide more sophisticated knowledge on how to properly check URLs. We opted for an Android smartphone app since in particular smartphone users are more likely to access phishing websites than desktop users. We decided to focus on the mobile browser rather than checking URLs before clicking on a link, e.g. with the aid of a preview function. Checking the URL previews would have the advantage that phishing could be detected before even clicking on a link. Yet, well-crafted URLs can still deceive users because URL previews are cropped in case they are too long. Additionally, not all email clients offer the preview functionality, e.g. Android's standard email client (e.g. version 4.4.2). We applied several learning principles [7], such as exercise, effect and primacy, to optimize learning effects. Gamification elements[5] like lives, levels, achievements, and leaderboards were also implemented to increase motivation. We followed a user-centered design, including an initial user survey to get an idea of the users' preferences with regard to an educational app. The results of our survey confirmed previous findings by Volkamer et al. [8] that for a German audience (adults at least) a rather neutral game based approach would be best accepted. Furthermore, we involved potential users in early stages by asking them to evaluate app texts before integrating them into the final game.

2   Game Design

The app entails two introductory parts and the game with ten levels mainly covering URL spoofing tricks.

2.1   Introduction Parts

Part 1 – Raise Awareness of Spoofed Messages, Links, and Websites: First, users are made aware of how simple it is to spoof messages. This is done by enabling them to send themselves with the *NoPhish* app an email from a sender address they provide in a corresponding form; and with a content they provide there as well. After submitting the form, *NoPhish* requests the users to check their email inbox. The sender of the received email is the one just chosen by the user. Furthermore, the email contains a link with the displayed text "https://www.google.de/" and users are asked to follow the link to search for "Phishing". However, clicking on this link redirects the users back to the app. Thereby, users learn by experience that they should not trust displayed link texts. At the end the user is told that faking websites is simple as well. Finally, in the app the user is informed that this kind of forgery is not only possible with emails, but also with, e.g. social networks, SMS or instant messaging systems.

Part 2 – Access Address Bar and View Entire URL: Due to the lack of space a mobile browser generally hides the address bar with its URL. Furthermore, the

---

[5] http://badgeville.com/wiki/Game_Mechanics

URL has to be scrolled in order to entirely view it. This part teaches the users how to access and view the entire URL in the mobile browser. The explanations how to do so are supported with corresponding screenshots. This part includes an exercise. Here, users are required to access the URL of a website they are forwarded to by *NoPhish*. Note, forwarding happens in a way that users first have to scroll up (which is necessary to make the generally hidden address bar of a mobile browser reappear). On top of the page, there is a text field, where they are asked to enter the last four characters of the URL. Then, they are asked to identify the first word of the URL (check one out of four provided possibilities). Once submitted the app checks the users' answers and can thereby ensure that they managed to access and view the entire URL. The users are forwarded to *NoPhish* as soon as they successfully complete the exercise.

2.2 Gaming Part

The gaming part is split into ten levels with increasing difficulty. Each level consists of two parts: an introductory block and the actual exercise. For the introduction of URL spoofing tricks the introductory block consists of a reminder, which provides a summary of previous levels (cf. Figure 1(a)) and the introduction of a new URL spoofing trick. The exercise is designed in a playful manner, i.e. users start with three lives, represented by hearts, and can collect points for correct answers and lose points and lives for wrong ones. Users receive direct feedback on their decision, e.g. they are immediately told why their answer was wrong. The next level is achieved if and only if a predefined amount of phishing and legitimate URLs have correctly been identified. To simulate the "behavior" of the address bar in mobile browsers, the entire URL as such is not displayed

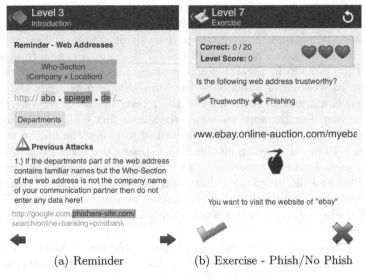

(a) Reminder   (b) Exercise - Phish/No Phish

Fig. 1. NoPhish Screenshots

but only parts of it. The user needs to scroll to the start of the URL in order to decide about the legitimacy of the displayed URL (cf. Figure 1(b)).

Level 1 – Structure of a URL: It is essential for people to achieve the capability of parsing a URL properly before learning different URL spoofing tricks. Especially the identification of the domain (first- and second-level domain) in a given URL is a key aspect which needs to be covered extensively. Therefore, the users start learning to identify the domain of a URL in level 1. To explain the different parts, we do not use technical terms such as URL, domain, subdomain, protocol and only provide details users need to know to successfully detect phishing URLs. The focus of this level is the domain, the *Who-Section* as we refer to it in *NoPhish*. During the exercise the users are asked to tap on the *Who-Section*.

Levels 2-8 – URL Spoofing Tricks: In levels 2-8 various URL spoofing tricks (cf. Table 1) are addressed. In level 2, we also explain IP addresses by using the analogy of house addresses. During the exercises, URLs together with the name of the website the users are supposed to visit are displayed (cf. Figure 1(b)). Users are asked to decide whether the URLs are legitimate or phishing ones. The URLs where selected from the top Alexa domains for Germany. The corresponding attack was then applied to a legitimate URL from the set whenever needed. Note, that in all levels both, HTTP and HTTPS URLs are displayed to the user, i.e. legitimate as well as phishing URLs can use HTTPS. Everytime the users correctly identify a phishing URL, *NoPhish* asks them to tap on the *Who-Section*. Depending on how often the user correctly identifies the Who-Section the frequency of asking to tap on the *Who-Section* decreases or increases.

Table 1. URL Spoofing Tricks – Levels – Assignment

URL Spoofing Tricks	Level
a) IP address, no brand (e.g. http://130.82.162.6/)	Level 2
b) Random/unrelated/trustworthy domain, no brand (e.g. https://marketchippy.com/ or http://www.account.com/login)	Level 3
c) Random/unrelated/trustworthy domain, brand in subdomain (e.g. http://paypal.kjdhsbc.com/signin)	Level 4
d) Random/unrelated/trustworthy/IP domain, brand in path (e.g. http://online-payment.com/www.paypal.com/)	Level 5
e) Derivated domains (e.g. https://www.facebook-login.com/)	Level 6
f) Introducing typos (e.g. http://www.twittter.com/)	Level 7
g) Replacing Character(s) (e.g. http://www.arnazon.com/)	Level 8

Level 9 – HTTPS: In this level, we introduce and explain the difference between HTTP and HTTPS. This level also includes an exercise.

Level 10 – Final Remarks: Here, users are made aware of some special cases: E.g. it is not generally secure to arbitrarily click on links as they could download malicious software. Additionally, the users are informed about further potential URL spoofing tricks that have not been exercised: e.g. homograph attacks. Also, the users are explained that they might encounter URLs which look very phishing-like, but actually are legitimate, e.g. https://www.paypal-community.com. Finally, *NoPhish* briefly introduces extended validation certificates.

3   Conclusion and Future Work

In the scope of this work, we have designed and implemented an anti-phishing education app – *NoPhish*. The detection of phishing URLs is realized as a game, where the user can win or lose points or lives. We already conducted a user study which showed very promising results. However, as knowledge retention is essential, we intend to run a corresponding retention study in three months with the same participants. We plan to publish the results of both parts of the study together. In future, we also plan to assess how such an education app can best be distributed. An idea would be to utilize embedded learning [9] where simulated phishing emails are sent to users. Whenever users fall for such an email they could be proposed to download the education app. Furthermore, the game could be extended by asking users to build legitimate or phishing URLs themselves. *NoPhish* is available upon request as it still in the user study stage. Once the user study is completed and new findings are integrated we plan to publish *NoPhish* in the Google Playstore.

Acknowledgements. This work was supported by CASED and EC SPRIDE.

References

1. Ramzan, Z.: Phishing attacks and countermeasures. In: Handbook of Information and Communication Security, pp. 433–448. Springer, Heidelberg (2010)
2. Aaron, G., Rasmussen, R., Routt, A.: Global phishing survey: Trends and domain name use in 2h2013. Anti-Phishing Working Group (2014)
3. Sheng, S., Magnien, B., Kumaraguru, P., Acquisti, A., Cranor, L.F., Hong, J., Nunge, E.: Anti-phishing phil: The design and evaluation of a game that teaches people not to fall for phish. In: SOUPS, pp. 88–99. ACM (2007)
4. Dhamija, R., Tygar, J.D., Hearst, M.: Why phishing works. In: SIGCHI. ACM (2006)
5. Lin, E., Greenberg, S., Trotter, E., Ma, D., Aycock, J.: Does domain highlighting help people identify phishing sites? In: SIGCHI, pp. 2075–2084. ACM (2011)
6. Li, T., Han, F., Ding, S., Chen, Z.: Larx: Large-scale anti-phishing by retrospective data-exploring based on a cloud computing platform. In: ICCCN, pp. 1–5. IEEE (2011)
7. Thorndike, E.L.: The fundamentals of learning. Teachers College Bureau of Publications (1932)
8. Volkamer, M., Stockhardt, S., Bartsch, S., Kauer, M.: Adopting the cmu/apwg anti-phishing landing page idea for germany. In: STAST, pp. 46–52. IEEE (2013)
9. Jansson, K., von Solms, R.: Simulating malicious emails to educate end users on-demand. In: 2011 3rd Symposium on Web Society (SWS), pp. 74–80 (2011)

ROMEO: ReputatiOn Model Enhancing OpenID Simulator

Ginés Dólera Tormo[1], Félix Gómez Mármol[2], and Gregorio Martínez Pérez[1]

[1] Department of Information and Communications Engineering,
University of Murcia, Murcia, 30100 Spain
{ginesdt,gregorio}@um.es
[2] NEC Europe Ltd., Kurfürsten-Anlage 36, 69115 Heidelberg, Germany
felix.gomez-marmol@neclab.eu

Abstract. OpenID is a standard decentralized initiative aimed at allowing Internet users to use the same personal account to access different services. Since it does not rely on any central authority, it is hard for such users or other entities to validate the trust level of each other. Some research has been conducted to handle this issue, defining reputation framework to determine the trust level of a service based on past experiences. Deep analysis and validation need to be achieved in order to prove the feasibility of this framework. Our main contribution in this paper consists of a simulation environment able to validate the feasibility of that reputation framework and to analyze its behavior within different scenarios.

1 Introduction

OpenID [1] is an open technology standard defining a decentralized authentication protocol, allowing end-users to sign in to multiple websites with the same account. Hence, users maintain their private information in a single point, deciding who is able to obtain such information. Due to its decentralized nature, OpenID does not rely on any central authority validating the trust level of the entities involved in the authentication process. Thus, users can barely know whether a given service is trustworthy enough to share their private information.

A decentralized reputation framework to be integrated with OpenID was defined in [2]. It describes how the OpenID protocol can be enhanced to allow the OpenID provider to collect recommendations about a service, in order to provide useful information about that service to the users beforehand. However, there are several ways of computing the reputation in this environment, becoming a hard task to analyze their feasibility if they are only theoretically described.

Our main contribution in this paper is presenting a simulation environment, developed within NEC Laboratories Europe, able to analyze and validate the feasibility of reputation models integrated with OpenID, such as [2]. This simulator environment, entitled ROMEO (ReputatiOn Model Enhancing OpenID Simulator), allows evaluating, among others, the capability of adversaries to exploit the reputation framework. For instance, analyzing whether a service could unfairly increase its reputation by introducing biased recommendations [3].

S. Mauw and C.D. Jensen (Eds.): STM 2014, LNCS 8743, pp. 193–197, 2014.

The remainder of the article is organized as follows. Section 2 introduces threats to consider when analyzing this kind of systems. Section 3 describes the internal components defining the architecture of the simulator, whereas Section 4 presents its user interface. Finally, Section 5 presents some concluding remarks.

2   OpenID-Integrated Reputation Frameworks Threats

There are several aspects affecting the behavior of reputation frameworks, which any simulator should consider. Next, we list some relevant assumptions and threats to contemplate when developing an OpenID-based reputation framework.

- Relying parties may try to figure out the recommendation that each OpenID provider has about them.
- Relying parties could offer services with diverse qualities.
- Quality of the services offered by the relying parties could fluctuate.
- Relying parties could fake the list of potential recommenders by including just the recommenders providing better recommendations about them.
- A relying party could decide not to participate in the reputation framework.
- There could be malicious OpenID providers supplying inaccurate recommendations values trying to distort the reputation of a given relying party.
- Users could provide inaccurate or biased recommendations [4].
- The framework cannot assume unlimited resources.
- A malicious entity can present multiple identities, issuing a higher fraction of the recommendations of the system, as a kind of Sybil attack [5].

3   ROMEO Architecture Overview

Internal components of the simulator are shown in Figure 1. The architecture has been designed to allow easy extensibility, in order to validate any reputation computation engine that may be defined in the future targeting OpenID.

- **Reputation Authority.** This component is the entry point for requesting recommendations. Users or other OpenID providers can send queries to this module to obtain the recommendations about a relying party.
- **Rule Engine.** The Rule Engine component aims to influence the reputation computation process according to the defined rules. An example of rule is: *if the system is overloaded, only the last 25 recommendations are considered.*
- **Preferences Engine.** To provide customized recommendations, this component processes the preferences of the users to influence the weights of the recommendations of other users when computing the reputation score [2].
- **Reputation Manager.** The Reputation Manager coordinates the reputation computation. It sends the gathered recommendations to a specific Computation Engine to obtain an aggregated reputation value.
- **Reputation Store.** This component is in charge of maintaining recommendations gathered in the past. Additionally, this module may act as a cache by storing already aggregated reputation values during a certain period of time.

Fig. 1. General ROMEO architecture overview

- **Data Collector.** This component retrieves the list of potential recommenders from a given relying party and then asks each of these recommenders (i.e. other OpenID providers) for recommendations about the relying party.
- **Computation Engines.** These components are in charge of aggregating reputation values from the recommendations. As they follow a common interface, the Reputation Manager could decide which one to use on-the-fly [6].

4 Reputation Model Enhancing OpenID Simulator

ROMEO is a simulator created at NEC Laboratories Europe and aimed to evaluate reputation frameworks integrated with OpenID, such as [2]. It allows, among others, analyzing the capability of malicious users or entities (or groups of them) to exploit reputation system vulnerabilities, such as those presented in Section 2. Malicious users or entities mainly aim to distort the reputation of a given relying party by supplying biased recommendations. ROMEO evaluates how certain reputation computation engines behave against different scenarios and threats.

4.1 Scenario Elements

As shown in Figure 2, ROMEO presents a graphical user interface where different reputation-based scenarios and their properties could be defined. A scenario is composed of a set of simulated users interacting with a relying party, by using simulated OpenID providers. The scenario properties define the behavior of the elements in the framework, in order to model the aspects described in Section 2 defining, for instance, whether (and how) the relying party will vary its QoS. It also allows configuring the different reputation computation engines. As part of the scenario properties, we have included the following.

- Type of Users:
  - **Normal:** These users provide appropriate recommendations according to the relying party quality of service.
  - **Negative/Positive Raters:** These users always provides bad (negative raters) or good (positive raters) recommendations when giving feedbacks, regardless of the quality of the received service.
- Type of OpenID Providers:
  - **Normal:** These providers properly follow the reputation framework guides.

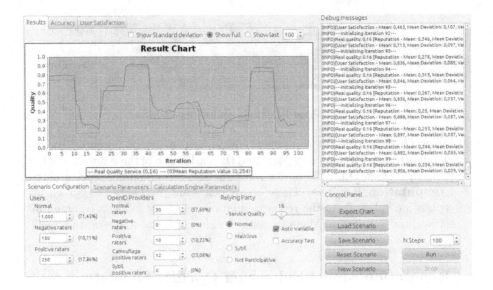

Fig. 2. ROMEO simulator graphical interface screenshot

- **Negative/Positive Raters:** These providers always give bad/good recommendations about the relying party, regardless of its real behavior.
- **Camouflaged Positive/Negative Raters:** Extending the previous one, these providers give good/bad recommendation, but only a $p\%$ of the times. The reminder $(100 - p)\%$, they act as normal raters.
- **Sybil Positive/Negative Raters:** These providers act as positive/ negative raters, although after a while, they replace their identity with a new one.
- Type of Relying Party:
    - **Normal:** The relying party properly follows the reputation protocol.
    - **Malicious:** The relying party includes in the recommenders list only the ones with better recommendations about itself.
    - **Sybil:** The relying party is disconnected and replaced with a new identity from time to time, reinitializing its associated reputation.
    - **Not Participative:** The relying party evades the recommender list.

Once defined the scenario, the simulation consists of executing a number of iterations. In each iteration, some of the simulated users ask their OpenID provider for the reputation of the relying party. Hence, the OpenID provider collects and aggregates recommendations using the elements described in Section 3. Depending on the reputation of the relying party, the users interact (or not) with the relying party. Finally, the users provide recommendations about the received service to their OpenID provider, which will be used for subsequent aggregation.

4.2   Visualization of Results

After running a simulation, ROMEO shows three charts, representing three different ways of analyzing the results. These charts are described in the following.

- **Results Chart.** The Results chart (Figure 2) compares the real relying party QoS with the reputation computed by the OpenID providers. This chart aims to evaluate the behavior of the reputation model against a specific scenario.
- **Accuracy Chart.** Taking into account that the users interact with the relying party with a probability p, being p the reputation given by its OpenID provider, this chart determines how many users interact with a given relying party. This chart is useful to compare different reputation computation engines regarding their accuracy when calculating reputation scores.
- **User Satisfaction Chart.** It indicates how satisfied the users are with the reputation values they receive. Users' satisfaction is higher if the reputation values fit the quality they receive from the service, according to their preferences. This chart aims to compare reputation models regarding the adaptation to users preferences.

5   Conclusions

The OpenID standard defines a decentralized authentication initiative. As such, OpenID does not rely on any central authority, which makes the trust of the involved entities hard to validate. Some research has been conducted to mitigate this problem. However, the proposed solutions need a deep analysis and validation. In this paper we have described a simulation environment able to evaluate the feasibility of reputation frameworks in this context, and analyzed their behavior within different scenarios. The simulator allows analyzing reputation models against reputation-related threats, involving malicious users or entities.

References

1. Recordon, D., Reed, D.: OpenID 2.0: a platform for user-centric identity management. In: Proceedings of the Second ACM Workshop on Digital Identity Management, DIM 2006, pp. 11–16 (2006)
2. Dólera Tormo, G., Gómez Mármol, F., Martínez Pérez, G.: Towards the Integration of Reputation Management in OpenID. Computer Standards & Interfaces 36(3), 438–453 (2014)
3. Gómez Mármol, F., Martínez Pérez, G.: Security Threats Scenarios in Trust and Reputation Models for Distributed Systems. Elsevier Computers & Security 28(7), 545–556 (2009)
4. Borg, A., Boldt, M., Carlsson, B.: Simulating malicious users in a software reputation system. In: Park, J.J., Lopez, J., Yeo, S.-S., Shon, T., Taniar, D. (eds.) STA 2011. CCIS, vol. 186, pp. 147–156. Springer, Heidelberg (2011)
5. Douceur, J.R.: The sybil attack. In: Druschel, P., Kaashoek, M.F., Rowstron, A. (eds.) IPTPS 2002. LNCS, vol. 2429, pp. 251–260. Springer, Heidelberg (2002)
6. Dólera Tormo, G., Gómez Mármol, F., Martínez Pérez, G.: Dynamic and flexible selection of a reputation mechanism for heterogeneous environments. In: Future Generation Computer Systems (June 2014)

Evaluation of Key Management Schemes in Wireless Sensor Networks

Filip Jurnečka, Martin Stehlík, and Vashek Matyáš

Faculty of Informatics
Masaryk University
{xjurn,xstehl2,matyas}@fi.muni.cz

Abstract. Evaluation of key management schemes is usually done analytically and by hand. As such, it is prone to mistakes and often focuses only on selected aspects of the schemes. In this paper we introduce our simulation framework for automated evaluation of key management schemes for wireless sensor networks. This framework contains a starting library of key management schemes.

1 Introduction

Wireless sensor networks (WSNs) provide a specific research area due to the higly limited resources of its nodes. Furthermore, these devices are not equipped with any tamper resistant hardware and thus an attacker can access a node and read out all its stored information, manipulate the node, etc.

Key management schemes (KMSs) are then the first building stone supporting security in these exposed systems. However, there are many proposed schemes, all proposed with different objectives and techniques in mind. Some taxonomies and evaluations of KMS properties have been established [8,9] to make it easier for developers and researchers to navigate through these schemes. However, encompassing comparative evaluation of multiple schemes is usually done analytically by hand. As such, the process is prone to mistakes and inconsistencies. An automated approach for evaluating KMS properties for WSN has been considered in [10] and in [7].

In this paper we present KMSforWSN [3] – our tool for automated evaluation of KMS properties in WSNs. KMSforWSN is a framework built on top of MiXiM [5], a WSN framework for Omnet++. Our work brings three major contributions:

1. KMSforWSN supports automated evaluation of KMS properties via detailed WSN specific simulation.
2. We propose a general experiment for evaluating a KMS for WSN.
3. We provide the first publicly available library of WSN specific KMSs.

2 Automatically Measurable KMS Evaluation Metrics

A *metric* is a precise numerical quantity that can be used to evaluate properties.

S. Mauw and C.D. Jensen (Eds.): STM 2014, LNCS 8743, pp. 198–203, 2014.
© Springer International Publishing Switzerland 2014

We suggest the following categorization of KMS evaluation metrics from the simulator point of view: 1. Well measurable metrics, 2. Not so well measurable metrics, and 3. Other metrics.

We suggest that the metrics in table 1 are well measurable on a simulator. Note that these are averaged values for a node in the network.

Table 1. Well measurable metrics

Metric	Unit
Communication overhead	number of bytes transmitted by a node
Connectivity	% of relevant links secured by a shared key
Network resilience	% of links compromised by a node-capturing attacker
Energy consumed	Joules used to compute and establish a shared key

Due to the difference of the underlying platform of a PC-based simulator from a wireless sensor node, we can not precisely measure memory requirements of the implementation or the timing of operations on a processor vastly faster than the microcontroller-equipped mote. However, we can measure these values and compare them to results for other schemes.

The set of *Not so well measurable metrics* is listed in table 2.

Table 2. Not so well measurable metrics

Metric	Unit
Memory requirements	number of bytes being stored by a node
Processing speed	seconds to compute a shared key
Scalability	function of other metrics evaluated on various-sized networks
Latency	seconds to establish a shared key between two nodes

All other characteristics such as *Extensibility, Node revocation*, etc. fall into the *Other metrics* category, mainly due to the fact that they depend on the implementation.

3 Framework Structure

MiXiM povides underlying functionality offering all the necessary environment models, reception and collision models, connectivity support and a strong protocol library. KMSforWSN extends MiXiM by three groups of components: 1. KMS library, 2. KMS evaluation support, and 3. KMS support modules.

KMSforWSN is built on top of MiXiM. Although the underlying settings can be modified heavily, MiXiM is required for running KMSforWSN.

3.1 Key Management Scheme Models

KMSforWSN provides the first publicly available library of implemented KMSs. So far, we have five implemented KMSs based on symmetric cryptography. These are: 1. Master key pre-distribution, 2. Pairwise pre-distribution, 3. BROSK [6], 4. Random pre-distribution (EG) [2], and 5. PIKE [1].

An advantage of building a KMS library is that with clever use of inheritance we can actually build a clearly defined taxonomy for KMSs in WSNs. Furthermore, implementing a proposal can serve as a form of review.

3.2 Evaluation Models

In our simulation, evaluation models are part of a global compound module called KMSEvaluator. We provide the following evaluation modules:

Connectivity Evaluator – We compute the successful connectivity ratio for the global (a secured path between two nodes), node (a shared secret between two nodes), and local (a shared secret between neighbours) connectivity.
Memory Evaluator – We measure the amount of stored data (keys and additional information) by a KMS and the size of the KMS implementation itself.
Processing Speed Evaluator – We measure the absolute and simulation timings of: 1. pre-deployment phase keying material generation, 2. key establishment process by every single node, and 3. completion of initialization phase.
Resiliency Evaluator – For evaluating the resiliency we defined our attacker model in [4], where additional discussions on the module logic are also provided.
Other Measured Metrics – The MiXiM framework modules provide statistics on the *communication* as well as *energy consumed*.

We see *scalability* as a function of multiple parameters. Therefore, it is measured using multiple runs on various sizes of the network. That way we can observe impact of the network size on individual metrics.

4   Proposed Universal Experiment

Our experiment highlights the most important life stages of a KMS equipped WSN. Such an experiment has several advantages: 1. evaluation of one's own proposal, 2. comparison to other implemented KMSs, 3. reduction of the time and space required to describe the experiment and its settings in the future, and 4. enrichment of a library of KMSs with own implementations. The experiment executes as follows:

1. Nodes are pre-loaded with information from a trusted entity and deployed.
2. If the KMS requires it, an initialization phase is executed.
3. The first custom stage tries once on each node to establish a secured link.
4. The second custom stage tries on each node to establish secured links with all the nodes in the network it does not share keys with yet.

After each stage, all valid metrics are evaluated.

We propose three baseline sizes of network in terms of number of nodes in order to be able to evaluate scalability of the KMS. Additionally, we propose to use two different network densities, in the form of deployment area size.

Furthermore, we propose two general deployment strategies. First is the uniform random distribution. However, due to the high chance of creating disconnected graphs our second strategy divides the deployment area into equally sized squares, where nodes are distributed uniformly inside each of these squares.

So far we do not consider a base station to be required for our experiments, but if for some future KMSs a BS would be needed, we envision its position in the centre of the network.

5 Sample Evaluation

In the following text and graphs we present sample results of the proposed experiment on selected metrics. In the graphs, we label the x-axis values 1, 2, 3 and 4 according to the experiment stages described in the previous section.

In the Figure 1 we can observe the global connectivity ratio of each KMS. Obviously, master key pre-distribution and pairwise pre-distribution show the same results of 100% connectivity within each graph component. In the larger sparse networks with multiple disconnected graph components in the random uniform deployment scenario, the average connectivity decreases.

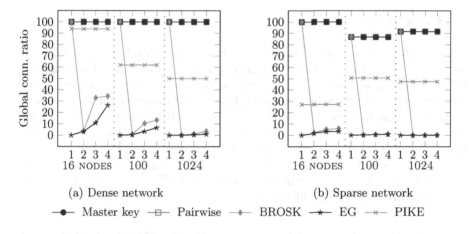

(a) Dense network   (b) Sparse network

━●━ Master key ━▫━ Pairwise ━◆━ BROSK ━✳━ EG ━✕━ PIKE

Fig. 1. Global connectivity ratio of KMSs after each experiment step

Figure 2 illustrates the average memory requirements per node in terms of number of keys. The EG scheme shows that it does increase the number of keys only slightly, by generating new keys between nodes that share multiple of the pre-distributed keys. Yet, the connectivity in the previous graphs increased over the course of the experiment. That indicates frequent collisions during the initialization phase while exchanging indexes of stored keys. With each index being transmitted the resulting message grows which induces collisions and lost packets. In turn, this results in a small global connectivity of the scheme in our experiments.

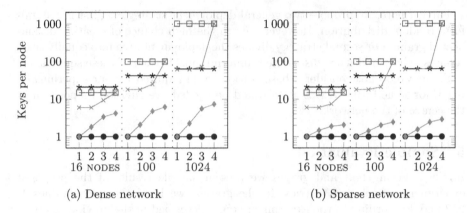

(a) Dense network   (b) Sparse network

Fig. 2. Average number of keys per node

Other metrics can be evaluated in similar fashion. Some of these are directly supported by Omnet++ or MiXiM, some of them are added in our evaluation framework. For sample results on network resiliency, see our previous paper [4].

6   Conclusions

We have presented our key management scheme evaluation framework for wireless sensor networks, called `KMSforWSN`. It provides an automated way of evaluating the main characteristics of KMSs while supporting standard simulator features such as repeatability, execution for whole domains of parameters, etc.

Alongside the framework we include the basis for KMS library for WSNs that has been missing. As of writing this paper, the released revision 7 contains five KMSs, however we envision this number to grow rapidly in the future.

We have described benefits brought by our framework and its structure. We have proposed a general experiment for evaluating KMSs that tries to include most of an arbitrary KMS's lifecycle.

Acknowledgement. This work was supported by the GAP202/11/0422 project of the Czech Science Foundation.

References

1. Chan, H., Perrig, A.: Pike: peer intermediaries for key establishment in sensor networks. In: INFOCOM 2005: Proceedings of 24th Annual Joint Conference of the IEEE Computer and Communications Societies, vol. 1, pp. 524–535 (2005)
2. Eschenauer, L., Gligor, V.D.: A key-management scheme for distributed sensor networks. In: Proceedings of the 9th ACM Conference on Computer and Communications Security, CCS 2002, pp. 41–47. ACM, New York (2002)

3. Jurnečka, F., Stehlík, M., Matyáš, V.: Key Management Schemes for WSNs (2014), https://sourceforge.net/projects/kmsfwsn/ (accessed July 14, 2014)
4. Jurnečka, F., Stehlík, M., Matyáš, V.: On node capturing attacker strategies. In: Security Protocols XXII. LNCS, Springer, Heidelberg (2014)
5. Köpke, A., et al.: Simulating wireless and mobile networks in OMNeT++ the MiXiM vision. In: Simulation Tools and Techniques for Communications, Networks and Systems, Simutools 2008, pp. 71:1–71:8. Brussels, Belgium (2008)
6. Lai, B., et al.: Scalable session key construction protocol for wireless sensor networks. In: IEEE Workshop LARTES, p. 7 (2002)
7. Özdemir, S., Khalil, O.: Performance evaluation of key management schemes in wireless sensor networks. Gazi University Journal of Science 25(2), 465–476 (2012)
8. Roman, R., et al.: Sensekey – simplifying the selection of key management schemes for sensor networks. In: Proceedings of the 2011 IEEE WAINA, pp. 789–794. IEEE Computer Society, Washington, DC (2011)
9. Simplício, M.J., et al.: A survey on key management mechanisms for distributed wireless sensor networks. Computer Networks 54(15), 2591–2612 (2010)
10. Vu, T.M., Williamson, C., Safavi-Naini, R.: Simulation modeling of secure wireless sensor networks. In: Proceedings of the 4thInternational ICST Conference on Performance Evaluation Methodologies and Tools, VALUETOOLS 2009, pp. 30:1–30:10. Brussels, Belgium (2009)

Efficient Java Code Generation
of Security Protocols Specified in *AnB/AnBx*

Paolo Modesti

School of Computing Science, Newcastle University, UK
paolo.modesti@newcastle.ac.uk

Abstract. The implementation of security protocols is challenging and error-prone. A model-driven development approach allows the automatic generation of an application, from a simpler and abstract model that can be formally verified. Our AnBx compiler is a tool for automatic generation of Java code of security protocols specified in the Alice&Bob notation. In contrast with existing tools, it uses a simpler specification language and computes the consistency checks that agents have to perform on reception of messages. Moreover, the tool applies various optimization strategies to achieve efficiency both at compile and run time.

Keywords: security protocols, code generation, applied formal methods.

1 Introduction

The implementation of security protocols is challenging and error-prone, as experience has shown [1] that even widely used and heavily tested protocols like TLS and SSH need to be patched every year due to low-level implementation bugs. The critical aspect is that the high-level security properties of a protocol must be hard-coded explicitly, in terms of low-level cryptographic operations and checks of well-formedness. To counter this problem, in this work we consider a model-driven development approach that allows automatic generation of an application, from a simpler and abstract model that can be formally verified. We present the *AnBx Compiler and Code Generator*[1], a tool for automatic generation of Java code of security protocols specified in the simple Alice&Bob (*AnB*) notation [2], suitable for agile prototyping. Despite being intuitive, *AnB* is semi-formal because it contains a lot of implicit concepts. In particular, it does not say explicitly which (defensive) consistency checks on the received data need to be performed to verify that the protocol is running according to the specification. It is important to recognize that while some checks on reception are trivially derived from the narrations (verification of a digital signature, comparison of agent's identities), others are more complex and managing them can be a challenging task even for an expert programmer.

In addition to the main contribution of an end-to-end *AnB* to Java compiler, we also present an improved way to compute the checks on reception with respect to a previous solution proposed by Briais and Nestmann [3]. This allows

---

[1] Available at http://www.dais.unive.it/~modesti/anbx/

S. Mauw and C.D. Jensen (Eds.): STM 2014, LNCS 8743, pp. 204–208, 2014.

reducing the compilation time (in one case even from days to seconds), preventing space state explosion problems in the optimization phase, and increasing the execution speed. The tool also supports the *AnBx* language [4], an extension of *AnB* to be employed for a purely declarative modelling of distributed protocols.

2   The *AnBx* Compiler

The automatic Java code generation of security protocols comprises several phases. A detailed description of the architecture of the tool, which is developed in Haskell, is given in [5] and can be summarized as follows:

Pre-processing and Verification $AnBx \rightarrow AnB \rightarrow$ (verification)

The *AnBx* protocol is lexed, parsed and then compiled to *AnB*, a format suitable for verification with the external tool OFMC [6], a state of the art model checker. The compiler can also read protocols directly in *AnB*. *AnBx* and its translation to *AnB* have already been described in [4,7].

Front-End $AnB \rightarrow ExecNarr \rightarrow Opt\text{-}ExecNarr$

If the protocol is deemed safe by the model checker, the *AnB* specification can be compiled into an *executable narration* (*ExecNarr*), a set of action that gives an interpretation on how the protocol participants are expected to execute the protocol. The core of this phase is the automatic generation of the consistency checks derived from the static information of protocol narrations. The *optimized executable narration* (*Opt-ExecNarr*) goes further in this direction and applies some optimization techniques, including common subexpression elimination (CSE), which in general are useful to generate efficient code.

Back-End $Opt\text{-}ExecNarr \rightarrow$ (protocol logic) + (application logic) $\rightarrow$ *Java*

The final result of the compilation is the generation of the Java source code from the *Opt-ExecNarr*. The previous phases are fully language independent and do not require any adaptation in case another programming language is used. But even in the back-end we postponed any language dependent decision in order to increase the compiler's portability and simplify the re-targeting.

3   Executable Narrations and Optimization

The computation of the checks on reception is done by extending and refining the ideas proposed in [3]. In short, three kinds of checks are considered in formulas on received messages: *equality* $[E = F]$ on expressions denoting the comparison of two bit-streams, E and F; *well-formedness* $[E]$ denoting the verification of whether the projections and decryption contained in E are likely to succeed; *inversion* $inv(E, F)$ denoting the verification that E and F evaluate to inverse messages. Since consistency checks operate on *(message,expression)* pairs, the representation of the agent's knowledge must be generalized. The underlying idea is that a pair (M, E) denotes that an expression E is equivalent to the message M. For this reason is it necessary to introduce the notion of *knowledge sets*, and two operations on them: *synthesis,* reflecting the closure of knowledge sets using message constructors, and *analysis,* reflecting the exhaustive recursive decomposition of knowledge pairs as enabled by the currently available knowledge.

The compilation of an action $A \to B : M$ checks that M can be synthesized by the agent A, instantiate a new variable x and adds the pair (M, x) to the knowledge of agent B. The consistency formula $\Phi(\mathcal{A}(K'_B))$ of the analysis of the updated knowledge K'_B defines the checks to be performed by B at run-time.

Performance Issues. A preliminary version of our compiler [7] implemented verbatim the method proposed in [3], extending only the *analysis* and *synthesis* rules in order to support cryptographic functions which were not available in [3], HMAC and Diffie-Hellman key agreements in particular. Unfortunately, especially with some industrial-size protocols, it turned out to be very inefficient. In our experiments [Table 1 (a)], we found it challenging to work with the original specification of the e-commerce protocols SET [8] (we considered the unsigned variant denoted SETv2 in which the customer does not possesses asymmetric keys) and 3KP [9]. A clear symptom of inefficiency was the fact that these protocols required very long time to be compiled (around 1 hr and 55 min for 3KP and almost 6 days for SETv2 on a Windows 7 64-bit machine, CPU Intel Core i7-3770 3.40 GHz, 8 GB RAM, JDK 7.0.45 64-bit, Haskell Platform 2013.0.0.2). In contrast, the revised versions specified in *AnBx* performed better, thanks to the fact that *AnBx* can express security properties at the channel level and this implies, in the concrete implementation, a reduced number of nested encryption layers and MACs, compared to the original specification.

Moreover, we noticed that some of the computed checks were failing anyway. It turned out that the reason of this discrepancy was the different behavior, in the abstract and concrete model, of the cryptographic primitives. In fact, given two identical messages and encryption keys, a non-deterministic encryption scheme returns two different ciphertexts which are indistinguishable by an observer. This nice (in the real world) property was not properly captured by the model.

Optimization. To address this issue, the key point is to observe that, if an agent knows the correct decryption key, he will deconstruct the ciphertext using the *analysis* rules. In this case, he will only store the decrypted message in his own knowledge, forgetting the ciphertext. A significant exception is represented by forwarding channels. For example, in SET and iKP the merchant must forward a message originating from the customer but secret for the acquirer, and such expression is stored in the knowledge as an encrypted term. Assuming a non-deterministic cipher scheme, when an agent will need to build a new ciphertext involved in an equality check, the check will fail because the term will differ from the one to be compared with. Therefore, if we prevent the agent from using the *synthesis* rules modelling encryption when computing the checks, we basically avoid computing any check which requires synthesizing new terms using symmetric and asymmetric encryption. It is important to underline that this does not undermine the robustness of the application because we just prune checks failing due to the over approximation of the abstract model.

Table 1. Exp. results: (a) as in [3] w/o opt (b) opt (c) opt+cse (*at compile time)

Protocol	Compile Time (sec)			Exec. Time (sec)			Mem. usage* (MB)		
	(a)	(b)	(c)	(a)	(b)	(c)	(a)	(b)	(c)
2KP (orig)	97.75	2.80	2.25	1.08	0.97	0.81	3.46	4.80	8.24
2KP (AnBx)	1.03	0.17	0.13	1.01	1.17	0.95	0.91	1.06	0.88
3KP (orig)	6,945.43	13.23	13.20	100.85	1.34	0.83	411.52	16.08	33.64
3KP (AnBx)	8.88	0.16	2.25	1.26	1.44	0.91	1.05	1.03	1.04
SETv2 (orig)	513,827.20	2.89	3.04	4.05	3.94	1.11	262.07	5.93	7.91
SETv2 (AnBx)	0.84	0.06	0.05	1.08	1.25	0.89	0.74	0.80	0.83
H530	1.89	1.75	2.70	1.96	1.88	1.79	10.14	9.12	5.31
Google SSOv2	1.33	0.03	0.02	1.07	0.95	0.90	0.68	0.71	0.75
Kerberos PKinit	0.37	0.36	0.36	1.32	1.12	0.94	1.35	1.53	1.88

From the practical point of view [Table 1 (b)], we were able to reduce the compile time for 3KP, from 1 hr 55 min to just 13 sec, decreasing the peak memory usage (measured by the Profiler of the Haskell Compiler 7.6.3) from 411 MB to just 16 MB. The execution time was also cut from 100 sec to just 1.34 sec. This large difference is explained by the fact that the standard algorithm [3] computes more than 10,000 checks (but most of them are failing), while our version generates about 50 checks. For the protocol SETv2, the good news is that it can now be compiled in 3 sec while before it required almost 6 days. Peak memory usage was also decreased from 262 MB to just 6 MB. The execution time diminished just from 4.05 sec to 3.94 sec. This is interesting because in this case the check set is not heavily pruned as in 3KP. Indeed our changes allows detecting the checks more efficiently than before.

Common Subexpression Elimination (CSE). We identify the set of cryptographic operations, which in general are computationally expensive, and optimize the code to reduce the overall execution time, introducing variables storing partial results, and making a reordering with the purpose of minimizing the number of cryptographic operation performed. In terms of performance gain [Table 1 (c)], CSE and reordering allowed us to cut further the execution time by 72% for SETv2, 38% for 3KP, but less than 5% for H530.

4   Related Work and Conclusions

With respect to the tools proposed in the past, our compiler generates Java code which includes the checks on reception. We think this is very important for building defensive implementations of security protocols and it has a practical impact. However, this makes difficult to compare the compile time performance with other tools because in [10,11,12] the checks must be written manually. In [13] is used a notion of "receivability" which only models the ability to decrypt the received messages but does not compute other checks. In contrast to the tools that require process calculi as input language [10,11,12], we use a more intuitive language *AnB*, making our tool suitable for a larger audience of developers. In addition, our abstract specification is the most compact. Using SPI requires long specification files [11] and type annotations, [13] requires type annotations as well. Instead, we use a simple naming convention to make the protocol specification extremely succinct and the tool delegates the duty to generate well-typed code to the type system. Future work could take several directions. It would be important to make a formal proof of the soundness of the translation process along with extending the tool to generate interoperable code.

Acknowledgments. Part of this work was carried out while the author was a Ph.D. candidate at Università Ca' Foscari Venezia, under the valuable supervision of Prof. Michele Bugliesi. This work was partially supported by the EU FP7 Project n. 318424, "FutureID: shaping the Future of Electronic Identity". The author wishes to thank Thomas Groß for his helpful discussions and comments.

References

1. Avalle, M., Pironti, A., Sisto, R.: Formal verification of security protocol implementations: a survey. Formal Aspects of Computing 26(1), 99–123 (2014)
2. Mödersheim, S.: Algebraic properties in Alice and Bob notation. In: International Conference on Availability, Reliability and Security (ARES 2009), pp. 433–440 (2009)
3. Briais, S., Nestmann, U.: A formal semantics for protocol narrations. Theoretical Computer Science 389, 484–511 (2007), doi:10.1016/j.tcs.2007.09.005
4. Bugliesi, M., Modesti, P.: AnBx - Security Protocols Design and Verification. In: Armando, A., Lowe, G. (eds.) ARSPA-WITS 2010. LNCS, vol. 6186, pp. 164–184. Springer, Heidelberg (2010)
5. Modesti, P.: Efficient Java code generation of security protocols specified in AnB/AnBx. Technical Report CS-TR-1422, Newcastle University (2014)
6. Basin, D., Mödersheim, S., Viganò, L.: OFMC: A symbolic model checker for security protocols. Int. Journal of Information Security 4(3), 181–208 (2005)
7. P. Modesti: Verified Security Protocol Modeling and Implementation with AnBx. PhD thesis, Università Ca' Foscari Venezia, Italy (2012)
8. Bella, G., Massacci, F., Paulson, L.C.: Verifying the SET purchase protocols. Journal of Automated Reasoning 36(1), 5–37 (2006)
9. Bellare, M., et al.: Design, implementation, and deployment of the iKP secure electronic payment system. IEEE JSAC 18(4), 611–627 (2000)
10. Pozza, D., Sisto, R., Durante, L.: Spi2Java: Automatic cryptographic protocol Java code generation from spi calculus. In: Proceedings of the 18th AINA. IEEE (2004)
11. Backes, M., Busenius, A., Hriţcu, C.: On the development and formalization of an extensible code generator for real life security protocols. In: Goodloe, A.E., Person, S. (eds.) NFM 2012. LNCS, vol. 7226, pp. 371–387. Springer, Heidelberg (2012)
12. Tobler, B., Hutchison, A.: Generating network security protocol implementations from formal specifications. Cert. and Security in Inter-Org. E-Service, 33–54 (2005)
13. Millen, J., Muller, F.: Cryptographic protocol generation from CAPSL. Technical Report SRI-CSL-01-07, SRI International (2001)

Author Index